T0330285

A Research Agenda for Human Resource Management

Elgar Research Agendas outline the future of research in a given area. Leading scholars are given the space to explore their subject in provocative ways, and map out the potential directions of travel. They are relevant but also visionary.

Forward-looking and innovative, Elgar Research Agendas are an essential resource for PhD students, scholars and anybody who wants to be at the forefront of research.

Titles in the series include:

A Research Agenda for Management and Organization Studies
Edited by Barbara Czarniawska

A Research Agenda for Entrepreneurship and Context
Edited by Friederike Welter and William B. Gartner

A Research Agenda for Cities
Edited by John Rennie Short

A Research Agenda for Neoliberalism
Kean Birch

A Research Agenda for Human Resource Management
Edited by Paul Sparrow and Cary L. Cooper, CBE

A Research Agenda for Human Resource Management

Edited by

PAUL SPARROW

Lancaster University Management School, UK

CARY L. COOPER, CBE

Alliance Manchester Business School, University of Manchester, UK

Elgar Research Agendas

 Edward Elgar
PUBLISHING

Cheltenham, UK • Northampton, MA, USA

Published by
Edward Elgar Publishing Limited
The Lypiatts
15 Lansdown Road
Cheltenham
Glos GL50 2JA
UK

Edward Elgar Publishing, Inc.
William Pratt House
9 Dewey Court
Northampton
Massachusetts 01060
USA

A catalogue record for this book
is available from the British Library

Library of Congress Control Number: 2017939818

This book is available electronically in the **Elgar**online
Business subject collection
DOI 10.4337/9781785362965

ISBN 978 1 78536 295 8 (cased)
ISBN 978 1 78536 296 5 (eBook)

Typeset by Servis Filmsetting Ltd, Stockport, Cheshire
Printed and bound in Great Britain by TJ International Ltd, Padstow

Contents

About the editors

Paul Sparrow is Emeritus Professor of International HRM at Lancaster University Management School and was Director of the Centre for Performance-led HR from 2006 to 2016. In 2016 he was awarded the USA's Society for HRM Michael R. Losey Award for lifetime achievement in human resource research and research contributions that impact the HR management field. He is regularly voted amongst the Most Influential HR Thinkers by *Human Resources* magazine, listed from 2008 to 2012 and 2014–2016. His research interests include cross-cultural and international HRM, HR strategy and the employment relationship. He has several writing collaborations from which his latest books are on: *Globalizing HRM* (Routledge, 2004); *Strategic Talent Management* (Cambridge University Press, 2015); *Do We Need HR?* (Palgrave Macmillan, 2015); *International HRM: Contemporary HR Issues in Europe* (Routledge, 2016); and *Human Resource Management, Innovation and Performance* (AIAA, 2016).

Cary L. Cooper is the 50th Anniversary Professor of Organisational Psychology and Health at the Alliance Manchester Business School, University of Manchester. He is president of the following organisations: CIPD, Relate, British Academy of Management and Institute of Welfare. He is also the author/editor of over 160 books and several hundred scholarly articles; the Editor-in-Chief of the Wiley-Blackwell *Encyclopedia of Management* (now in its 3rd edition), Founding Editor of the *Journal of Organizational Behavior* and co-editor of the *Journal of Organizational Effectiveness*. He received his CBE and Knighthood from the Queen for services to organisational health and the social sciences respectively in 2001 and 2014.

Contributors

John W. Boudreau is Professor of Management and Organization at the University of Southern California's Marshall School of Business. He is recognised for breakthrough research on human capital, talent, and sustainable competitive advantage. His large-scale and focused field research studies the future of the global HR profession, HR measurement and analytics, decision-based HR, executive mobility, HR information systems, and organisational staffing and development. He has published more than 50 books and articles, and his research has been featured in *Harvard Business Review*, the *Wall Street Journal*, *Fortune*, and *BusinessWeek*. Professor Boudreau serves as Research Director for Marshall's Center for Effective Organizations. He advises numerous organisations, including early-stage companies, global corporations, government agencies, and non-profit organisations.

Chris Brewster is Professor of International Human Resource Management at Henley Business School, University of Reading, UK; and at Nijmegen University in the Netherlands. He had substantial experience as a practitioner and gained his doctorate from the London School of Economics before becoming an academic. He researches in the field of international and comparative HRM; and has published some 25 books and more than 150 articles. He has taught in many countries around the world. In 2002 Chris Brewster was awarded the Georges Petitpas Memorial Award by the practitioner body, the World Federation of Personnel Management Associations, in recognition of his outstanding contribution to international human resource management. In 2006 Chris was awarded an Honorary Doctorate by the University of Vaasa, Finland.

Susan Cartwright is Professor of Organisational Psychology and Well Being and Director of the Centre for Organisational Health and Well-Being at Lancaster University. She is interested in the area of occupational stress and organisational health and well-being. Her work has produced a number of innovative and best practice examples of organisational development initiatives to reduce stress and promote health, as well as leading to the development of a widely used stress screening tool, "ASSET" (with C.L. Cooper). Other areas of research interest include: the impact of change, particularly the human aspects of mergers and acquisitions on organisational productivity, commitment, employee satisfaction and well-being, expatriation, innovation, health and culture, training evaluation, emotional intelligence, the meaning of work and older workers.

Wayne F. Cascio is a Distinguished University Professor at the University of Colorado, and he holds the Robert H. Reynolds Chair in Global Leadership at the University of Colorado Denver. He has served as president of the Society for Industrial and Organizational Psychology (1992–1993), Chair of the SHRM Foundation (2007), the HR Division of the Academy of Management (1984), and as a member of the Academy of Management's Board of Governors (2003–2006). He has served as an editor of the *Journal of International Business Studies* (JIBS). He has authored or edited 28 books on human resource management, including *Managing Human Resources* (10th edn, McGraw-Hill, 2016), *Short Introduction to Strategic Human Resource Management* (with John Boudreau, Cambridge University Press, 2012), *Investing in People* (with John Boudreau, 2nd edn, Prentice Hall, 2011), and *Applied Psychology in Human Resource Management* (with Herman Aguinis, 8th edn, Pearson, 2013). He is a two-time winner of the best-paper award from the *Academy of Management Executive* for his research on downsizing. In 2010 he received the Michael R. Losey Human Resources Research Award from the Society for Human Resource Management, received the Distinguished Scientific Contributions Award from the Society for Industrial and Organizational Psychology in 2013, and in 2016 the World Federation of People Management Association's Lifetime Achievement Award. He is an elected Fellow of the National Academy of Human Resources, the Academy of Management, the American Psychological Association, and the Australian HR Institute.

Allan H. Church is the Vice President Global Talent Assessment and Development at PepsiCo. He is responsible for leading the talent development and capability building agenda for PepsiCo's Global Groups (that is, Global Beverages, Global Snacks, and Global Nutrition), global marketing, strategy, operations, information systems, and the corporate functions. In addition, he is responsible at the enterprise level for building executive talent assessment and development capabilities to strengthen the company's c-suite leadership pipeline. Allan joined

PepsiCo in December 2000. Previously he spent nine years as an external OD consultant working for W. Warner Burke Associates and several years at IBM in the Communications Measurement and Research, and Corporate Personnel Research departments. On the side, he has served as an Adjunct Professor at Columbia University and as Chair of the Mayflower Group. Currently he is a Visiting Faculty Scholar at Benedictine University, a member of the Executive Committee of the Conference Board's Council of Talent Management, and SIOP's Publications Officer. Allan received his PhD in Organisational Psychology from Columbia University. He is a Fellow of the Society for Industrial-Organisational Psychology, the American Psychological Association, and the Association for Psychological Science.

Johan Coetsee is a Senior Lecturer in Organisation and Human Resource Management in Newcastle Business School (NBS) at Northumbria University and is involved in executive education. Before joining NBS, Johan held a number of senior positions in academia and industry. His background is in chemical, manufacturing, banking and organisational development. His main academic interests are in change management and creating organisational readiness for change. In particular, this professional expertise has been put into practice by designing and delivering executive and masters level programmes for senior and executive managers from a range of organisations.

David G. Collings is Professor of Human Resource Management and Associate Dean for Research at Dublin City University (DCU). He received his PhD from Limerick University. Prior to joining DCU, he held faculty positions at the National University of Ireland, Galway and the University of Sheffield. He was also Visiting Professor at King's College London. He is Senior Consulting Editor at the *Journal of World Business*. He is the former editor of the *Human Resource Management Journal* and the *Irish Journal of Management* and permanent Chair of the EIASM workshop on talent management. He has been named by *HR Magazine* as one of the Most Influential International Thinkers in the field of HRM three times (2014–2016). His research and teaching focuses on talent management and global staffing. He has consulted with a number of leading global organisations in these areas. His speaking and consulting engagements include Airbus, the Danish Confederation of Industry, Enterprise Ireland, KPMG, Medtronic, Mercer, Stryker and many others. He is currently supervising a number of PhD students in areas such as international staffing, subsidiary innovation, HRM and performance, and born global firms. He has taught and delivered executive education in the US, UK, Iceland, Finland, France, Denmark and Singapore.

Patrick C. Flood is Professor of Organisational Behaviour and Co-Director of the Leadership and Talent Institute at Dublin City University. He received his PhD from the London School of Economics. He previously worked at London Business School and the University of Limerick and has held visiting appointments at the Cambridge Judge Business School; University of Maryland, Australian Graduate School of Management, Irish Management Institute, Capital University and Northeastern University, PRC. His key specialties include: top team vision and strategy development, executive education on leadership and change, leadership programme development, and organisational change planning. He has provided executive education to many companies such as Intel, Pirelli, Adidas, Pernod Ricard, Enterprise Ireland, Teagasc, ESBI and over 100 fast growth and new venture teams. He maintains close working relationships with practitioners in industry and is a regular industry conference speaker. Patrick is a current Fellow of the Academy of Social Sciences (FAcSS) and a former Fulbright, British Council FCO and EU HUMCAP scholar. He holds both teaching and research excellence awards from two universities. He is author of over 100 publications; his books include *Change Lessons from the CEO* (Wiley, 2013); *Persuasive Leadership* (Wiley, 2010); *Effective Top Management Teams* (Silver Lake, 2000); *Managing Strategy Implementation* (Wiley, 2000); and *Managing without Traditional Methods* (Addison Wesley, 1997).

Jamie A. Gruman is an Associate Professor of Organisational Behaviour at the College of Business and Economics, University of Guelph. He serves as the Graduate Coordinator in the Organizational Leadership stream of the PhD in Management. He has previously taught in both the Psychology Department and the Odette School of Business at the University of Windsor, and in the Psychology Department and the Department of Management at the University of Toronto. He is a founding member, and serves as Chair of the Board of Directors of the Canadian Positive Psychology Association. He completed his doctoral internship at Jackson Leadership Systems, a consulting firm specialising in leadership assessment and development. His research has been widely covered. In Canada he has been profiled and quoted in print and online magazines such as *MoneySense* magazine, *Chatelaine*, and *Canadian Business*, trade publications such as *HR Professional*, newspapers such as *The Globe and Mail* and *National Post*, and has appeared on CTV's Canada AM, Global News, Report on Business Television and has been syndicated on CBC radio. He has consulted and delivered seminars for Fortune 500 corporations, public, and not-for-profit agencies including General Motors, The Canadian Federal Government, and The Children's Wish Foundation.

Anthony Hesketh is a Senior Lecturer at Lancaster University Management School. His research interests cover: the construction, articulation and evaluation of *executive* strategy making; the relationship between strategy, leadership and organisational performance; the management of talent, especially examination of human capital management architectures and measurement; cultural political economy, semiotic materialism, critical realism and related methodologies; and managerial labour markets. His books include *The Mismanagement of Talent* (Oxford University Press, 2004) and *Explaining the Performance of HR* (Cambridge University Press, 2008). He played an important role in helping establish the Centre for Performance-Led HR at Lancaster – which had amongst its members some of the UK's most influential HR directors. He was also a founding member of the HROA Europe Board and sits on a number of advisory boards in the HR outsourcing space.

Kaifeng Jiang is an Assistant Professor of Management and J. Donnelly Fellow in Participatory Management at Mendoza College of Business, University of Notre Dame. He received his PhD in Industrial Relations and Human Resources from Rutgers University in 2013. His primary research interests focus on the effects of human resource management practices on employee, team, and organisational outcomes. Related interests include leadership, work teams, and organisational climate. Kaifeng regularly presents his research at conferences of Academy of Management (AOM) and Society for Industrial and Organizational Psychology (SIOP). His research work has been evidenced in top-tier publications, such as the *Academy of Management Journal*, the *Journal of Applied Psychology*, *Organizational Behavior and Human Decision Processes*, and *Personnel Psychology*. Kaifeng is an Associate Editor of *Human Resource Management Journal* (2016–2019) and serves on the editorial boards of *Academy of Management Journal*, *Journal of Applied Psychology*, *Personnel Psychology*, *Management and Organization Review*, and *International Journal of Human Resource Management*.

Jason Kautz (MBA, Canisius College, 2013) is at the University of South Carolina, Columbia with expertise in Organizational Psychology. He is a PhD student in the management department at the University of South Carolina's Darla Moore School of Business. His primary interests include workplace aggression (specifically social undermining), collective employee attitudes, selection, turnover, and advanced statistical methods. His most recent research focuses on emergent phenomena and the linkage between individual level characteristics and group level characteristics.

Dave Lepak has the Douglas and Diana Berthiaume Endowed Chair in Management at the Isenberg School of Management at the University of Massachusetts Amherst. He received his PhD in Business Administration from the Pennsylvania State University in 1998. Before joining the University of Massachusetts he was Professor of Human Resource Management at Rutgers University from 2008 to 2016, Professor of Management at University of Bath from 2007 to 2008, Associate Professor of Human Resource Management at Rutgers University from 2003 to 2007, and Assistant Professor of Management at University of Maryland College Park from 1998 to 2003. He is Editor of the *International Journal of Human Resource Management*, and Chairperson, HR Division of the Academy of Management. His research interests cover: the strategic management of human capital; individual interpretations and reactions to HRM practices; international HRM; and strategic HRM. He received the Scholarly Achievement Award, Human Resources Division, Academy of Management in 2010.

Cai-Hui (Veronica) Lin, PhD, is a Lecturer at Queen's Management School, Queen's University, Belfast. Cai-Hui's research focuses on strategic human resource management, creativity, innovation, and research methods. Her work has appeared in *Human Resource Management, British Journal of Management, Human Resource Management Journal* and in a number of books. Cai-Hui teaches at both undergraduate and postgraduate levels.

Anthony McDonnell is Professor of Management at the Cork University Business School, University College Cork, Ireland. Prior to joining UCC, Anthony was Head of the Management Department, Director of the Centre for Irish Business and Economic Performance and Reader in Management at Queen's University Belfast. Anthony is currently the (Co)Editor-in-Chief of *Human Resource Management Journal* and Adjunct Senior Research Fellow at the University of South Australia. His primary research interest and area of expertise is in the areas of talent management and international management, and more specifically, the HRM approaches of MNCs across countries.

John McMackin is a Lecturer in HRM and Organisational Behaviour at Dublin City University Business School and Chairperson of the School's MSc in Leadership and Organisational Behaviour programme. He has been associated with the School since 1996 and lectures on a range of HR topics with a particular focus on performance management, change management and leadership development. He has recently resumed academic work after an extended period in School management and consulting. His current research focuses on the application of change management techniques to the implementation of Lean practices. His work has been published in outlets such as *Academy of Management Review, Applied Cognitive Psychology* and *Human Resource Management Journal.*

Wolfgang Mayrhofer is Full Professor and head of the Interdisciplinary Institute of Management and Organisational Behaviour, WU Vienna, Austria. He previously held full-time positions at the University of Paderborn, Germany, and at Dresden University of Technology, Germany. He conducts research in comparative international human resource management and leadership, work careers, and systems theory and management and has received national and international rewards for outstanding research and service to the academic community. Wolfgang Mayrhofer has widely published, serves as editorial or advisory board member of several international journals and research centres and regularly consults with organisations in the for-profit and non-profit world.

Lilian Otaye-Ebede has a PhD in Human Resource Management (HRM) and Organisational Behaviour. She currently works as a Senior Lecturer in HRM – Research with Liverpool Business School, Liverpool John Moores University (LJMU). Her research interests are in the areas of strategic human resource management, employee relations, diversity management, international HRM and employee well-being. Her research explores the influence of HR strategies, practices, knowledge and capabilities on performance. Prior to joining LJMU, she worked as a Post-Doctoral Research Associate with the Centre for Performance-Led HR at Lancaster University. She also worked at Aston University, Birmingham as a Sessional Lecturer at the Business School; Research Associate on a project sponsored by the British Safety Council; and with the Aston Centre for Human Resources. She is currently an editorial board member of the *Journal of Organizational Effectiveness: People and Performance* and is a member of the British Academy of Management (BAM), Academy of Management (AOM), and the Nigerian Institute of Management (NIM).

Robert E. Ployhart is the Bank of America Professor of Business Administration in the management department at the University of South Carolina's Darla Moore School of Business. His PhD was from Michigan State University in 1999. His primary interests include human capital resources, staffing, recruitment, and advanced statistical methods. His most recent research focuses on the intersection of psychology with organisational strategy. Rob has been Associate Editor of the *Journal of Applied Psychology* and is a Fellow of the Society for Industrial and Organizational Psychology, the American Psychological Association, and the Association for Psychological Science.

Alan M. Saks is a Professor of Organizational Behavior and HR Management in the Department of Management at University of Toronto, Scarborough. He holds a cross-appointment to the Organizational Behaviour area at the Rotman School of Management and the Centre for Industrial Relations and Human Resources. He conducts research on organisational entry and the school-to-work transition such as job search, recruitment, and the socialisation and on-boarding of new hires. He has also studied and written about the transfer of training, employee engagement, and workplace spirituality. His teaching includes courses in Organizational Behaviour, Research Methods in Industrial Relations and Human Resources, Training and Development, and Human Resource Planning and Strategy.

Karin Sanders is Professor Organizational Behavior and Human Resource Management at the University of New South Wales Australia Business School, Sydney, Australia and is Director of the Centre of Innovation and Entrepreneurship (CIE; UNSW). Her research focuses on the process approach of HRM, in particular the impact of employees' perceptions and attributions of HRM on their attitudes and behaviours, such as their informal learning activities. She has published in journals like *Academy of Management Learning & Education, Organization Studies, Human Resource Management, Journal of Vocational Behavior, Group & Organization Management, International Journal of HRM* and *Human Resource Management Journal*.

Helen Shipton is Professor of Human Resource Management and Director of the Centre of People, Innovation and Performance at Nottingham Business School, Nottingham Trent University. She has published widely in several areas: human resource management, innovation and performance, how HRM influences creativity and innovation and performance – especially from a multi-level perspective, leadership development and leadership development evaluation, and international perspectives on HRM and performance. Helen holds a Visiting Professorship at the School of Management, Australian School of Business, University of New South Wales, Australia.

Adam Smale is Professor of Management and Business Administration and Head of the HRM Research Group in the Department of Management in the University of Vaasa. His research interests focus on international HRM, how multinational firms manage their human and knowledge resources on a global scale, and the types of challenges they face. He has published over 20 articles, several award-winning, on HRM, talent management and knowledge transfer in multinational corporations in leading journals and sits on the editorial board of the *Journal of Organizational Effectiveness: People and Performance* and the *Nordic Journal of Business*.

Huadong Yang is currently a Senior Lecturer in Organisational Behaviour and HRM at the University of Liverpool Management School (ULMS). Before joining ULMS, he taught at the University of Twente in the Netherlands and at Birkbeck, University of London. Dr Yang has also held a Senior Visiting Fellow position at the Australian School of Business at UNSW (Australia) and a Visiting Fellow position at the School of Public Administration, Renmin University of China. He received his PhD degree in Organisational Psychology from the University of Groningen in the Netherlands. He did his undergraduate and graduate study in psychology in China. He conducts his research in the areas of Conflict Management, Cross-Cultural Psychology and Human Resource Management.

1 Introduction: the future research agenda for HRM

Paul Sparrow and Cary L. Cooper

1.1 The genesis of this book

Why do we need to think about the future HRM research agenda? In part, there is a need to ensure that we simply catch up with the recent past. Before we even think about some of the technical changes and disruptive technologies that are now nearly upon us, it is evident that in the last 10 years the HRM function has already seen many significant and important changes. The agenda for those who lead the function has been one of building the capabilities deemed necessary in their function to help organisations survive and prosper in a very competitive environment. The strategic competence of organisations and their top teams has been questioned, as has been the role and purpose of organisations in society. Where they have been successful – and debate continues as to just how successful or not HR directors have been at transforming their function – HR directors have had to develop considerable strategic insight into their organisation. They have tried to focus their function on the need to look "into" the organisation, and its strategy, and help ensure the effective execution of change, as part of a team of other senior leaders. As such, they have had to evidence the contribution that people management can have to business challenges such as innovation, productivity, lean management, customer centricity, and the globalisation of operations and organisation capabilities. This has in turn required that they understand the complexity of their organisation's business models and the different options that exist in terms of organisation design. Even where they have developed potentially useful insight, or challenge, to existing strategic thinking, they have faced the challenge of having to engage the rest of the Board with their ideas and understanding. Not all Boards listen to HR, and not all HR teams understand the needs of the Board.

When it comes to what HR functions do, although the territory and range of activities is very wide, two over-riding debates or narratives have come to shape much of their activity. The first narrative has been around the notion of talent management. Deep and challenging questions have been asked about what makes people talented (or not) in this complex world, with various events such as the global financial crisis testing the confidence and trust in many HRM practices. HR directors have often quietly been "reconfiguring" their talent systems, or face calls from researchers to do this, looking critically at the leadership models that sit beneath them, and asking whether their organisation (and its practices) is creating, developing, deployed, measuring and evaluating the right sorts of human capital. The second narrative has been around the need to forge a clear link, and line of sight, from the strategy and the changes in business model that it often entails, and the engagement of the workforce. Clever business models that can make eminent business sense may be seen as inappropriate by employees and other stakeholders, with the solution needing to be not a simple re-presentation of the strategy, but creating a much deeper process that ensures that people believe and trust in the strategy, have a sense of fairness, and are therefore willing to engage and contribute. In short, HR directors also have to look "out" to the world of work, and to understand the social and technical changes taking place outside their organisation that will impact the way that employees within the organisation behave. We see the re-emergence of societal debates about things such as pension provision, executive reward, low pay, the access of all employee segments to careers, and quality work, the nature of diversity and role of key groups, such as women on boards, the global sourcing of work, change in the pattern of social mobility, and the potential implications of what has been called the 100 year life. Each of these social trends is driven by different ways of thinking about fairness, and it is becoming ever more apparent that what is fair for one employee segment might be seen as inherently unfair for another.

HR is at an inflexion point. The developments discussed throughout the book raise questions about the sorts of practices and processes that we give attention to as practitioners, and the sort of research that HR academics need to engage in to ensure both their relevance and rigour. HR practitioners are well aware that their function is continuing to develop and evolve. Their existing centres of expertise continue to change. Questions are being raised as to whether some of their expertise may be hollowed out, taken over by other functions or general line managers, or externalised. Some of their knowledge needs to be "joined together" in different ways, as practitioners find themselves working with other management functions or specialists on projects or change programmes that are aimed at building organisational effectiveness. There are also many people "competing" to offer important services. External consultants or outsourced and third-party organisations are themselves trying to add to the value that they can offer to organisations or policy makers. We see the growth of many value-adding specialist houses offering discretionary services, from areas such as HR analytics to business intelligence. HR service providers are becoming fewer in number, offer multi-tower HR–IS–Finance services, and are moving up the value-chain of services. Many third-party services operate through direct interfaces with line managers. Many of the technologies and data technologies used to promote employee engagement – such as crowdsourcing and social media – are becoming corporate, used across several management functions.

The book argues that we are seeing a new organisational effectiveness context for the HR function, and the questions now being asked about effectiveness often extend beyond any one organisation. Business models are increasingly collaborative, embedding organisations in networks that flow back through supply chains and into national governments, institutions and partners. We can no longer divorce what we do inside our organisations, or with our strategies, from their corporate and social impact.

HR is then at a crossroads. It is being pulled in several directions. We might find that it retreats from some of the challenges facing organisations now and in the future, and choose to concentrate on its traditional administrative and process-managing work. There will be a need for someone to manage core people-related functions such as recruitment and selection, training, pay and rewards, and so forth for quite some time to come. But when we look at what is happening in organisations we see some significant changes taking place. Organisations are beginning to "defunctionalise" themselves, as they try to address challenges that are both complex and cross-disciplinary. Many of these challenges are however still very people centric, that is, without the successful management of people the challenges will not be met. There is an opportunity for HRM researchers and practitioners alike to take on some of the intellectual leadership that is needed. This will not be easy. It means that we need to ask questions about the syllabus that should be taught to practitioners, and the knowledge models, theories and methods that HRM researchers should also start to employ.

1.2   The structure of the book

In order to help us think about these issues, we have opened up discussion of the future HRM agenda to academics from the leading HR research centres from around the world. They have been encouraged to lay out what they see as the current state of knowledge, and the future challenges for research and practice, in their respective areas of study.

We have organised the book into four topics:

- The role of HR strategy, structure and architecture;
- The role of key HR processes;
- Key performance enablers; and
- Key performance outcomes.

1.2.1   Strategy, structure and architecture

The debate begins in Chapter 2 by Dave Lepak, Kaifeng Jiang and Robert E. Ployhart on HR Strategy Structure and Architecture. This chapter reminds us that the field of strategic HRM – itself a relative newcomer in academic terms – has gone through various incarnations in a relatively short time. They trace this evolution to show how the field was initially dominated by the field of industrial and organisational psychology, but that slowly attention has shifted from an initial focus on core HR practices and processes, to questions about the HR system as a whole. We now think about how best to combine core practices into an effective architecture, and how to manage this portfolio depending on the technical, sector, country, strategic, and performance context. As a result, we have developed better insight into different employee segments, each with their varying needs and varying levels of strategic centrality. One of the refinements that began to occur was an attempt to look at the impact of HRM across levels, to try and show for example how individual and unit level factors influenced subsequent organisational performance, and the role played by important mediating factors such as commitment and well-being. They show how we began to understand that effective performance often only occurs if it is allowed to emerge, and that this emergence of a link between HRM and performance is a consequence of both bottom-up as well as top down processes. As such, they argue that it is far more sensible to think of strategic HRM as a system. There are several ways in which we might try to analyse this system. They place the attention that has been given to the link between abilities, motivations and opportunities (AMO model), or the role of various employee-organisation relationships and bonds, in this context.

Dave Lepak, Kaifeng Jiang and Robert E. Ployhart show how this rapid evolution of the field is continuing. As they look to the future, they see *four* shifts, each of which will move our attention away from analysing the impact of HRM at the level of what we might have erroneously assumed to be a unified organisation. First, we should give far more attention to the different patterns of strategic execution often seen across work groups within a single organisation. We need now to understand the characteristics of leaders, managers, groups and individuals that help to amplify the positive impacts that HRM can have, and that lead to more effective performance. Second, and broadly as a consequence of the first shift above, we need to give far more attention to those factors that promote group work. Third, we need to understand how factors such as team cognition, team diversity, team demographics and composition, and team efficacy, all impact effectiveness. And fourth, we need to understand the linkages between these issues, so that we can explain how group-level factors can help transfer the impact of organisation-level HR systems to produce individual-level outcomes, or how individual-level outcomes can be aggregated upwards to contribute to group-level and organisation-level outcomes.

Interestingly, Dave Lepak, Kaifeng Jiang and Robert E. Ployhart also draw attention to the importance of time (something that is also done in the last chapter of the book on globalisation by Chris Brewster, Adam Smale and Wolfgang Mayrhofer). In terms of HR strategy, we need to understand how fast or how long it can take for change to occur. We also need to know the role of important system design qualities over time – such as the role of consistency versus flexibility. Without knowing such things, we can miss or understate the importance of key variables and factors in the causal link between HRM and performance. This means that in terms of research methodology we need to encourage research that uses longitudinal datasets and better controls for prior factors that might predispose an organisation to perform in one way versus another. It means that we need to stop assuming linear effects, and better understand whether the effects of HR systems diminish or grow over time. To do this we need better experimental control, as it can be hard to test for variation in live organisational contexts. There is then a place for experimental designs and simulations.

Finally, Chapter 2 makes a call – one that will be seen in most of the chapters throughout this book – that we adopt multidisciplinary theories and lenses in our research. They point to the way in which researchers began to blend ideas from human capital theory with those that come from the field of strategy and a resource-based view of the firm, and how this has led to the current attention that is being given the different forms of human capital and the enabling processes that transform individual knowledge, skill, ability, and other characteristics (the KSAO model) into unique, unit-, operations- and firm-level resources.

1.2.2   Key HR processes

The next three chapters then give attention to a series of important HRM processes that might be considered to shape the quality of human capital open to an organisation. The first two of these chapters cover the process of talent management and the third examines the process of selection, assessment and turnover.

In Chapter 3 on Talent Management, David G. Collings, Anthony McDowell and John McMackin evaluate the current state of the literature on talent management and establish the key trends in the research that has taken place in this area. They show how the topography of the area has been constantly evolving. Given the relative recent development of talent management as an academic field (it has been a concern of practice for much longer) the early attention academic enquiry focused on defining what talent management actually means. Initially, there was a temptation for there to be some simple rebranding of human resource management as talent management, for some simplistic arguments that talent might be categorised as A, B and C players and that organisations needed to load themselves with A players to be effective, or develop talent pools of high performing and high potential employees capable of moving into future senior leadership roles. We then saw some more sophisticated attempts to shift the talent management agenda towards also thinking about positions with the potential for significant variation in output and value added between a high performer and an average performer, that could be defined by their centrality to organisational strategy combined (this perspective is also developed in Chapter 4 by Wayne F. Cascio, John W. Boudreau and Allan H. Church). They also draw attention to some fundamental differences in philosophy that can dominate both the research and practice of talent management. For example, the level of exclusivity of talent programmes has been one of the central debates in the literature. Yet there has been little precision in academic studies or amongst practitioners around the definition of what it is that makes people "talent".

They also argue that researchers need to look across several different strands of research. For example, the parallel literature on star employees is moving beyond its initial focus on talent as high potentials and/or high performers, to a more nuanced understanding of what makes people talented or not in a particular organisational context. It is differentiating between research that treats talent as a subject (where every individual's strengths should be harnessed for the organisation's benefit, the motivational effects associated with being classified as talent, and the attention that must therefore be given to the role of objective, fair, and transparent processes of identification), and research that treats talent as an object (where attention is given to the ability, competence, performance, and behaviours of a subset of the workforce that makes them comparatively more important than everyone else in terms of the value they add to corporate performance).

They advocate an acceptance that, at least in terms of strategy, a more exclusive approach might be needed. While accepting that we must beware a possible "elitist" underpinning of differentiated talent management systems, and ensure that attention to the role of key individuals does not come with any suggestion that those in non-critical roles receive no investment, the focus of research must help organisations to make informed decisions around the optimum level of talent required in critical job roles. They also argue that by looking at the interplay between critical roles and talent in isolation, we can avoid the limitations of early research that segmented employees into A- B- and C- players. Roles serve to moderate the value that can be created by any individual. They show where talent can have the greatest impact on important organisational outcomes.

They note that the literature on talent management could at best be described as in early adolescence, but given the recent proliferation of special issues on the topic the knowledge base is changing fast. The field is phenomenon-driven, still suffers from limited theoretical grounding, and the quality, focus and sophistication of some of the empirical work remains open to question. As a result is still developing in a haphazard way.

They identify three key trends that they feel will drive the talent agenda from both a research and practice perspective over the coming years.

They point to the interface between our models of talent management, and performance management. Despite there being little empirical evidence that organisations are actually moving away from ratings in performance management, we need to better understand how to identify talent in the absence of performance ratings. They suggest a research agenda that explores how a changed understanding of performance may influence talent management systems and processes, and how this may translate into sustainable organisational effectiveness and performance. They caution that we need to move away from the assumption that performance is normally distributed amongst employees in organisations. In terms of strategic value, there is an emerging view that performance does not in fact follow a normal distribution, but is rather subject to a Paretin or power distribution. As they point out, this means that there are potentially more stars than a normal distribution would suggest, owing to there being a longer "tail".

If so, this has implications for where the "mean" of performance really lies in the workplace, and the skew created by star performers might equally mean that a far greater percentage of performers fall below the mean. Forcing a normal distribution on performance scores might also result in a number of high performers being designated as average. Both of these implications would be discomforting and demoralising for many HR practitioners and employees alike, who assume a normal distribution. It also would have implications for errors in the resourcing process, a topic that is looked at in Chapter 5 by Robert E. Ployhart and Jason Kautz.

In Chapter 3 David G. Collings, Anthony McDonnell and John McMackin also highlight the importance of context in future talent management research. We should expect to see some shifting boundaries of talent management research in light of growth in contingent work and what has been called the gig economy. Assessing the quality and quantity of talent available through these atypical relationships will be challenging. But we also need to understand how what they characterise as alternative talent platforms can provide access to high quality talent globally, how organisations or networks might maximise the deployment of core employees to focus on key tasks, how to provide access to talent and skills when attempting to scale up across these different platforms, and how to engage this talent and maximise their contribution and rewards for sustainable organisation performance.

Having noted the importance of understanding context and the link between key roles and the scope for individual talent, they note that the nature of roles themselves can be subject to other mantras. What happens for example to the contribution that talent can make as organisations "lean" their processes? They sketch out a research agenda that might be able to understand talent management in the context of what they call a lean talent agenda. As David G. Collings, Anthony McDonnell and John McMackin note in Chapter 3, there are important questions around risk and compliance in these contingent workforces. This leads us nicely to the next chapter.

In Chapter 4, Wayne F. Cascio, John W. Boudreau and Allan H. Church develop the discussion of talent management by using a risk optimisation lens. They argue that organisations now need to reframe their talent management systems in ways that hedge risk and uncertainty. They introduce the notion of human capital risk – which they define as the uncertainty arising from changes in a wide variety of workforce and people-management issues that affect a company's ability to meet its strategic and operating objectives. There are some important gaps in our research knowledge in terms of understanding how to manage such risk. For example, existing research on leadership-succession planning reveals little that helps us understand or predict the antecedents, consequences, and moderating and mediating factors that relate talent systems to improvements in risk-optimised talent decisions.

They advocate a process through which organisations prepare a portfolio of talent that is optimised against an uncertain future. Rather than focus on identifying and then systematically building future capabilities using internal processes and tools, we need to better understand how future scenarios are constantly shifting, the risks inherent in the current talent base given this, and the options that are available to alleviate those risks as the scenarios materialise. Despite the strategy literature being littered with examples of firms that failed to react appropriately to developments in their external environments, top teams still seem to be ill prepared to face outside threats. The focus of succession planning needs to be on agility and embracing uncertainty rather than trying to reduce it. It needs to be on optimising the balance between risk and opportunity. In future, success, they argue, will be determined not so much by the validity and execution quality of succession systems, but rather by the ability of the organisation to nurture a sufficient variety of options aligned against multiple future scenarios.

Whilst Chapter 3 signals that our concepts of potential tend to be too narrowly defined, Chapter 4 explains why this is so. It argues that for both researchers and practitioners alike, the concept of "potential" remains only vaguely defined. It is subject to significant differences of interpretation and generally fails to consider talent readiness to adapt to a changing future. Potential is defined too narrowly, as a general proxy for individual readiness to advance through a linear career path to one or more upper-level positions as they currently exist. We need to take a much more contingent approach, asking potential for what?

They also highlight two implications for practice: what this means for measuring candidate "potential"; and what the implications are for the ownership rights and decision accountability for talent development. The chapter argues that we need to take a more holistic view of potential and apply it throughout the entire talent-management process. They use a leadership potential framework to demonstrate how organisations might take a more comprehensive and holistic view to framing the identification and prediction of future leadership success. They signal some of the cognitive capabilities, learning orientations, and individual motivations and drive that might form more appropriate attributes to concentrate on. We also know very little about the antecedents, moderators, and consequences of cross-unit talent optimisation.

However, as Wayne Cascio, John Boudreau and Allan Church warn us, researching risk optimisation will not be easy. They note that we need four things: improved HR information/talent management systems, databases, and managerial tools for planning different staffing scenarios and downstream implications; changes in the mindsets of leaders, the culture of organisations, reward systems, accountability; changes in our concepts of what talent management and succession planning are supposed to be about; and changes in the capabilities of HR professionals. Their chapter raises a number of challenges for HR practice. The current focus of practice, which is solely on "incumbents in roles", is limiting. Talent gap analysis processes are too linear and mechanistic, estimates of bench strength are over-optimistic based on assessments of potential for historic role structures and performance contexts, and models of success are not grounded in theory and research.

The talent management agenda outlined in Chapters 3 and 4 is also helping selection and turnover researchers to recast some of their own research efforts in order to focus on collective human capital resources, selection becomes the mechanism through which such resources are built and acquired, and turnover represents the erosion of such resources. In Chapter 5, Robert E. Ployhart and Jason Kautz apply a human capital management lens to research on selection, assessment and turnover. The chapter provides a review of contemporary research on selection and retention. They look at these two core but interdependent HRM processes – selection and retention – in the context of the talent management research agenda. It shows that after over a century of scholarly research devoted to understanding how to make the most accurate selection decisions, the core focus of selection research remains fixated on identifying selection practices and techniques that produce scores with high validity, low subgroup differences, are cost-effective, and are acceptable to candidates, and there is reasonably shared consensus around many key points. We know for example that the validity for many types of these scores is generalisable across different contexts and cultures, that cognitive ability is highly related to job performance across these contexts and cultures, and that the relationship becomes stronger as the complexity of the job increases. We know that cognitive ability is rarely itself a sufficient predictor for job performance, and that in general terms hiring talent from the outside costs more money and delivers worse performance than hiring from the inside. Similarly, in terms of turnover, we know that there are negative consequences of turnover on nearly all performance indicators, but that low to moderate levels of turnover may be beneficial to an organisation in removing low-performers. Therefore, there is a curvilinear relationship between turnover and performance, and a need to optimise its management. This relationship is seen through a number of research lenses: the loss for valuable knowledge, skills, and abilities (the KSAO model introduced in Chapter 2 by Dave Lepak, Kaifeng Jiang and Robert E. Ployhart); operational disruption and loss of important information flows; and human resource accounting for the true costs of turnover. The chapter shows that some new concepts are beginning to shape the field. For example, researchers now consider the role of organisational embeddedness, that is, the fit between the employee and the organisation, the social links created through the job, and the sacrifice associated with leaving.

Rob Ployhart and Jason Kautz characterise our understanding of basic principles of selection and retention as impressive, but also warn that there are signs that selection and retention research have not kept pace with changes in business over the last 15 or so years. For them, these changes relate to globalisation, business, and competition. The effect of cultural influences on most predictor methods is still largely unknown, and we are faced with an interesting paradox: selection practices differ considerably across cultures, but the knowledge, skills, abilities and other factors (KSAO) assessed in many selection practices are equivalent. We should not assume that cultural differences in practice do not translate into cultural differences in selection effectiveness because the validity of key selection techniques seems to be invariant. We need more research that directly compares various predictor methods and the corresponding scores from those methods, across cultures, before we can definitely know what the role of culture may be on selection practice and outcomes. We also know even less about the impact of cultural differences on retention practices and outcomes.

Similarly, despite the fact that technology plays an important role in understanding turnover (because the platforms that record data such as social media usage or postings can be used to predict behaviour), there has been very little scientific examination of the use of technology for selection and retention. Chapter 4 on risk optimisation and talent management noted that an agile organisational strategy becomes particularly critical in a VUCA world, but in such environments it is impossible to predict the future. The challenge of this environment for selection and retention research is to recognise that organisational strategies will change quickly, so selection and retention must become more nimble if organisations are to effectively implement strategy. Robert E. Ployhart and Jason Kautz argue this will require a major shift in research focus. Most selection and retention research has been conducted at the individual level, but future research will have to build on recent advancements that study selection and retention at the unit or firm levels, and will have to incorporate theory and research from organisational strategy. They discuss some interesting findings on there being a link between investments in selection and training and the recovery of firm productivity (a topic picked up in Chapter 10) and profit and recovery from the global financial crisis. This reinforces their point that future research is needed that links selection practices to business strategy and the broader economic conditions in which firms operate. We see efforts now to examine the flow of collective human capital resources over time – what they call the human capital resource pipeline.

1.2.3   Key performance enablers

The book then addresses a series of important factors that may be characterised as performance enablers in four chapters: employee engagement; well-being; the role of leadership; and the choices made about the HR analytics to be used, and the assumptions these make about value.

The first of these is examined in Chapter 6 by Alan M. Saks and Jamie A. Gruman when they review the relationship between engagement and HRM. They pick up on the agenda that Dave Lepak, Kaifeng Jiang and Robert E. Ployhart traced back to the mid-2000s in Chapter 2, which is the need to link HR practices to the attitudes, behaviours, and performance of individual employees, and then back to firm performance. Although study of employee engagement is nowhere near as mature a field as that seen in the previous chapter on selection and retention, there is now a growing body of work and this research has identified various antecedents and consequences of engagement and has shown how engagement mediates relationships between various antecedents and intermediate performance outcomes. There is however a gap in both the research and practitioner literature when it comes to understanding how HRM practices and systems can be configured to enhance employee engagement. Alan M. Saks and Jamie A. Gruman review research on HRM and employee engagement, using the ability–motivation–opportunity or AMO model of HRM introduced in Chapter 2 by Dave Lepak, Kaifeng Jiang and Robert E. Ployhart as one of the dominant theories to capture the employer–employee relationship. They review research on HRM and employee engagement within each of the three HRM dimensions of the AMO model – skill-enhancing, motivation-enhancing, and opportunity-enhancing HRM practices.

Linking back to the previous chapter, for example, selection practices can be used to predict which job applicants are most likely to become engaged. The evidence reviewed in Chapter 6 shows that person–organisation fit perceptions are positively related to engagement. Training opportunities and socialisation act as skill enhancing HRM practices and important predictors of employee engagement. We also know about the importance of many opportunity-enhancing practices such as voice, job design and job enrichment. Alan M. Saks and Jamie A. Gruman argue that we know less, however, about potentially motivation-enhancing practices, other than the likely importance of practices that improve the level and accuracy of expectations (such as various aspects of performance management). Linking back to the discussion of the overall HR architecture in Chapter 2, positive perceptions of HRM practices are positively related to engagement, and engagement mediates the relationship between HRM practices and specific work outcomes such as innovation (this performance outcome is discussed in more detail in Chapter 11). Much of the evidence about links between HRM and employee engagement, however, remains fragmented. To guide future empirical work, they develop an integrative model that links various HRM practices to a series of important processes – such as meaningfulness, safety, resources, support, trust, fairness and perceptions of fit, and suggest that these in turn may be predictors of employee, team and/or collective engagement.

The second key performance enabler is examined in Chapter 7 on HRM and workplace well-being. Susan Cartwright reminds us that the issue of workplace health and well-being has received increasing attention from researchers, employers and policy makers throughout the developed economies. She points out that the human resource function is likely to come under increasing future pressure to develop and comply with human capital reporting standards (a topic picked up later in this section by Anthony Hesketh in Chapter 9). The function will have to account for the value of their employees and their collective knowledge, skills, abilities and capacity to develop and innovate.

Organisations and governments therefore continue to look for evidence-based ways of dealing with well-being. The chapter provides some trends that show why it is right that they do so, noting the brake it places on productivity. It argues that we need to broaden the meaning of well-being beyond its traditional and legislative concerns with health status from a medical perspective. We know quite a lot about features of the job which contribute to well-being – these include job demands, control, role clarity, security, pay and equity, and wider factors such as co-workers, HR practices, and aspects of the workplace environment more generally.

However, once we broaden our understanding and interpretation of well-being, it is clear that the relationship between human resource management (HRM) and employee well-being is complex. It is also full of paradoxes and inherent conflicts. On the one hand HRM practices can positively enhance employee well-being and result in gains in organisational performance, but on the other hand, HRM can also work to the benefit of corporate performance through work intensification, and so adversely impact on employee well-being.

Susan Cartwright examines the evidence from systematic reviews of flexible working to reveal these paradoxes. She examines some of the ways in which organisations can prevent and address the occurrence of ill health and promote health, well-being and performance. Strategies have not been as effective as they might, with organisations and policy makers focusing on whatever is reasonably practicable to prevent work-related ill health, in ways that cause as little disruption as possible, rather than the more disruptive positive promotion of well-being. This has narrowed attention on the reduction of incidence of ill health, and the management and support of employees who have developed medical conditions or have been injured at work. These initiatives are of course important, and are reviewed in the chapter, but we need also to draw upon positive psychology, and look at the promotion of well-being at work and the role of organisational initiatives directed at helping individuals to feel happy, competent and satisfied in their roles (this builds upon the previous chapter on employee engagement). The chapter addresses questions of responsibilities for this, and the choice of processes open to organisations as they proactively accept that it is in their best interests to take steps to monitor, address and modify workplace policies, practices and job characteristics that may adversely impact on health and which employees are powerless in their ability to change or control.

Given the need for changes in responsibility – something seen throughout this book – then it is important that we think about the nature of leadership and the agenda that this creates for HRM. In Chapter 8 on Leadership Models, Patrick C. Flood and Johan Coetsee show how the volume of leadership research has increased exponentially over the past 10 years, resulting in the development of a range of leadership theories and approaches. Whilst Chapter 4 raises questions about our definitions of leadership potential and the nature of succession programmes, Chapter 8 argues that there also remains a lack of understanding about the importance of underlying leadership models. We know much about how leaders are perceived and qualities in leaders that may be important, but far less about how leaders go about changing processes in individuals, groups, or organisations, and make their organisations more effective. The chapter explains the main approaches that are currently taken – such as leader-centric approaches, traits and behaviours of leaders, ethical and relational approaches, follower-centric approaches, team leadership and identity-based approaches. We also suffer from too narrow a focus in the current research – it is characterised by the over-use of a leader-centric approach (the romance of leadership), retrospective and single time survey measures, single level and single method approaches, and a lack of longitudinal studies.

In order to address these limitations, and move leadership research forward, the chapter argues that we need to re-examine the assumptions and paradigms we currently use in the study of leadership, as well as our methodologies. It lays out some new paradigms of leadership, and explains the methodologies that will enhance our understanding of what is a complex phenomenon. The chapter signals two important areas of research that now need to be addressed: First, to understand leadership as it is conducted in a context of strategic collaboration at the industry and firm level, and predicated on more collaborative cultures at the top of the organisation; and second, the role of HR directors as coaches of their organisations.

In Chapter 9, the final chapter of this section, Anthony Hesketh addresses the issue of value, and the role of big data in helping to establish this. It explores why and how most researchers continue to think the answer lies in organisations (and key functions within them such as the HR function) using more of the same analytical techniques. There remains an apparent insecurity established in the discourse of human resources executives when faced with the prospect of engaging with senior members of the boardroom. The chapter shows that there is an almost-unquestioned narrative emerging that we need data-driven decision-making. HR analytics defined typically as a more systematic application of predictive modelling using inferential statistics to existing HR people-related data – follows in this mould. It is intended to inform judgements about the possible causal factors that drive key HR-related performance indicators. He is critical of this, observing that predictive analytics, at least those used in HR, rests on the use of traditional statistical techniques, such as regression and advanced modelling techniques, with which generations of statisticians and operational research students are highly familiar. What is new is the volume and speed at which such statistical techniques can be applied. Whilst "big data" has now become commonplace as a business term, he reminds us of the recent calls for there to be much more published management scholarship that tackles the challenges of using such tools. The chapter responds to this call by presenting a case for why we need to complicate the field, and functions need to complicate themselves, to move forward. One of the problems that we face is that when data are "big", then everything becomes statistically "significant". To avoid being seduced by such reductionism, we need to use alternative, meta-theoretical approaches, and their associated techniques. The chapter argues there is a wider malaise in both research and practice as to what constitutes knowledge in general, and what counts as analytical evidence of *causality* in driving business outcomes. To make this clear, the chapter examines and critiques much of the research that is used to argue for the relationship between human resources management and performance. For Anthony Hesketh, the way forward is not to reject the quantitative form that is offered by analytics, but to move towards a purer form of what he calls "analytical argumentation" via a new form of analysis.

1.2.4   Key performance outcomes

The final three chapters of the book place HRM in its business context, and look at arguably the three most important performance challenges facing HR directors over the next few years: productivity, innovation, and globalisation.

In the aftermath of the global financial crisis, we see a lot of attention being given to productivity. In Chapter 10, Paul Sparrow and Lilian Otaye-Ebede address the challenges for the field of HRM created by this drive for productivity. Productivity may be thought of as one form of organisational resilience, but HRM researchers have only made limited inroads into the topic of productivity. This is unfortunate, because HR directors are likely to be tasked with contributing to fundamental workforce and business model transformations aimed at reversing what is now a serious productivity problem at national level.

In many areas HRM research – such as dealing with performance challenges including innovation, customer centricity, lean management – the demand-pattern for professional knowledge both inside organisations for practitioners, and for the academics studying these issues, is changing. Chapter 10 demonstrates this when it looks at the issue of productivity. It shows that the HR function has not been directly involved in helping the organisation think through the best ways to respond to the productivity challenge, except in some traditional sectors such as manufacturing. The HR function also tends to think in relatively narrow terms – looking to individual-level productivity activities such as building workforce skills, managing employee engagement to keep skilled employees delivering, and designing performance management systems and incentives systems such as performance-related pay to maintain control over the implementation of work. Yet, in order to be able to hold their own as a field of management, HR practitioners and researchers alike need to skill themselves up and integrate knowledge from other fields in order to be able to demonstrate the complex people and organisational issues that will need to be resolved if firms and nations are to deal with the productivity challenge.

It argues that the study of performance drivers, or their enablers, presents both a "multi-level" and a "horizontal" problem. These challenges require different interventions at national (macro), organisational (meso), and task or business process (micro) level. They are also horizontal. Within any one organisation, the solution often sits "above" and "across" the traditional management functions, such as HRM. The challenges can only be properly understood and solved by cross-functional action and focus inside the organisation, but also connections to, and coordination across, people beyond the organisation (partners, supply chain, governments).

The chapter outlines two challenges – developments in national and organisational level productivity – and explains some of the main factors involved in organisation level productivity. It links the national and organisational agendas by drawing attention to areas such as the role of skills in improving productivity. The chapter uses a range of different productivity challenges across several sectors – such as supermarkets, fast food, oil and energy, aerospace, nuclear sector, healthcare, and on-demand business models – to demonstrate this. The examples are used to demonstrate the highly idiosyncratic nature of productivity strategies needed. It identifies three important contextual factors that HRM research will have to take into account: the role of time in the HRM–productivity challenge; the relationship between productivity, HRM, and risk; and the importance of understanding the most appropriate level of analysis question in examining the relationship between HRM and productivity. Finally, it argues that we need much better use of human capital metrics and HR analytics so that organisations, and important stakeholders such as the financial community, can get a better fix on the true health and future value of an organisation. The discussion of various productivity recipes in this chapter is also another example of the importance of the need for HRM researchers to understand the role of time, raised in Chapter 2. The examples given all show the subtle but crucial changes taking place in the way in which the organisations have to think about their effectiveness, and without an understanding of the evolutions or revolutions taking place in these productivity equations, practitioners and researchers alike can be blinded to the most appropriate solutions.

Of course, one of the key enablers of increased productivity will need to be innovation. In Chapter 11, Helen Shipton, Veronica Lin, Karin Sanders and Huadong Yang examine the relationship between innovation and HRM. Whilst the value of innovation at a corporate level, and of technical experts and R&D units, is well understood, we do not know that much about how organisations can leverage the insights and creativity of those performing day-to-day jobs. Yet this employee segment represents an unfathomable well of ideas. They examine the literature on recognising, leveraging and releasing the creative and innovative behaviours of employees across specialisms, and across levels of the hierarchy. They operationalise innovation as the intentional introduction of ideas that are valuable and novel within a specific context as their point of departure, and develop a four-stage conceptualisation to break it down into substages. The first two of these are individual: problem identification, and idea generation. The next two are collective in nature: idea evaluation and implementation.

The chapter identifies two areas that they believe would benefit from more focused attention. The first is distinguishing between environments where creativity and innovation is overtly required, as opposed to job roles where creative outcomes, while valuable, are not expressly called for as part of the job. In the same way that the job performance literature distinguishes between in-role versus extra role behaviours, there may be different (hidden) predictors of expected versus unexpected creative and innovative outcomes – different motivators for each type of job. They look at the impact that HRM can have on both of these sets of employees.

The second under-researched area is the effect that HRM has on individual creativity (idea generation) and the more collective process of innovation implementation. They highlight the top-down implications of HRM for job roles where creativity is expected versus those where there is no express requirement. In contexts where creative and innovation-oriented behaviours are discretionary, informal, workplace learning is likely to be at a premium. Innovation is often a by-product of other workplace goals. Common to both types of job, however, is the process of bottom-up emergence. HRM can play a very important role in facilitating this. They look at the way in which HRM can support and underpin employees' efforts not just to generate ideas, but also to work with others to foster their implementation.

In the final chapter, the book brings in an International HRM perspective. Chapter 12 on Globalisation and HRM by Chris Brewster, Adam Smale and Wolfgang Mayrhofer reminds us that all of the HR strategies and processes that are examined in this book are carried out in an increasingly globalised context. HRM is one of the least globalised of all the management functions, and regardless of whether the overall level of economic globalisation advances, slows down or retreats, there will be a process of catch up and realignment within the practice of HRM. Our understanding of HRM increasingly needs to take an international and comparative view, and this truism becomes particularly stark when we look at the significance of globalisation for HRM. As international integration and the growing interconnectedness of business increases, the outcome might be to strengthen the specific advantage of particular locations or subsidiaries, or it might be to increase standardisation around the globe. Standardisation in turn might take place between regions, countries or country clusters, or it may take place within MNEs, as they attempt to harmonise HRM practices and ensure local responsiveness as well as consistency across their foreign operations. HRM policies might diffuse around the world at all of these levels. However, most HRM research is still conducted in single countries.

Globalisation is examined in in the context of two of the main streams of research in IHRM: comparative HRM (CHRM), which examines the commonalities and differences in HRM between regions and nations; and HRM in multinational enterprises (MNEs), which examines the HRM policies and practices of organisations operating across national boundaries, particularly the management of MNE subsidiaries and knowledge transfer. There is a global/local tension not only in international business in general, but also across the extensive research in the field of IHRM. They examine the debates behind the "globalisation thesis", which have focused on long-term developments towards convergence or divergence at the macro level of nation states, and the meso level of organisational practices. The chapter reminds us that the convergence thesis has not remained uncontested, with counter evidence coming from both cultural and institutional researchers.

To structure the review, both the comparative and MNE research are further broken down against the notions of context, time and process. These concepts are familiar to the business strategy literature, though less so to HRM researchers. In general business literature context is often captured by the notion of contingency, such as differences in management processes created by the size of the business, the sector(s) in which it operates, the geography. Context is often framed as a tension, or duality, between attempts to create HRM standardisation, and the constraints imposed by the local environment.

We know a fair amount about how the desire of MNEs to standardise their HRM is often restricted by local contextual constraints that require them to compromise, but far less about how the local contextual norms and arrangements regarding HRM are influenced by MNEs and MNE subsidiaries. We also know much about the headquarters' view of HRM in MNEs, but are beginning to see more research adopting the subsidiary perspective and examining the contextual antecedents of reverse HRM transfer.

Reflecting the call made in Chapter 2 for us to incorporate and better understand the role of time – a call generally made in the interests of better theory building – Chris Brewster, Adam Smale and Wolfgang Mayrhofer incorporate this into their analysis. Time is very important to the CHRM stream (if country differences are decreasing, for example, then there is less value in studying them). But the existing MNE research is mainly cross-sectional, and it is almost impossible to make inferences about patterns of standardisation or differentiation over time. This said, we are now seeing some insightful, longitudinal, qualitative work mainly in the form of case studies, and this is revealing the important role played by power relations and micro-political processes in determining the use and effectiveness of different HRM control mechanisms over time.

However, they note that in addition to the role of context and time, very little attention has been given to the role of process – the means and mechanisms through which management operates – particularly in the international HRM field. This "process school", as they call it, is drawing on the strategy-as-practice perspective in the strategy literature. We are seeing more attention now being given to how HRM practices, practitioners in a broad sense, and praxis interact and shape the way people-related decisions within organisations are made, implemented and enacted. We are seeing more emphasis being given to the role of key actors at higher levels, and the role of psychological processes at the individual level through which employees attach meaning to HRM.

As a final comment, we hope that this book serves to challenge, to stimulate and motivate, and to shape the HRM research agenda over the forthcoming years. We have drawn together a community of leading researchers who seem to be of one mind. The field of HRM is going to be one of the most exciting and challenging areas of management research.

2 HR strategy, structure and architecture

Dave Lepak, Kaifeng Jiang and Robert E. Ployhart

2.1 Introduction: the evolution of strategic HRM research

The field of strategic HRM has gone through various incarnations over its relatively short history as an area of focus in the broader human resource management field. The purpose of this chapter is to look back over the evolution of strategic HRM research and review where we are in the field. We then shift our focus to reflect on some current exciting areas of research and forward into areas of research that are critical to continue to push the field forward. The field of strategic HRM has gone through many different stages as a field of study. As a starting point, we can think of the emergence of the field as a shift in focus. Historically, human resource management researchers examined various HR practices linked to practical initiatives and processes such as selection, training, compensation, performance management, job design, and voice to name a few. Drawing heavily on industrial/organisational psychology, the emphasis was on the impact of these organisational initiatives on employees and work groups within the workplace as well as employee's experiences and reactions to the exposure to those practices. With this starting point, the field of strategic HRM made several shifts in focus that evolved into newer ways to looking at some important issues within organisations.

2.1.1 Thinking at the unit level

Several aspects of this research shifted in the earlier days of strategic HRM to help define what was meant by strategic HRM. First, key questions related to unit or organisational performance gained prominence producing a series of small subgroups in the field. Examining the unit level performance effects stemming from selective staffing (for example, Koch and McGrath, 1996; Terpstra and Rozell, 1993) or pay for performance plans (for example, Banker et al., 1996; Shaw, Gupta and Delery, 2001) as examples helped usher in the notion of "strategic" HRM – tying to understand how these practices impacted important unit or organisational outcomes of interest.

Second, while HR practices were examined in isolation as key areas of inquiry, some strategic HRM scholars switched orientation to examine how multiple HR practices operated in concert (for example, Arthur, 1994; Huselid, 1995). The underlying logic for focusing on bundles of HR practices or HR systems is that employees are not exposed to HR practices in isolation but rather, are exposed to multiple practices simultaneously. So the effectiveness of selection practices rests, in part, on the competitiveness of the compensation system or the nature of the job design in place. Failure to account for the internal alignment of these HR practices within a system provides misleading information about the real impact of any HR practice. This remains a key defining aspect of strategic HRM research.

A third defining attribute of strategic HRM research in the mid-1990s was a focus on context. Just as a single HR practice's effect cannot be understood without information into the presence/absence/nature of other practices, different bundles of HR systems were expected to be more or less effective in different contexts. Researchers have focused on many contexts such as technology (Kintana, Alonso and Olaverri, 2006), industry (Datta, Guthrie and Wright, 2005), strategy (Youndt et al., 1996), and country (Lertxundi and Landeta, 2011) to dig deeper to understand when different HR systems are likely to positively and/or negatively impact important organisational outcomes.

2.1.2   An architectural perspective

As the field continued to progress with the evolving strategic HRM focus on HR systems, higher level outcomes, and contingencies, a slightly different emphasis emerged with researchers adopting an architectural perspective within strategic HRM. This architectural perspective explores three interrelated issues – how companies structure their portfolio of internal and external employment arrangements, why some employees within organisations are exposed to high investment human resource systems but others are not, and the performance implications associated with how companies structure their HR architecture.

Lepak and Snell (1999) developed a theoretical framework for how companies make decisions regarding the allocation of work among internal and external employees as well as how they deploy HR systems to manage these different groups of workers. This framework recognises that not all employees are equally valuable to a company's success – different employees within an organisation contribute towards company goals in different ways. Second, companies rely on external labour – temporary employees, contractors, and other contingent workers – in conjunction with a full-time workforce to meet their strategic needs. Third, differences in the role of employees as well as whether or not they are internal or external may account for variability in the use of different HR systems within companies. Lepak and Snell (2002) found support for the HR architectural perspective and Lepak et al. (2007) found that industry impacts how companies structure their HR architecture by influencing the relative level of high investment HR system use for core employees. These findings are particularly important because they suggest that existing research that focuses only on one group of employees in their sampling designs, or research that fails to isolate HR system use for different employees groups, may be inaccurate in their assessments of the use and effects of high investment HR systems. Lastly, Lepak, Takeuchi and Snell (2003) examined the firm level performance benefits associated with how firms structure their portfolio of employment arrangements. The results indicate that extensive use of core knowledge-based employees and/or short-term contract workers is positively associated with enhanced firm performance. Interestingly, these results indicate that an increased reliance on non-core job-based employees and long-term external workers is associated with diminished firm performance.

2.1.3   Digging deeper – multi-level

While researchers continued to explore more traditional strategic HRM and variability in how employees are managed, the mid-2000s witnessed a shift to bring back in more psychological aspects to the research. This integration sought to link HR practices to the attitudes, behaviours, and performance of individual employees, and then back to firm performance. The current iteration of this work is picked up in Chapter 6 on employee engagement by Alan M. Saks and Jamie A. Gruman.

Several theoretical frameworks were published that began to develop the conceptual linkages (Bowen and Ostroff, 2004; Lepak et al., 2006).

Adjacent developments in multi-level theory and empirical methods (Kozlowski and Klein, 2000) further stimulated advancement of multi-level HR research by providing frameworks that could be applied to HR topics.

One focus of this research sought to establish cross-level effects where firm or unit-level HR practices influence individual level employees. This work was primarily focused on mediational processes within strategic HRM models. For example, Takeuchi et al. (2007) examined the role of collective human capital and establishment social exchange norms as key factors that are influenced by HR systems which, in turn, predicted establishment performance. Takeuchi, Chen and Lepak (2009) examined the impact of HR systems on employee perceptions of perceived organisational support which, in turn, impacted important employee satisfaction, commitment, and emotional exhaustion. Nishii, Lepak and Schneider (2008) focused on employee attributions of their organisations' intentions and found that the attributions employees make regarding why certain HR practices are used, even if those attributions differ from stated managerial intentions, impact how employees behave on the job. Liao et al. (2009) found that managers and employees differed in their perceptions of the employee's exposure to HR practices and that employee's perceptions directly impact the extent to which employees demonstrate high levels of customer service in banks.

The second focus of multi-level HR research sought to explore bottom-up effects where employee characteristics and behaviour combine in different ways to create new, higher-level constructs. This bottom-up process is known as *emergence,* and several studies sought to understand how HR practices might shape the emergence of employee characteristics and behaviour. Most of the research on emergence has focused on human capital resources, which are discussed shortly.

2.1.4   Revisiting what HR systems really are

Just as multi-level modelling continues to occupy a greater point of emphasis within the field, several researchers have focused a bit more on the HR system itself and have sought to decompose systems into key underlying mechanisms that drive employee attitudes and behaviours. One model is the AMO model (Jiang et al., 2012a) that refers to aligning HR practices with the three components of employee performance. The logic is that some practices such as selection training and recruitment operate by influencing the abilities (A) of workers are oriented toward (A). Other practices such as compensation, rewards, and performance management are more oriented toward influencing employee motivation (M) to display certain attitudes or behaviours on the job. Still other practices are oriented toward the opportunities (O) employees have to contribute which are influenced by practices such as job design, work design, voice and participation. Jiang et al. (2012b) found that skill-enhancing HR practices were more positively related to human capital and less positively related to employee motivation than motivation-enhancing practices and opportunity-enhancing practices. Moreover, the three dimensions of HR systems were related to financial outcomes both directly and indirectly by influencing human capital and employee motivation as well as voluntary turnover and operational outcomes in sequence.

Another model to decompose HR systems is based on the employee–organisation relationship framework (Tsui et al., 1997). This approach divides HR systems into practices reflecting inducements and investments offered to employees (for example, training and job security) and those reflecting employer expectations on employee performance (for example, pay-for-performance and performance appraisal). Shaw et al. (2009) found that two dimensions of HR systems have different impacts on employee quit rates such that HR inducements and investments help reduce quit rates of both good- and poor-performers, whereas expectation-enhancing practices reduce good-performer quit rates and enhance poor-performer quit rates.

2.2   Looking ahead

2.2.1   Group-level HRM

Traditional strategic HRM research has paid primary attention to HR systems and their performance effects at the organisation level of analysis. Even though work groups and teams have drawn substantial research attention of management scholars (Kozlowski and Bell, 2003) and serve as important work contexts for employees, limited efforts have been exerted to study HR systems in work groups. To enrich future research in this area, we suggest the following directions.

First, more efforts are needed to understand the variance in HR systems across work groups. Researchers have acknowledged the discrepancies between designed HR systems and implemented HR systems and recognised the role of group or first-line managers in implementing HR systems (Nishii and Wright, 2008). Due to the difference in group managers' abilities and motivation to deliver HR systems, it is reasonable to expect that HR systems designed at the organisational level are implemented to different levels in work groups. For example, using a sample of 51 teams of a Korean company, Pak and Kim (in press) found that 33 per cent of the variance in employee experience of HR systems resided between work teams within the same company. This finding shows that work groups account for a significant amount of variance in HR systems. In order to enhance the influence of designed HR systems on group outcomes, it is important to explore the causes of the variance in HR systems across work groups. Jiang (2013) focused on group managers' abilities and motivation to implement HR systems and found that managers who are willing to take HR responsibilities tend to perceive HR systems as planned by organisations and those with more skills and experiences in implementing HR systems are more likely to make employees have similar perceptions of HR systems to managers' own perceptions. Future research can delve into the group-level variance in HR systems by examining other individual differences of group managers or group characteristics.

Second, research attention is needed to identify HR practices that are especially critical for promoting group work. The traditional strategic HRM research focuses on the role of HR systems in promoting employees' abilities, motivation, and opportunities to complete their work in general. However, the past research has not specified what HR practices contribute more to group performance versus individual performance. In order to establish a strong relationship between HR systems and group outcomes, we recommend researchers to develop group-based HR systems and examine how the group-based HR systems are related to group outcomes beyond general high-performance work systems. For example, rather than selecting the best all-around candidate in general, group-based HR systems may emphasise employees' abilities to collaborate and work in teams. Similarly, group-based HR systems may focus on team building and interpersonal relations in addition to improving employees' job skills and abilities in general. Lepak and Snell (2002) have provided some insights into group-based HR systems by proposing a collaborative HR configuration. Chuang, Jackson and Jiang (2016) recently conceptualised and developed an HR system for knowledge-intensive teamwork and set an example for examining HR systems for other types of work groups in the future.

Third, we encourage more research to examine how and when HR systems are related to outcomes at the group level of analysis. Team researchers have proposed and examined several key factors that may affect team effectiveness, including team cognition (DeChurch and Mesmer-Magnus, 2010), team diversity (Joshi and Roh, 2009), team compositions (Bell, 2007), team processes (LePine et al., 2008), team efficacy and potency (Gully et al., 2002), and team conflict (De Dreu and Weingart, 2003). These studies provide opportunities for strategic HRM research to explore how group-level HR systems affect team effectiveness, especially through the mediators that are not commonly examined at the organisation level of analysis. Moreover, strategic HRM researchers can examine how HR systems operate with other critical antecedents of team effectiveness to affect group outcomes. For example, Jiang, Chuang and Chiao (2015) examined the influence of high-performance work systems on customer knowledge and service climate in small service units and found that service leadership substitutes for the positive influence of HR systems on both variables. Future research can look into other factors such as team characteristics and task characteristics to understand the conditions under which HR systems are more likely to improve group outcomes.

Fourth, because traditional strategic HRM focuses on why and how HR systems affect organisational performance and the emerging multi-level HRM research emphasises the cross-level influence of HR systems on individual outcomes, strategic HRM scholars can explore how the group-level factors transfer the impact of organisation-level HR systems on individual-level outcomes and how the individual-level outcomes can be aggregated to contribute to group-level and organisation-level outcomes. Jiang, Takeuchi and Lepak (2013) developed a three-level mediation model involving organisation-, group-, and individual-level analysis and provided a starting point for researchers to examining the mediating role of group-level factors in the cross-level relationship between HR systems and outcomes at different levels.

2.2.2   Time issues in strategic HRM research

Theoretical models of the HR systems–performance relationship suggest that it takes time for organisations to design and implement HR systems, which also need time to influence employee and firm performance (for example, Becker and Huselid, 1998; Lepak et al., 2006). However, the temporal dynamics of the relationship between HR systems and performance outcomes has received little attention and several scholars have expressed the concerns of ignoring temporal issues in strategic HRM research (for example, Lepak et al., in press; Ployhart and Hale, 2014; Wright and Haggerty, 2005). For example, Ployhart and Hale (2014) noted that failing to understand the temporal dynamics makes it difficult to know whether and why the changes in HR systems are related to changes in performance outcomes, and also leaves it unclear about how fast or how long it will take for change to occur. The answers to these questions will not only contribute to theoretical understanding of the causal relationship between HR systems and performance outcomes but also provide more meaningful and actionable implications for managerial practices.

To enrich our understanding of time issues in strategic HRM research, we join other scholars (for example, Lepak et al., in press; Ployhart and Hale, 2014; Wright and Haggerty, 2005) to offer the following directions. First, we encourage more studies on how the changes in HR systems lead to changes in performance outcomes over time. Some recent studies have started to look into this question by using some unique longitudinal datasets (Kim and Ployhart, 2014; Piening, Baluch and Salge, 2013; Shin and Konrad, 2017). For example, using 359 firms with over 12 years of longitudinal firm-level data, Kim and Ployhart (2014) examined whether and why staffing and training influence firm profit growth. By controlling for prior profit in random coefficient growth models, they drew more rigorous conclusions about the causal relationships between the two HR practices and firm profit growth and found that the relationships may differ as a function of economic conditions. Future research can follow this approach to examine the influence of a broader set of HR practices on organisational performance over time. Researchers can also explore the dynamic mediating process by examining how the changes in HR systems are related to the changes in organisational performance through the changes in employee outcomes.

Second, more efforts are also needed to explore the functional form of HR effects over time. Researchers can examine whether the adoption of HR systems has a constant and linear effect on performance outcomes as time passes, or whether the effects of HR systems diminish or grow over time. This may require a field experimental design to examine how performance outcomes change over time after the adoption of HR systems. For example, Banker et al. (1996) examined the impact of work teams on manufacturing performance and found that quality and labour productivity improved over time after the formation of work teams. This study only examined the linear relationship between time after the adoption of work teams and performance outcomes. Future research can contribute to this stream of research by exploring the nonlinear relationship and examining whether additional investments in HR systems may change the performance effects of HR systems over time.

Third, we expect more studies to examine how patterns of change in HR systems are related to performance outcomes. Previous research has proposed different ways for maximising the performance effects of HR systems. On the one hand, researchers have suggested that organisations need to ensure the consistency in HR practices in order to create a strong system to direct employee attitudes and behaviours over time (for example, Bowen and Ostroff, 2004). On the other hand, scholars have suggested that flexibility in HR systems is required to help organisations to adapt to diverse and changing environment (for example, Wright and Snell, 1998). Based on the two perspectives, it is important to understand whether firms should maintain stability or flexibility in HR systems. It is also critical to know whether firms should make continuous incremental changes or episodic radical changes and when firms should make the changes in order to achieve the flexibility in HR systems.

Fourth, future research also needs to study whether the components of HR systems have different impact on employees in certain periods of time. For example, Lepak et al. (in press) proposed that staffing practices may have a strong effect on employees soon after they join a company but the effect may decrease over time. However, employees may be affected by certain pay schemes and/or benefit programmes throughout their career in the company. Providing empirical evidences for these arguments is helpful for organisations to understand when to make investments in specific HR practices to generate greater return on HR investments.

2.2.3   Strategic human capital – a multidisciplinary lens

With the swing of the pendulum, more recently we have witnessed the emergence of a distinct area of research that overlaps with more mainstream strategic HRM research. In this newer area of focus researchers continue to examine "human capital" within the workplace but have done so by blending economics, strategy, HRM, and psychology in the study of strategic human capital. In some ways this is a natural extension of the architectural perspective in that it focuses on the relative contributions different employees (human capital) make towards organisational competitiveness. But within this newer focus, there are several interesting areas of research that continue to push what we know about managing human capital strategically.

Most HR research prior to the late 1990s adopted frameworks that were grounded in Becker's (1964) human capital theory. Research from this perspective gives primary attention to the distinction between generic and specific forms of human capital. Generic human capital is transportable across organisations (for example, cognitive ability), whereas specific human capital is tied to a specific context (for example, firm, work group). Starting with Lepak and Snell (1999), the focus began to shift and recognise different forms of human capital that could exist in different employee groups. This work also began to blend human capital theory (from economics) with resource-based theory in strategy (for example, Barney, 1991) to emphasise the role of human capital for generating competitive advantage. Together, research was beginning to shift from directly linking HR practices to firm performance, to connecting HR practices to firm performance and competitive advantage through human capital resources (for example, Lepak et al., 2006).

The second generation of this research began to take a closer look at the nature of the human capital construct. Specifically, Ployhart and Moliterno (2011) developed a conceptual model explaining how employee knowledge, skill, ability, and other (KSAO) characteristics come to form into human capital resources. Their framework is inherently multi-level and argues that human capital resources emerge from the KSAOs of individual employees. However, human capital resources are not the simple aggregation of individual KSAOs. Rather, there is an emergence enabling process that exists, where the nature of the task environment interacts with emergent states (for example, climate, shared knowledge). The emergence enabling process transforms the individual KSAOs into unique, unit-level resources. Importantly, the human capital resources that emerge are shaped by HR policies and practices.

Concurrent to these theoretical advancements, there had been a sufficient amount of empirical research that enabled narrative and empirical summaries of the human capital literature. Nyberg et al. (2014) summarised over 150 articles on human capital and concluded that there was considerable evidence linking human capital to firm performance. Crook et al. (2011) meta-analysed over 60 empirical studies and found a moderate correlation with firm performance outcomes. However, in a path model, the effect of human capital on operational performance was nearly three times larger (0.32) than the direct effect on firm performance (0.10). Thus, at this point there is pretty consistent theoretical and empirical evidence to suggest human capital is strategically valuable and contributes to firm performance.

2.3   Conclusions

In conclusion, the current evolution of research that we have outlined in this chapter can be seen to be bringing together multiple theoretical disciplines to develop a more comprehensive understanding of human capital. This type of research is important because scholars trained in different disciplinary foundations frequently accept assumptions within one's domain but reject assumptions from other domains, prohibiting a holistic view of human capital (Nyberg and Wright, 2015; Wright, Coff and Moliterno, 2014). Ployhart et al. (2014) integrated theoretical perspectives on human capital from economics, strategy, sociology, and psychology, to provide a typology that distinguishes KSAOs, human capital, human capital resources, and strategic human capital resources. This framework further reconciles some nagging difficulties with applying human capital theory (Becker, 1964) to a more strategic and resource-based view; phenomena the original theory was not intended to explain. In doing so, their paper concludes by noting that nearly all collective human capital resources will be firm-specific because they are based on combinations of individuals within a particular firm and context.

Research on strategic human capital continues to expand in new directions. For example, there is growing attention paid to star employees, who are hypothesised to generate above-normal performance, have broad visibility, and high social capital (Call, Nyberg and Thatcher, 2015; Tzabbar and Kehoe, 2014). Stars present an interesting set of challenges for human capital research: although they are strategically important, they may also capture most of the value they create, and hence not contribute strongly to organisational value capture. Another area that is receiving growing attention is the research on turnover. It is increasingly recognised that turnover represents the erosion of human capital resources (for example, Nyberg and Ployhart, 2013; Park and Shaw,

2013). Research is starting to show that turnover can negate the positive benefits of human capital resources (for example, Kim and Ployhart, 2014). Hence, a final area of research has begun to focus on talent pipelines and the flows of talent into and out of organisations (Reilly et al., 2014; Brymer, Molloy and Gilbert, 2014). This research thus recognises that human capital is a resource that is dynamic and multi-level.

References

Arthur, J.B. 1994. Effects of human resource systems on manufacturing performance and turnover. *Academy of Management Journal*, 37(3): 670–687.

Banker, R.D., Lee, S.Y., Potter, G. and Srinivasan, D. 1996. Contextual analysis of performance impacts of outcome-based incentive compensation. *Academy of Management Journal*, 39(4): 920–948.

Barney, J.B. 1991. Firm resources and sustained competitive advantage. *Journal of Management*, 17(1), 99–120.

Becker, B.E. and Huselid, M.A. 1998. High performance work systems and firm performance: A synthesis of research and managerial implications. In G.R. Ferris (ed.) *Research in Personnel and Human Resources Management* (vol. 16: 53–101). Stamford, CT: JAI Press.

Becker, G.S. 1964. *Human Capital.* New York: Columbia University Press.

Bell, S.T. 2007. Deep-level composition variables as predictors of team performance: A meta-analysis. *Journal of Applied Psychology*, 92(3): 595–615.

Bowen, D.E. and Ostroff, C. 2004. Understanding HRM–firm performance linkages: The role of the "strength" of the HRM system. *Academy of Management Review*, 29(2): 203–221.

Brymer, R.A., Molloy, J.C. and Gilbert, B.A. 2014. Human capital pipelines: Competitive implications of repeated interorganizational hiring. *Journal of Management*, 40(2): 483–508.

Call, M.L., Nyberg, A.J. and Thatcher, S. 2015. Stargazing: An integrative conceptual review, theoretical reconciliation, and extension for star employee research. *Journal of Applied Psychology*, 100(3): 623–640.

Chuang, C.H., Jackson, S.E. and Jiang, Y. 2016. Can knowledge-intensive teamwork be managed? Examining the roles of HRM systems, leadership, and tacit knowledge. *Journal of Management*, 42(2): 524–554.

Crook, T.R., Todd, S.Y., Combs, J.G., Woehr, D.J. and Ketchen Jr, D.J. 2011. Does human capital matter? A meta-analysis of the relationship between human capital and firm performance. *Journal of Applied Psychology*, 96(3): 443–456.

Datta, D.K., Guthrie, J.P. and Wright, P.M. 2005. Human resource management and labor productivity: Does industry matter? *Academy of Management Journal*, 48(1): 135–145.

DeChurch, L.A. and Mesmer-Magnus, J.R. 2010. The cognitive underpinnings of effective teamwork: A meta-analysis. *Journal of Applied Psychology*, 95(1): 32–53.

De Dreu, C.K. and Weingart, L.R. 2003. Task versus relationship conflict, team performance, and team member satisfaction: A meta-analysis. *Journal of Applied Psychology*, 88(4): 741–749.

Gully, S.M., Incalcaterra, K.A., Joshi, A. and Beaubien, J.M. 2002. A meta-analysis of team-efficacy, potency, and performance: Interdependence and level of analysis as moderators of observed relationships. *Journal of Applied Psychology*, 87(5): 819–832.

Huselid, M.A. 1995. The impact of human resource management practices on turnover, productivity, and corporate financial performance. *Academy of Management Journal*, 38(3): 635–672.

Jiang, K. 2013. Bridging the gap between reality and perception: Managers' role in shaping employee perceptions of high performance work systems (Doctoral dissertation, Rutgers University, Graduate School–New Brunswick).

Jiang, K., Chuang, C.H. and Chiao, Y.C. 2015. Developing collective customer knowledge and service climate: The interaction between service-oriented high-performance work systems and service leadership. *Journal of Applied Psychology*, 100(4): 1089–1106.

Jiang, K., Lepak, D.P., Han, K., Hong, Y., Kim, A. and Winkler, A.L. 2012a. Clarifying the construct of human resource systems: Relating human resource management to employee performance. *Human Resource Management Review*, 22(2): 73–85.

Jiang, K., Lepak, D.P., Hu, J. and Baer, J. 2012b. How does human resource management influence organizational outcomes? A meta-analytic investigation of the mediating mechanism. *Academy of Management Journal*, 55(6): 1264–1294.

Jiang, K., Takeuchi, R. and Lepak, D.P. 2013. Where do we go from here? New perspectives on the black box in strategic human resource management research. *Journal of Management Studies*, 50(8): 1448–1480.

Joshi, A. and Roh, H. 2009. The role of context in work team diversity research: A meta-analytic review. *Academy of Management Journal*, 52(3): 599–627.

Kim, Y. and Ployhart, R.E. 2014. The effects of staffing and training on firm productivity and profit growth before, during, and after the Great Recession. *Journal of Applied Psychology*, 99(3): 361–389.

Kintana, M.L., Alonso, A.U. and Olaverri, C.G. 2006. High-performance work systems and firms' operational performance: The moderating role of technology. *The International Journal of Human Resource Management*, 17(1): 70–85.

Koch, M.J. and McGrath, R.G. 1996. Improving labor productivity: Human resource management policies do matter. *Strategic Management Journal*, 17(5): 335–354.

Kozlowski, S.W.J. and Bell, B.S. 2003. Work groups and teams in organizations. In W.C. Borman, D.R. Ilgen and R.J. Klimoski (eds) *Handbook of Psychology (vol. 12): Industrial and Organizational Psychology* (pp. 333–375). New York: Wiley.

Kozlowski, S.W.J. and Klein, K.J. 2000. A multilevel approach to theory and research in organizations: Contextual, temporal, and emergent processes. In K.J. Klein and S.W.J. Kozlowski (eds) *Multilevel Theory, Research, and Methods in Organizations* (pp. 3–90). San Francisco, CA: Jossey-Bass.

Lepak, D.P., Jiang, K., Kehoe, R. and Bentley, S. in press. Strategic HR and organizational performance. To appear in N. Anderson, D.S. Ones, H.K. Sinangil and C. Viswesvaran (eds) *Handbook of Industrial, Work and Organizational Psychology* (2nd edition). London: Sage.

Lepak, D.P., Liao, H., Chung, Y. and Harden, E. 2006. A conceptual review of human resource management systems in strategic human resource management research. In J. Martocchio (ed.) *Research in Personnel and Human Resource Management* (pp. 217–271). Stamford, CT: JAI Press.

Lepak, D.P. and Snell, S.A. 1999. The human resource architecture: Toward a theory of human capital allocation and development. *Academy of Management Review*, 24: 31–48.

Lepak, D.P. and Snell, S.A. 2002. Examining the human resource architecture: The relationships among human capital, employment, and human resource configurations. *Journal of Management*, 28(4): 517–554.

Lepak, D.P., Takeuchi, R. and Snell, S.A. 2003. Employment flexibility and firm performance: Examining the interaction effects of employment mode, environmental dynamism, and technological intensity. *Journal of Management*, 29(5): 681–703.

Lepak, D.P., Taylor, S.M., Tekleab, A.G., Marrone, J.M. and Cohen, D. 2007. Examining variability in high investment human resource system use across employee groups, establishments, and industries. *Human Resource Management*, 46(2): 223–246.

LePine, J.A., Piccolo, R.F., Jackson, C.L., Mathieu, J.E. and Saul, J.R. 2008. A meta-analysis of teamwork processes: Tests of a multidimensional model and relationships with team effectiveness criteria. *Personnel Psychology*, 61(2): 273–307.

Lertxundi, A. and Landeta, J. 2011. The moderating effect of cultural context in the relation between HPWS and performance: An exploratory study in Spanish multinational companies. *The International Journal of Human Resource Management*, 22(18): 3949–3967.

Liao, H., Toya, K., Lepak, D.P. and Hong, Y. 2009. Do they see eye to eye? Management and employee perspectives of high-performance work systems and influence processes on service quality. *Journal of Applied Psychology*, 94(2): 371–391.

Nishii, L.H., Lepak, D.P. and Schneider, B. 2008. Employee attributions of the "why" of HR practices: Their effects on employee attitudes and behaviors, and customer satisfaction. *Personnel Psychology*, 61(3): 503–545.

Nishii, L.H. and Wright, P. 2008. Variability at multiple levels of analysis: Implications for strategic human resource management. In D.B. Smith (ed.) *The People Make the Place* (pp. 225–248). Mahwah, NJ: Lawrence Erlbaum Associates.

Nyberg, A., Moliterno, T., Hale, D. and Lepak, D.P. 2014. Resource-based perspectives on unit-level human capital: A review and integration. *Journal of Management*, 40(1): 316–346.

Nyberg, A.J. and Ployhart, R.E. 2013. Context-emergent turnover (CET) theory: A theory of collective turnover. *Academy of Management Review*, 38(1): 109–131.

Nyberg, A.J. and Wright, P.M. 2015. 50 years of human capital research: Assessing what we know, exploring where we go. *Academy of Management Perspectives*, 29(3): 287–295.

Pak, J. and Kim, S. in press. Team manager's implementation, high performance work systems intensity, and performance: A multilevel investigation. *Journal of Management*.

Park, T.Y. and Shaw, J.D. 2013. Turnover rates and organizational performance: A meta-analysis. *Journal of Applied Psychology*, 98(2): 268–309.

Piening, E.P., Baluch, A.M. and Salge, T.O. 2013. The relationship between employees' perceptions of human resource systems and organizational performance: Examining mediating mechanisms and temporal dynamics. *Journal of Applied Psychology*, 98(6): 926-947.

Ployhart, R.E. and Hale, D. 2014. Human resource management is out of time. In A.J. Shipp and Y. Fried (eds) *Time and Work: How Time Impacts Groups, Organizations and Methodological Choices* (vol. 2, pp.76-96). London: Psychology Press.

Ployhart, R.E. and Moliterno, T.P. 2011. Emergence of the human capital resource: A multilevel model. *Academy of Management Review*, 36(1): 127-150.

Ployhart, R.E., Nyberg, A.J., Reilly, G. and Maltarich, M.A. 2014. Human capital is dead; long live human capital resources! *Journal of Management*, 40(2): 371-398.

Reilly, G., Nyberg, A.J., Maltarich, M. and Weller, I. 2014. Human capital flows: Using context-emergent turnover (CET) theory to explore the process by which turnover, hiring, and job demands affect patient satisfaction. *Academy of Management Journal*, 57(3): 766-790.

Shaw, J.D., Dineen, B.R., Fang, R. and Vellella, R.F. 2009. Employee–organization exchange relationships, HRM practices, and quit rates of good and poor performers. *Academy of Management Journal*, 52(5): 1016-1033.

Shaw, J.D., Gupta, N. and Delery, J.E. 2001. Congruence between technology and compensation systems: Implications for strategy implementation. *Strategic Management Journal*, 22(4): 379-386.

Shin, D. and Konrad, A.M. 2017. Causality between high-performance work systems and organizational performance. *Journal of Management*, 43(4): 973-997.

Takeuchi, R., Chen, G., and Lepak, D.P. 2009. Through the looking glass of a social system: Cross-level mediating effects of high performance work systems on employee attitudes. *Personnel Psychology*, 62(1): 1-29.

Takeuchi, R., Lepak, D.P., Wang, H. and Takeuchi, K. 2007. An empirical examination of the mechanisms mediating between high performance work systems and performance of Japanese organizations. *Journal of Applied Psychology*, 92(4): 1069-1083.

Terpstra, D.E. and Rozell, E.J. 1993. The relationship of staffing practices to organizational level measures of performance. *Personnel Psychology*, 46(1): 27-48.

Tsui, A.S., Pearce, J.L., Porter, L.W. and Tripoli, A.M. 1997. Alternative approaches to the employee–organization relationship: Does investment in employees pay off? *Academy of Management Journal*, 40(5): 1089-1121.

Tzabbar, D. and Kehoe, R.R. 2014. Can opportunity emerge from disarray? An examination of exploration and exploitation following star scientist turnover. *Journal of Management*, 40(2): 449–482.

Wright, P.M., Coff, R. and Moliterno, T.P. 2014. Special Issue Editorial: Strategic human capital: Crossing the great divide. In *Special Issue: Strategic Human Capital*. Edited by P.M. Wright, R. Coff and T.P. Moliterno. *Journal of Management*, 40(2): 353-370.

Wright, P.M. and Haggerty, J.J. 2005. Missing variables in theories of strategic human resource management: Time, cause, and individuals. *Management Revue*, 18: 164-173.

Wright, P.M. and Snell, S.A. 1998. Toward a unifying framework for exploring fit and flexibility in strategic human resource management. *Academy of Management Review*, 23(4): 756–772.

Youndt, M.A., Snell, S.A., Dean, J.W. and Lepak, D.P. 1996. Human resource management, manufacturing strategy, and firm performance. *Academy of Management Journal*, 39(4): 836–866.

3   Talent management

David G. Collings, Anthony McDonnell and John McMackin

3.1   Introduction

Talent management (TM) has arguably brought the people agenda into focus for the C-suite to a degree far greater than has been the case in the past. The current interest in talent management is generally traced to the publication of a report on the "War for Talent" by a group of McKinsey consultants in the mid-1990s (Chambers et al., 1998). The hype created by this report was legitimised by high profile advocates such as the then CEO of General Electric Jack Welch. Over the past two decades the interest in talent management has not diminished (Collings, Mellahi and Cascio, 2017; Sparrow, Scullion and Tarique, 2014). While from an academic perspective there is more consistency in terms of how talent management is defined (Gallardo-Gallardo et al., 2015) there is not universal agreement around its conceptual and intellectual boundaries. There is equally a lack of clarity of how to operationalise talent management within the practitioner community. For example, 93 per cent of CEOs surveyed in a recent study recognised the need to change their talent strategies. However, when asked how well-prepared HR was to engage with these key challenges, only 34 per cent felt that HR was sufficiently ready and 9 per cent said it was not prepared at all to lead this effort (PwC, 2014).

This chapter aims to evaluate the current state of the literature on talent management to establish the key trends in extant research in the area. Having reviewed this literature we identify three key trends which we argue are likely to drive the talent agenda from a research perspective and also in practice over the coming years. The three areas we focus on are:

1. Identifying talent in the absence of performance ratings;
2. The shifting boundaries of talent management in light of the gig economy; and
3. The lean talent agenda.

Clearly this list is not exhaustive but it represents three of the key issues that we consider as potentially driving the talent agenda moving forward.

3.2   Review of the talent management literature

The importance placed on managing talent by organisational leaders can explain the burgeoning interest in the area over the past decade (see for example the multiple special issues at the *Asia Pacific Journal of Human Resources, International Journal of Human Resource Management, Journal of World Business*). While the literature is at best described as in early adolescence, the base is fast changing. However, the development has been rather haphazard owing to a lack of consensus on the parameters or boundaries of the field (Cappelli and Keller, 2014; 2017). Detailed reviews on the field of talent management have been written by Cappelli and Keller (2014), Dries (2013b), Gallardo-Gallardo et al. (2015), Lewis and Heckman (2006), McDonnell et al. (2017), and Thunnissen, Boselie and Fruytier (2013). This has led to talent management being viewed as largely phenomenon-driven with limited theoretical grounding (Dries, 2013b). Notwithstanding the criticisms around conceptual and theoretical development, empirically the field has more recently started to take hold with a notable increase in empirical work (McDonnell et al., 2017). However, the quality, focus and sophistication of some of the empirical work is open to question.

3.2.1   What is talent management?

As a relatively new field of academic enquiry it is unsurprising that the early attention focused on defining what talent management actually means (Lewis and Heckman, 2006; Collings and Mellahi, 2009; McDonnell et al., 2017). The lack of agreement led to almost every published paper opening with a statement along the lines of there being a "disturbing lack of clarity regarding the definition, scope and overall goals of talent management" (Lewis and Heckman, 2006). The field has moved on considerably since Lewis and Heckman's (2006) pioneering article that summarised three approaches to talent management evident in the academic and practitioner literature at that time. The first perspective they identified was a simple rebranding of human resource management as talent management. The rebranding viewpoint is still evidenced in some practitioner literature, although Cappelli and Keller (2014) have argued that the academic literature has advanced beyond this with clear attempts to differentiate between talent management and human resource management. The second perspective viewed talent management as focused on loading the organisation with A-players and managing poorly performing staff (or C-players) out of the organisation. This approach was pioneered by advocates such as Jack Welch at GE. The third approach they identified as foregrounding talent pools of high performing and high potential employees who had been identified to move into future senior leadership roles. Later work identified a fourth approach whereby talent management was viewed as being about the most pivotal or strategic positions (Collings and Mellahi, 2009). These positions are defined by their centrality to organisational strategy combined with the potential for significant variation in output or value added between a high performer and an average performer deployed in the role (Boudreau and Ramstad, 2007; Huselid, Beatty and Becker, 2005).

While the academic literature has not reached consensus on a single definition of talent management, Collings and Mellahi's (2009: 304) definition has been demonstrated to be the most widely adopted definition in the literature (see Gallardo-Gallardo et al., 2015). They define strategic talent management as:

> ... activities and processes that involve the systematic identification of key positions which differentially contribute to the organisation's sustainable competitive advantage, the development of a talent pool of high potential and high performing incumbents to fill these roles, and the development of a differentiated human resource architecture to facilitate filling these positions with competent incumbents and to ensure their continued commitment to the organisation.

This definition advocates a more exclusive approach to talent management with a focus on particular segments of the workforce. This stands in contrast to more inclusive approaches where all employees are considered as equally valuable to the organisation. The level of exclusivity of talent programmes has been one of the central debates in the literature thus far. While some challenge the perceived "elitist" underpinning of differentiated talent management systems, suggesting that those in non-critical roles receive no investment, the focus should be on making informed decisions around the optimum level of talent required in these roles (Huselid and Becker, 2011) and the appropriate level of HR investment for individuals in those roles. Indeed, given the broad recognition of the positive impact of investment in HR more widely, we advocate a high baseline investment in the organisation's workforce (Collings and Mellahi, 2013).

This definition also emphasises a focus on critical roles as opposed to talent in isolation which contrasts with the focus of early work on talent management which focused on A-players. Research has demonstrated the disproportionate contribution that high performing employees can make (for example, O'Boyle and Kroska, 2017) but the role one occupies may of course moderate the value that can be created. Collings and Mellahi's definition recognises that certain roles are more central or critical to organisational performance than others (Hunter, Schmidt and Judiesch, 1990). Roles characterised by centrality to organisational strategy and where there is significant variation in the output between an average and top performer are emphasised (Boudreau and Ramstad, 2007). So before focusing on individual talent, one needs to establish where talent can have the greatest impact on organisational outcomes. Focusing solely on individual stars risks an over-investment in areas or roles that don't have the potential to generate additionally value. A key challenge for organisations then centres on the capacity to identify the pivotal or strategic roles. In the context of pivotal positions, it is important that organisations consider roles outside of senior leadership (which are often pivotal) but to consider their strategic objectives in delineating the other strategic roles that may exist (McDonnell et al., 2016).

3.2.2 What is meant by talent?

In exploring the wider literature on TM, a separate line of literature has focused on the question of what constitutes talent in the context of talent management. Indeed, the talent management literature appears to have focused limited explicit attention on how talent is defined, with the predominant focus instead being on talent management practices and their impact on organisational outcomes. Tansley (2011) has noted that overall there appears to be little precision in academic studies and amongst practitioners around the definition of "talent". There is, however, a parallel literature on star employees which is apposite in this regard (see for example O'Boyle and Kroska, 2017 for an up-to-date review). For some, talent merely means people, while the term has also been used synonymously with high potentials and/or high performers. Recent reviews (Meyers, van Woerkom and Dries, 2013; Gallardo-Gallardo, Dries and González-Cruz, 2013) have considered the question of how talent is defined. Although there is wide variation in approaches, the key commonalities that emerge see talent viewed in terms of it being an object or a subject and the extent to which an inclusive or exclusive perspective is adopted (Gallardo-Gallardo, Dries and González-Cruz, 2013). The subject approach sees all employees viewed as talent (inclusive) whereby every individual's strengths should be harnessed for the organisation's benefit, vis-à-vis the elite approach that views a subset of the workforce as comparatively more important than everyone else in terms of the value they add to corporate performance. Under the object approach, talent emphasises individual characteristics (for example, ability, competence, performance, behaviours). From this perspective, talent can refer to natural ability or innateness; the mastery of particular competences; possessing commitment to the work at hand and to the organisation; and fit to the particular context as an individual may not perform in the same way across every situation or context (Gallardo-Gallardo, Dries and González-Cruz, 2013).

A key challenge for organisations is in establishing how they define talent and ensuring an objective, fair, and transparent process of identification is utilised. A failure in this regard may lead to negative outcomes with recent empirical work articulating the importance of transparency in talent identification (for example, Dries, 2013a; Gelens et al., 2014). One of the foremost implications from this research is that transparency in the identification process is imperative in improving perceptions around distributive justice amongst employees who are not identified as talents. Failure to do so may lead to a range of negative outcomes such as demotivation amongst those who did not make it into the talent management programme and/or view the processes as flawed and unfair. This is illustrated in Björkman et al.'s (2013) research on how those designated as "talent" compare with those who are not, on a range of outcomes. They found that individuals who perceive that they are viewed as a talent vis-à-vis those that were not, demonstrated greater commitment to improving their performance, had greater levels of organisational identification, lower turnover intention and were more supportive of the corporate objectives. Overall, there appeared to be a strong motivational effect associated with being classified as talent. However, the research is not conclusive on the positive impacts of exclusive approaches to talent management on employee outcomes and more research is certainly required on this topic (see for example Collings, Mellahi and Cascio, 2017; Meyers, De Boeck and Dries, 2017).

3.3   Talent management: a research agenda

The preceding review has highlighted how our understanding of talent management has progressed over the past two decades. While progress is evident, the topography of the area is constantly evolving and in this section we identify three key trends which we believe represent important elements of the research agenda in talent management.

3.3.1   Talent management in the context of performance management

The first issue which we consider is the changing landscape of performance management (PM). This is significant as almost every model of talent management is to a degree predicated on identifying high performing employees, often in collaboration with high potential (see Gallardo-Gallardo, Dries and González-Cruz, 2013 Nijs et al., 2014. Performance management and appraisal generally play key roles in informing these decisions. Following (Aguinis, 2013: 2) we define performance management as:

> ... a continuing process of identifying, measuring, and developing the performance of individuals and teams and aligning performance with the strategic goals of the organisation.

Performance management is almost universally recognised as a key HR practice. Reflective of this, most organisations around the world utilise performance management techniques to some extent; for example, a survey of almost 1000 professionals in Australia found that 96 per cent of companies implement some form of PM (Aguinis and Pierce, 2008).

However, it is clear that practitioners continue to struggle with designing a consistently effective PM process. A 2014 CIPD report found that almost a third of employees (30 per cent) believed their current PM system to be unfair. Recent findings from professional services firm Towers Watson, showed that nearly half (45 per cent) of the surveyed companies say their managers don't see the value in performance management. During 2015, over 50 major US employers including Netflix, Microsoft, Accenture and Deloitte, announced that they were undertaking a radical overhaul of their performance management processes, including, in many cases, discarding the traditional annual performance "rating" (Buckingham and Goodall, 2015). However, it is important to note that there is little empirical evidence of the extent to which organisations are actually moving away from ratings in performance management. Anecdotal evidence suggests that the trend is towards incremental changes in performance management rather than the wholesale changes suggested by the high profile organisations identified above. Nonetheless, while challenges around the accuracy of performance evaluations have long been recognised (see DeNisi and Smith, 2014) a shift away from the use of formal performance evaluations in the talent identification process raises important questions for talent management. For example, how is high performance conceptualised and calibrated? Who is best placed to evaluate this performance? How do organisations minimise the biases and challenges which are well recognised in traditional critiques of performance evaluation?

A second key theme around performance management which merits consideration is the nature and distribution of performance in organisations. In this regard, much of the literature on high performance and certainly tracing back to the McKinsey work on the "War for Talent" is premised on the idea that performance is normally distributed amongst employees in organisations. This suggests that the majority of employees perform at an average level while very few actually achieve levels of performance associated with being a star (Aguinis and Bradley, 2015; O'Boyle and Kroska, 2017). This thinking was central to practices such as forced performance distribution and is central to many tools of performance management. More recent research presents a strong case that performance does not in fact follow a normal distribution and rather is subject to a Paretin or power distribution (O'Boyle and Kroska, 2017). In simple terms this research suggests that around 20 per cent of employees generate about 80 per cent of output. This means that there are potentially more stars than a normal distribution would suggest owing to the longer "tail". This distribution also has significant implications for where the "mean" of performance lies in the workplace. The presence of star performers shifts the average to the right of the distribution compared to a normal distribution. Hence a far greater percentage of performers fall below the mean. This perspective highlights how, to date, PM has been operating under the assumptions of a normal distribution and has a number of implications for performance management. For example, forcing a normal distribution on performance scores might result in a number of high performers being designated as average. Obviously this could have significant demoralising effects. More broadly this suggests a research agenda in exploring how a changed understanding of performance may influence talent management systems and processes and how this may translate into sustainable organisational effectiveness and performance.

3.3.2   Talent management in the context of contingent employment

The challenges which organisations face in attracting the quality and quantity of talent required to deliver on their strategic intent are well recognised. Indeed, a report by the CBI in the UK identified talent retention and skills gaps as the second and third key challenges for businesses in London in 2016, topped only by uncertainty over the potential implications of Brexit at that time. While the McKinsey Global Institute predicts that by 2020 the global shortage of college-educated skilled workers could reach 40 million vacancies. These are real challenges for organisations and forcing many to re-evaluate how they manage their talent programmes. At a broader level there is also widespread recognition that the nature of business and employment are changing and significantly impacting on how organisations compete and deliver their strategy and mission (Boudreau, Jesuthasan and Creelman, 2015). Concomitantly, the futurist Jacob Morgan identifies five key trends which will shape the nature of work in the future. These include:

1. New behaviours – which affect how we collaborate and share information and challenge how employees work and what they expect from an organisation.
2. Technology – such as the shift to the cloud which reduces the requirement for colocation in technology deployment and upgrade. Collaboration platforms have important implications for connecting and engaging people any time, anywhere and on any device. Big data (see Chapter 9) also facilitates better decision-making, a trend which will increase exponentially with the emergence of the Internet of things.
3. The millennial workforce – have introduced new behaviours, approaches, attitudes and expectations about the nature of the workplace which arguably spill over to other generations.
4. Mobility – employment is much less location dependent. Remote

working allows employees to work and collaborate regardless of location.

5. Globalisation (see Chapter 12) – means talent doesn't need to be local. Talent markets operate on a global basis and technology facilitates global collaboration.

These and other trends have challenged organisations to become nimble and competitive and to seek out expert talent in a variety of ways that fall outside the traditional employment model (Bidwell et al., 2013). These trends question the traditional talent model of relying solely on full time employees which it is argued was a response to the needs of a particular historical period (Younger and Smallwood, 2016). Indeed, the business case for contingent workers is supported by some preliminary research evidence that the use of outsourcing and contingent work has benefited employers (see Bidwell et al., 2013). However, the research on this is limited and we do need further study around the potential negative impacts of these relationships.

Therefore, another key trend which we identify relates to the shifting boundaries of talent management and particularly the emergence and increased potential of the so-called gig economy. As will be made clear in the next chapter, there are important questions around risk and compliance in these contingent workforces, how to effectively manage and lead in these contexts all require further elaboration. However, there are also some interesting insights from research concerns the quality and quantity of talent available through atypical relationships. While it is difficult to have an accurate sense of the scale of these atypical arrangements, European data suggest that approximately 32 per cent of workers had some sort of a contingent work arrangement (Maselli, Lenaerts and Beblavy, 2016). Other estimates are even higher ranging up to 50 per cent (Younger, Patterson and Younger, 2015). Some 7.4 per cent of the US population constitute independent contractors alone (Bidwell and Briscoe, 2009). UK data suggests that the freelance workforce there has expanded from 1.04 million workers in 1992 to 1.91 million in 2015 (Kitching, 2015). Hence there is a significant pool of labour available across the globe. This research confirms that individuals often pursue contractor type arrangements by choice bringing highly skilled and experienced contractors with in-demand skills into the labour market (Bidwell and Briscoe, 2009). Hence, from an organisational perspective these alternative talent platforms provide access to high quality talent globally, maximise the deployment of core employees to focus on key tasks, provide access to talent and skills when scaling, facilitate agility in accessing skills as required, and also help costs. We know far less about how to engage this talent and how to maximise their contribution to sustainable organisation performance (c.f. Boudreau, Jesuthasan and Creelman, 2015; Younger and Smallwood, 2016).

3.3.3   Talent management in the context of lean management

The final theme which we identify resonates with the increasing shift towards lean organisation. We have noted the importance of understanding the link between key roles and the scope for individual talent. However, the nature of roles themselves can be subject to other mantras. What happens to the contribution that talent can make as organisations "lean" their processes? Lean is an operational strategy which originated in the car manufacturing industry. A system that was initially solely applied within Toyota, the Toyota Production System (Ohno, 1988) has developed into "lean" and has been widely adopted by manufacturing business globally. In more recent years the lean promise of increasing productivity and quality while reducing cost has led to widespread adoption of lean practices in a wide range of business contexts, notably software development and financial services but also in contexts as diverse as emergency departments (Fillingham, 2007) and business schools (Radnor and Bucci, 2010). Since operations typically account for a high proportion of employees in any organisation, an understanding of the HR and talent implications of lean is a key question for practitioners and researchers alike which remains underexplored. Furthermore, the potential of insights from talent management to inform lean strategies has heretofore been neglected.

In considering talent management in the context of lean, one key challenge for researchers concerns the development of a shared definition of lean. In particular, conceptual confusion arises from the range of terms used to describe different aspects of lean. At a high level, lean can be defined as a "multidimensional approach to manufacturing which encompasses a wide range of management practices within an integrated socio-technical system dedicated to minimising waste" (Shah and Ward, 2007: 791).

For those not familiar with the concept, we suggest that lean can best be understood in terms of three levels of abstraction – lean philosophy, lean methods and lean tools and activities. At the highest level, lean is a philosophy of work – a set of values, an approach. Rejecting manufacturing philosophies based on economies of scale and large-scale production, Ohno (1988: ix) maintained that productivity was created through flow. Lean methods are used to realise an organisation's lean philosophy. Examples of lean methods include six sigma (developed first by Motorola in the 1980s), agile, scrum, lean startup, and lean software development (see Shah and Ward, 2007 for a review). So lean is not six sigma or lean/agile, but six sigma and lean/agile are lean. They are lean methodologies. They are context specific implementations of a lean operational strategy.

Finally, lean tools are used to implement lean methods. Examples of lean tools include 5s (organising the work area); Kanban boards (used to improve productivity by offering a live visual image of the work flow to regulate supply and demand); and root cause analysis.

Enhanced conceptual clarity and the widespread adoption of lean practices have generated interest from HR researchers more widely in the implications of lean adoption for employees and the people who manage them. One key insight from this literature is the requirement for the talent management strategy to be aligned with a lean operational strategy in order for lean to deliver sustainable value for the organisation (Liker and Morgan, 2006: 12). The logic underpinning this argument is compelling. Adoption of lean practices imposes specific behavioural requirements on employees and managers that in many cases are radically different from expectations of these roles in more traditional operational environments. Key employee and managerial implications of a lean operational strategy include interdependent teamwork, decision-making at team level based on customer feedback, cross training for depth and breadth of technical skills, continuous learning and innovation, and customer focus. The critical importance of aligning talent management systems with the behavioural requirements of a lean environment is now also recognised by practitioners:

> Getting people matters right is essential for any serious lean-management effort, for ultimately much of the point of a transformation is to help people achieve more – build their capabilities, increase their capacity, intensify their engagement, and develop deeper connections between purpose and meaning. Accordingly, in conversations with business and HR leaders at some of lean management's most experienced organisations, a consistent theme has been the importance of HR both to the transformation process and to the changes' long-term sustainability (McKinsey & Co., 2014: 80).

There is a tradition of research on people issues in lean environments. Interestingly, McDuffie's (1995) seminal work on bundles of HR practices was conducted in automotive plants using lean practices. It is now widely accepted that piecemeal adoption of HR practices may in fact lead to "deadly combinations" of HR practices that neutralise each other – for example, team based work design combined with individual performance management and rewards (Becker et al., 2007). More broadly there has been some HR focused research in the lean context. For example, Martínez-Jurado, Moyano-Fuentes and Gómez (2013) found that five areas of HR practice – training, communication, rewards, job design and work organisation – were of particular importance in the introduction of lean practices in a case study of the aeronautics industry. De Treville and Antonakis (2006) assessed the relationship between lean practices and job design. Cullinane et al. (2014) investigated the implications for employee motivation and well-being of operating in a high involvement, fast paced, lean environment. Applying Bakker and Demerouti's (2007) Job Demands–Resources model, they found that the relatively high level of job demands in a lean environment may require higher levels of job resources in order to sustain employee motivation and well-being. However, this research is premised on a relatively standardised approach to HR, with little attention to differentiation in talent management thus far. This means there is potentially much value left on the table in lean environments owing to the failure to understand the potential value of differentiated talent management systems. We propose that a significant opportunity now exists for the development of a talent management research agenda that will address the question: What talent management strategies are required to support the successful and sustainable implementation of lean? More specifically, what combinations, bundles or systems of talent management practices are needed to support the behaviours of managers and employees required for sustainable lean transformation? What roles are of most central importance to performance in a lean operating environment? What leadership and managerial competencies are needed for high performance in a lean environment? How can talent with these competencies be attracted, retained, motivated and developed?

3.4   Conclusions

Talent management has become one of the hottest topics in management research and practice over the past two decades. However, the area has struggled to gain academic legitimacy over that time owing to concerns over its conceptual and intellectual boundaries. This is not unusual in areas that have their roots in practice. However, our understanding of the topic has certainly advanced over more recent years as the quality and quantity of empirical evidence in the area has begun to improve (Collings, Mellahi and Cascio, 2017; McDonnell et al., 2016; Sparrow, Scullion and Tarique, 2014). However, as an academic field of enquiry there is much scope for further development.

In this chapter we have pointed to three key issues which could inform the research agenda for the area moving forward. Specifically, we point to the requirement to better understand the measurement of performance as an input into talent management decisions in organisations which are reframing their performance management practices, and particularly those which are moving away from performance ratings. Second, we point to the changing boundaries of organisations and the shift to the gig economy. While this offers great potential for expanding the available talent pool and offers organisations greater agility in addressing talent priorities they also bring risks. We require academic work to build on early insights (see Boudreau, Jesuthasan and Creelman, 2015; Younger and Smallwood, 2016) around the issues of risk and compliance in the context of these contracted talent relationships and how organisations manage the recruitment, retention and engagement in these non-traditional talent marketplaces. Finally, given the proliferation of lean methodologies in organisations, we flag the failure to consider questions of talent management in these contexts as a key gap in our understanding of talent management and as a potential limitation in the implementation of lean methodologies.

As talent management has maintained a strong profile amongst c-suite leaders in organisations for over two decades and there is little to indicate that this interest is likely to diminish in the near future, there is a strong requirement for further empirical work in this field. Thus the current chapter is a call to action for a research agenda which reflects the key challenges which organisations are facing in the talent space.

References

Aguinis, H. (2013). *Performance Management: Pearson New International Edition.* London: Pearson Higher Education.

Aguinis, H. and Bradley, K.J. (2015). The secret sauce for organizational success. *Organizational Dynamics*, 44: 161–168.

Aguinis, H. and Pierce, C. A. (2008). Enhancing the relevance of organizational behavior by embracing performance management research. *Journal of Organizational Behavior*, 29(1): 139–145.

Bakker, A.B. and Demerouti, E. (2007). The job demands-resources model: State of the art. *Journal of Managerial Psychology*, 22: 309–328.

Becker, B., Huselid, M., Pickus, P. and Spratt, M. (2007). HR as a source of shareholder value: Research and recommendations. *Human Resource Management*, 36(1): 39–47.

Bidwell, M. and Briscoe, F. (2009). Who contracts? Determinants of the decision to work as an independent contractor among information technology workers. *Academy of Management Journal*, 52(6): 1148–1168.

Bidwell, M., Briscoe, F., Fernandez-Mateo, I. and Sterling, A. (2013). Changing employment relationships and inequality: Causes and consequences. *Academy of Management Annals*, 7(1): 61–121.

Björkman, I., Ehrnrooth, M., Mäkelä, K., Smale, A. and Sumelius, J. (2013). Talent or not? Employee reactions to talent identification. *Human Resource Management*, 52(2): 195–214.

Boudreau, J.W., Jesuthasan, R. and Creelman, D. (2015). *Lead the Work: Navigating a World Beyond Work and Employment.* New York: Wiley.

Boudreau, J.W. and Ramstad, P.M. (2007). *Beyond HR: The New Science of Human Capital.* Boston, MA: Harvard Business School Press.

Buckingham, M. and Goodall, A. (2015). Reinventing performance management. *Harvard Business Review*, 93(4): 40–50.

Cappelli, P. and Keller, J.R. (2014). Talent management: Conceptual approaches and practical challenges. *Annual Review of Organizational Psychology and Organizational Behavior*, 1: 305–331.

Cappelli, P. and Keller, J.R. (2017). The historical context of talent management. In D.G. Collings, K. Mellahi and W.F. Cascio (eds) *The Oxford Handbook of Talent Management* (Chapter 2). Oxford: Oxford University Press.

Chambers, E.G., Fouldon, M.F. Handfield-Jones, H., Hankin, S. and Michaels III, E. (1998). The war for talent. *The McKinsey Quarterly*, 3: 44–97.

Collings, D.G. and Mellahi, K. (2009). Strategic talent management: A review and research agenda. *Human Resource Management Review*, 19(4): 304–313.

Collings, D.G. and Mellahi, K. (2013). Commentary on: "Talent – innate or acquired? Theoretical considerations and their implications for talent management", *Human Resource Management Review*, 24(3): 322–325.

Collings, D.G., Mellahi, K. and Cascio, W.F. (eds) (2017). *The Oxford Handbook of Talent Management.* Oxford: Oxford University Press.

Cullinane, S-J., Bosak, J., Flood, P. and Demerouti, E. (2014). Job design under lean manufacturing and the quality of working life: A job demands and resources perspective. *The International Journal of Human Resource Management*, 25: 21.

DeNisi, A. and Smith, C.E. (2014). Performance appraisal, performance management, and firm-level performance: A review, a proposed model, and new directions for future research. *Academy of Management Annals*, 8(1): 127–179.

de Treville, S. and Antonakis, J. (2006). Could lean production job design be intrinsically motivating? Contextual, configurational, and levels-of-analysis issues. *Journal of Operations Management*, 24(2): 99–123.

Dries, N. (2013a). Special issue: Talent management, from phenomenon to theory. *Human Resource Management Review*, 23: 267–271.

Dries, N. (2013b). The psychology of talent management: A review and research agenda, *Human Resource Management Review*, 23: 272–285.

Fillingham, D. (2007). Can lean save lives? *Leadership in Health Services*, 20(4): 231–241.

Gallardo-Gallardo, E., Dries, N. and González-Cruz, T.F. (2013). What is the meaning of "talent" in the world of work? *Human Resource Management Review*, 23(4): 290–300.

Gallardo-Gallardo, E., Nijs, S., Dries, N. and Gallo, P. (2015). Towards an understanding of talent management as a phenomenon-driven field using bibliometric and content analysis. *Human Resource Management Review*, 25(3): 264–279.

Gelens, J., Hofmans, J., Dries, N. and Pepermans, R. (2014). Talent management and organisational justice: Employee reactions to high potential identification. *Human Resource Management Journal*, 24(2): 159-175.

Hunter, J.E., Schmidt, F.L. and Judiesch, M.K. (1990). Individual differences in output variability as a function of job complexity. *Journal of Applied Psychology*, 94: 48–61.

Huselid, M.A. (1995). The impact of human resource management practices on turnover, productivity, and corporate financial performance. *Academy of Management Journal*, 38(3): 635–672.

Huselid, M.A., Beatty, R.W. and Becker, B.E. (2005). "A players" or "A positions"? The strategic logic of workforce management. *Harvard Business Review*, December, 110–117.

Huselid, M.A. and Becker, B.E. (2011). Bridging micro and macro domains: Workforce differentiation and strategic human resource management. *Journal of Management*, 37: 421-428.

Kitching, J. (2015). Tracking UK freelance workforce trends 1992-2015, in A.E. Burke (ed.) *The Handbook of Research on Freelancing and Self-Employment* (pp. 15-28). Online: CRSE.

Lewis, R.E. and Heckman, R.J. (2006). Talent management: A critical review. *Human Resource Management Review*, 16(2): 139-154.

Liker, J. and Morgan, J. (2006). The Toyota way in services: The case of lean product development. *Academy of Management Perspectives*, 20(20): 5-20.

Martínez-Jurado, P., Moyano-Fuentes, J. and Gómez, P. (2013). HR management during lean production adoption. *Management Decision*, 51(4): 742-760.

Maselli, I., Lenaerts, K. and Beblavy, M. (2016). Five things we need to know about the on-demand economy. CEPS Essays. Brussels, Centre for European Policy Studies.

McDonnell, A., Collings, D.G., Mellahi, K. and Schuler, R.S (2017). Talent management: An integrative review and research agenda. *European Journal of International Management*, 11(1): 86-128.

McDonnell, A., Gunnigle, P., Lavelle, J. and Lamare, R. (2016). Beyond managerial and leadership elites: "Key group" identification and differential reward architectures in multinational companies. *The International Journal of Human Resource Management*, 27(12): 1299-1318.

McDuffie, J.P. (1995). Human resource bundles and manufacturing performance: organisational logic and flexible productions systems in the world auto industry. *Industrial and Labour Relations Review*, 48: 197-221.

McKinsey & Co. (2014). Guiding the people transformation: The role of HR in lean management. http://www.mckinsey.com/mgi/our-research (accessed 27 April 2017).

Meyers, M.C., De Boeck, G. and Dries, N. (2017). Talent or not: Reactions to talent identification. In D.G. Collings, K. Mellahi and W.F. Cascio (eds) *The Oxford Handbook of Talent Management* (Chapter 9). Oxford: Oxford University Press.

Meyers, M.C., van Woerkom, M. and Dries, N. (2013). Talent – innate or acquired? Theoretical considerations and their implications for talent management. *Human Resource Management Review*, 23(4): 305-321.

Nijs, S., Gallardo-Gallardo, E., Dries, N. and Sels, L. (2014). A multidisciplinary review into the definition, operationalization, and measurement of talent. *Journal of World Business*, 49(2): 180-191.

O'Boyle, E. and Kroska, S. (2017). Star performers. In D.G. Collings, K. Mellahi and W.F. Cascio (eds) *The Oxford Handbook of Talent Management* (Chapter 3). Oxford: Oxford University Press.

Ohno, T. (1988). *Toyota Production System: Beyond Large-Scale Production*. Cambridge, MA: Productivity Press.

PwC (2014). 17th *Annual Global CEO Survey: The Talent Challenge*. London: PwC.

Radnor, Z. and Bucci, G. (2010). Analysis of lean implementation in UK business schools and universities (PDF). Association of Business Schools.

Shah, R. and Ward, P.T. (2007). Defining and developing measures of lean production. *Journal of Operations Management*, 25: 785–805.

Sparrow, P., Scullion, H. and Tarique, I. (eds) (2014). *Strategic Talent Management*. Cambridge: Cambridge University Press.

Tansley, C. (2011). What do we mean by the term "talent" in talent management? *Industrial and Commercial Training*, 43: 266-274.

Thunnissen, M., Boselie, P. and Fruytier, B. (2013). A review of talent management: "Infancy or adolescence"? *International Journal of Human Resource Management*, 24(9): 1744–1761.

Younger, J., Patterson, S. and Younger, A. (2015). The big factors that attract the best freelancers. *Harvard Business Review*, 10 December.

Younger, J. and Smallwood, N. (2016). *Managing on Demand Talent*. Harvard, MA: Harvard Business Press.

4 Using a risk-optimisation lens: maximising talent readiness for an uncertain future

Wayne F. Cascio, John W. Boudreau, and Allan H. Church

4.1 Introduction

The previous chapter laid out the research agenda for talent management. We now develop this research agenda by adopting a risk optimisation lens. As was signalled in the previous chapter, the assumptions underlying typical talent-management and succession-planning systems will often become obsolete in a world of increasing uncertainty and an increasing pace of change. Given those scenarios, it will be vital to reframe talent management systems to hedge risk and uncertainty – a process through which an organisation prepares a portfolio of talent optimised against an uncertain future. It is analogous to changing investment strategies designed to optimise a balance of risk and return under uncertainty. Chapter 8 examines the topic of Leadership. Unfortunately, the published literature in leadership-succession planning reveals little research that describes or predicts the antecedents, consequences, and moderating and mediating factors that relate talent systems to improvements in risk-optimised talent decisions. We argue that succession-planning systems must relinquish a near-exclusive focus on identifying and then systematically building future capabilities using internal processes and tools. Rather, they should seek to understand constantly how future scenarios are shifting, the risks inherent in the current talent base, and the options available to alleviate those risks as the scenarios materialise. To illustrate the practical implications of seeing talent management as risk optimisation in an uncertain future, we examine two of the most visible and prominent elements of today's talent-management and succession-planning systems:

(1) measuring candidate "potential"; and

(2)   ownership rights and decision accountability for talent development.

We conclude by contrasting today's typical approaches in nine key areas of leadership succession to necessary approaches for a risk-optimised future.

4.2   From talent management to talent risk optimisation

Human capital risk refers to the uncertainty arising from changes in a wide variety of workforce and people-management issues that affect a company's ability to meet its strategic and operating objectives (Young and Hexter, 2011). Identifying and optimising human capital risks is important for many reasons, but particularly because human capital accounts for at least half of all operating costs in many companies. Based on the results of a survey conducted among global finance, HR and risk executives from *Fortune 1,000* companies, Ernst & Young (2008) identified four broad areas that comprise human capital risks: strategic, operational, compliance, and financial risks.

Strategic risks include people-related issues that limit the ability of an organisation to achieve its strategic objectives. Two of the most important risks in this category reflect the talent management domains of succession planning (for example, identifying and developing candidates for key leadership roles) and workforce planning (for example, identifying the right long-term talent capabilities needed for the future). Operational risks are those that affect an organisation's ability to meet its objectives through the efficient and effective use of talent (for example, internal controls, integrated talent management systems, performance management, and learning and development). Compliance risks refer to processes and controls to keep a company out of trouble (for example, regulatory compliance, fraud). Finally, financial risks are intrinsic to an organisation's financial management and reporting (for example, equity and incentive compensation, financial accounting and disclosure). All four of these risks are affected by decisions about talent management, of which important components are succession planning and leadership development.

This chapter takes as its departure point the premise that as organisations face increasing uncertainty and an increasing pace of change, it will be vital to reframe HR systems such as talent management more in terms of hedging risk and uncertainty than in terms of preparing the organisation for an anticipated future state. As Cascio and Boudreau (2012, 2014) noted, this requires more than the important tasks of supporting risk-mitigation processes such as legal compliance or meeting regulatory requirements to name successors to key positions. Rather, it ultimately involves reframing talent management, not only in terms of talent productivity and readiness, but as a process through which the organisation prepares a portfolio of talent optimised against an uncertain future. Such an approach requires accepting that rapid change may make current talent obsolete, and that today's processes of career and succession planning must evolve to also include the idea that such plans are not so much goals to be met as changing investment strategies designed to optimise a balance of risk and return under uncertainty. Such systems are much more akin to scenario planning than to gap analysis based on a single forecast. Indeed, fully integrated talent management systems will enable dynamic consideration of many talent and succession scenarios, as well as multiple possible career and development moves, something that is sorely lacking in most of today's systems.

Perhaps even more important is the need for research reflecting this perspective. The keys to such risk-optimised talent decisions certainly include improved HR information/talent management systems, databases, and managerial tools for planning different staffing scenarios and downstream implications that we will discuss. Equally key, however, are changes in the mindsets of leaders, the cultures of organisations, reward systems, accountability, and, ultimately, the basic concepts of talent management and succession planning. It will also require HR practitioners to have significantly greater analytics capabilities than they do today. We conducted a comprehensive literature review of talent management and succession planning for this chapter.[1] Based on that review, we conclude that little research exists that describes or predicts the antecedents, consequences and moderating and mediating factors that relate talent systems to improvements in risk-optimised talent decisions.

4.3   Talent and human capital risks affect organisational strategic success

Ernst & Young (2008: 1) characterised human capital risks as "one of the key business risks of our time". Risk-management language is already familiar to most boards of directors and senior executives. Both groups are well aware that investors as well as regulators in the United States take it very seriously, particularly in light of the Sarbanes–Oxley Act of 2002 and the Dodd–Frank Wall Street Reform and Consumer Protection Act of 2010.

In the context of human capital risks, here are the top five, as reported by Young and Hexter (2011):

(1) a shortage of critical skills within a company's workforce;
(2) compliance/regulatory issues;
(3) succession planning/leadership pipeline;
(4) the gap between current talent capabilities and business goals; and
(5) a shortage of critical skills in the external labor force.

With the exception of point 2 above, notice how all other major human capital risks reflect the availability of appropriate talent to achieve strategic business objectives. Yet there are serious threats to such availability, and those threats come from outside as well as inside an organisation.

In terms of outside threats, as military planners are fond of saying, "We live in a VUCA world" – volatile, uncertain, complex, and ambiguous. Johansen (2007) described each of these succinctly:

- *Volatility* – The nature and dynamics of change, together with the speed of change forces and change catalysts.
- *Uncertainty* – The lack of predictability, the prospects for surprise, and the sense of awareness of issues and events.
- *Complexity* – the multiplex of forces, the compounding of issues, and the chaos and confusion that surround an organisation.
- *Ambiguity* – The haziness of reality, the potential for misreads, and the mixed meanings of conditions; confusion over causes and effects.

What do these conditions imply for organisations?

The importance of anticipating and reacting aggressively to discontinuities is rising dramatically in our increasingly volatile world. That means monitoring trends, engaging in regular scenario-planning exercises, wargaming the effects of potential disruptions – and responding rapidly when competitive conditions shift (Dobbs et al., 2014).

In short, firms in all industries need to engage in regular processes of environmental scanning. The process begins by acknowledging that organisations operate in multiple environments: political, economic, sociocultural, technical, legal, and environmental (PESTLE). With respect to each of these areas, there are two key questions to address:

(1)   Which factors are likely to have the greatest impact on the ability of our organisation to achieve its short- and long-range objectives?

(2)   How might these effects change over the short and long terms?

From the perspective of talent supply and demand, the key challenge is to identify and then prioritise the people-related implications of developments in the PESTLE environments – and to do so on a regular, not episodic, basis (Cascio, 2015).

Sadly, the strategy literature is littered with examples of firms that failed to react appropriately to developments in their external environments. As Lei and Slocum (2014) note, yesterday's winners often morph into tomorrow's dinosaurs. As examples, consider Circuit City, Borders, Filene's Basement, Blockbuster, MCI Worldcom, and Tyco. Kodak failed to react to developments in digital photography. More recently, Intel announced a reduction of 11 per cent of its workforce – a consequence of the shrinking personal-computer market and the chip maker's failure to take advantage of the industry's transition to smartphones (Clark and Stynes, 2016). Intel, how can this be?

It seems to be a common problem that companies in the technology business that lead one generation of computing often struggle in the next. Thus neither Intel nor Microsoft gained a foothold in the mobile market, which was transformed after Apple, Inc. introduced the iPhone in 2007. More recently, sales of personal computers have been mainly declining since Apple's iPad emerged in 2010 (Clark and Stynes, 2016).

Uncertainty is the new normal, and vulnerability to change is an integral part of doing business. Conversely, remaining vibrant and competitive presents a permanent challenge, and to remain true to what one does best (Lei and Slocum, 2014). This is as true of business strategy as it is of leadership succession. In both cases the focus needs to be on agility and embracing uncertainty rather than trying to reduce it, optimising the balance between risk and opportunity (Cascio and Boudreau, 2014).

4.4   The traditional approach to leadership succession fails to optimise risk

This is a far cry from the traditional approach to leadership succession. Cappelli (2008, 2011) has provided a detailed history of succession planning. In the era of lifetime employment, popular until the mid-1980s, vacancies were easy to predict because employees did not quit and were rarely fired. Vacancies tended to come with retirements at mandatory retirement ages. A key assumption was that the supply of talent was entirely within the control of a company. Candidates, who were essentially raw material, were brought into a limited number of entry-level jobs, and then developed to fit the specialised needs of the company. Adjustments were made to the supply pipeline, principally by adjusting the rate at which candidates progressed from one job to another, to ensure that it matched demand in the future.

This approach to succession planning began to unravel after the recession of 1981–1982. Business and talent forecasts in the 1970s proved to be extremely inaccurate, as low economic growth combined with inflation to produce "stagflation". Talent pipelines continued to supply managers based on those inaccurate forecasts, leading to substantial surpluses of talent. The surpluses occurred during the worst recession at that point (1981–1982) since the Great Depression, and led to a decade of layoffs. As if those developments were not enough, uncertainty in the business environment increased dramatically with the advent of deregulation (for example, in airlines, trucking, and telecommunications) and the growth of international competition, which increased the number and sophistication of competitors around the world. In a nutshell, uncertainty became the new normal.

A singular focus on one future scenario extrapolates today's workforce into the future using past patterns of movement, attrition, and so on. Talent management and succession planning simply no longer have the luxury of pretending that assumptions made years in advance will hold long enough to enact traditional multi-year plans. Instead, success will be determined not so much by the validity and execution quality of succession systems, but rather by nurturing a sufficient variety of options aligned against multiple future scenarios. The existing paradigm assumed much more outcome certainty than will exist in the future, and thus fails to consider a sufficient variety of options aligned against multiple future scenarios.

This often unstated and unquestioned fundamental focus explains why typical talent systems exhibit shortcomings such as:

- Linear talent-gap analysis, with a mechanistic approach to completing the annual or episodic formal talent review or succession process, with success defined only as delivering a report to the CEO or Board of Directors and a reliance on slow-changing competency models (which assumes the future will be stable enough to be forecast yearly, and that the language and nature of work does not change once it is codified).
- Slates of potential candidates created for specific positions that often do not produce the candidate ultimately chosen. This may occur because conditions, role requirements, employee availability or structures have changed since the initial plan was made; individuals were placed on slates of candidates to provide a false sense of bench strength, versus representing true candidates for a role; or there was a lack of integrated planning across multiple slates of candidates that are impacted at the same time when decisions need to be made.
- Models of success used to evaluate talent based on incumbent leaders that are not multidimensional, not grounded in theory and research, or linked to future organisational success (because it is assumed that today's existing leaders and jobs will stay similar long enough to offer useful planning frameworks).

To adopt the metaphor of financial investing, most succession-planning systems would be similar to making financial investments by identifying one likely future scenario ten years ahead, then amassing a portfolio of financial instruments based on current assumptions, and setting a ten-year plan for nurturing those investments consistent with today's assumptions. Obviously, any reasonable group of leaders and investors would realise that the future is far too uncertain for this. Instead, they would constantly keep in mind multiple future scenarios, they would continuously alter them as new data emerged, and they would fluidly add and remove investments as the future emerged, optimising the balance between the current portfolio payoff versus readiness for future shifts.

Talent management researchers and leaders should encourage thinking beyond traditional incumbents, roles, and career paths, and instead begin with the idea that increasing VUCA means organisations must instead ask, "Are we optimising all possible types and sources of talent, to be properly hedged against the multiple futures and risks that our talent (and business) will face?" Success is, in part, defined by having the right mix of high-performing and high-potential incumbents in critical roles, but ultimately the idea of focusing solely on "incumbents in roles" is limiting. Succession-planning systems must evolve eventually from an almost exclusive focus on identifying and then systematically building future capabilities using internal processes and tools, to constantly understanding how future scenarios are shifting, the risks inherent in the current talent base, and the options available to alleviate those risks as the scenarios materialise. There needs to be a shift from a fixed approach to one that is more fluid in nature.

To illustrate the practical implications of seeing talent management as risk optimisation in an uncertain future, we take up two of the most visible and prominent elements of today's talent-management and succession-planning systems:

(1)   measuring candidate "potential"; and
(2)   ownership rights and decision accountability for talent development.

4.5   A risk-optimisation-based "blue print" for measuring "potential"

The concept of future "potential" is fundamental to most talent and succession systems, because it reflects the assessment of the likely future capacity of talent, and is a prerequisite for looking beyond present requirements to prepare for the future. As the previous chapter noted, the concept of "potential" remains only vaguely defined and subject to significant differences of interpretation. Also, it is typically not used to consider talent readiness to adapt to a changing future. Rather, it is a general proxy for individual readiness to advance through a linear career path to one or more upper-level positions as they currently exist. Table 4.1 shows the contrast between today and the needed future.

While most executives and human resources professionals would agree that the differentiation and segmentation of talent (that is, as having more or less potential for future growth) is central to effective talent-management and succession-planning processes, they are unlikely to agree on how to go about achieving those objectives. While

Table 4.1   Contrast between current and future needs in talent management systems

Today	Needed for the Future
• Potential is a generic concept	• "Potential for What?" is specific
• Vague distinctions between potential and performance	• Clear distinctions between potential and performance
• Vague definitions of type of leadership or skilled talent needed	• Specific and distinct leadership and skills in different organisational levels and positions
• Readiness defined on vague criteria that confuse general traits with specific capability	• Readiness clearly distinguishes general traits from specific capabilities
• Leaders define high-potentials on traits that are "like me"	• Leaders define high-potentials on traits that reflect an evolution from the current cadre

some organisations have more sophisticated talent identification and development programmes that use psychological assessment suites, such as at PepsiCo (Church and Silzer, 2014) or P&G (Conaty and Charan, 2010), the vast majority are using what have been called "like me" frameworks for selecting their best and brightest talent. In short, the more an individual manager shares the same background, interests, and career experiences as the senior leader choosing top talent, the more like them, and therefore "high-potential" they are.

This approach is ubiquitous in family-business succession plans, and it may work at times in the short term if conditions are highly stable (for example, in scenarios where only a single successor is desired or needed). However, it reflects an antiquated model, and it puts the organisation at risk for future survival. Today, increasingly complex, global organisations with shifting business models and multiple generations of employees entering and exiting need a framework and methodology for differentiating talent into those with more or less potential. Such a framework should be: (1) grounded in theory and research, not based on hunches or idiosyncrasies; (2) consistently understood and applied across the organisation; (3) flexible enough to allow application to different target roles (that is, answering the key question of potential for what?); and finally, (4) integrated into the broader talent-management strategy and processes. In addition, if formal measurement tools are to be used for informing talent decisions, such as promotions (which research suggests is increasingly the case with top development companies – Church and Rotolo, 2013), then (5) the validity of the approach also becomes particularly important. This is to protect the organisation from risk both with respect to (a) selecting the right candidates for the health of the business, as well as (b) protecting the organisation from having systemically biased processes and avoiding adverse impact and negative legal consequences downstream.

How do organisations define "high-potential" in the succession-planning process? Fully 64 per cent of large companies today use a levels-based approach such as "likely to advance two levels" as their definition of potential (Church et al., 2015). Others base their determination on current and past performance or other intangibles (Church et al., 2015; Silzer and Church, 2010). This rating of potential (typically a judgment) is then used in a nine-box framework that compares performance to potential. These judgments are often based on little more than a senior leader's perception of the individual. This may or may not reflect the individual's likelihood to make key contributions to specific future challenges, or to adapt readily should such challenges change. Moreover, the rating of potential is often based largely on current and past performance. In that case, current performance is reflected in both the rating of performance and the rating of future potential. The two dimensions become one, offering little value in assessing "potential" beyond "performance". Church and Waclawski (2010) have labelled this phemonema the performance-potential paradox, and further argue as a consequence that the nine-box model so commonly used in organisations today is not an effective means of differentiating talent against future needs of the business.

Many models of potential exist in practice, and, in particular, in the consulting industry. They tend to reflect the need to be understood, adopted, and sold to leaders steeped in traditional systems. Thus, they reflect the paradigm to focus either on what has worked in the past (that is, "like me") or to adopt the latest "silver bullet" tool or model of current best-practice organisations. They often apply these tools traditionally, focusing on a small portion of the talent pool, usually those in the top cadre.

Is there a better definition or way of thinking about potential, that is not only more evidence-based, but also more likely to serve to optimise risk and reflect the need for options to hedge against future changes?

The way forward is to take a more holistic view of potential and apply it throughout the entire talent-management process. One theoretical approach to conceptualising the landscape of leadership potential in organisations that allows this flexibility, and which is gaining recognition in the literature and in practice, is the *Leadership Potential BluePrint*, introduced by Silzer and Church (2009). Based on a comprehensive review and synthesis of the psychological literature and both internal and external talent-management programmes that have been implemented over the past 50 years, the *BluePrint* represents not a definition of high-potential per se, but a framework for organisations to take a more comprehensive and holistic view to framing the identification and prediction of future leadership success. It is currently used in assessment and development efforts at several large organisations, including Citi-Bank, Eli Lilly, and PepsiCo (Church and Silzer, 2014). It also has been cited as part of the underlying basis of other firms' consulting approaches (for example, Aon-Hewitt, 2013), as well as scholar-practitioner models and reviews of potential (for example, MacRae and Furnham, 2014; Piip and Harris, 2014; Silzer and Borman, 2017; Thornton, Johnson and Church, 2017). In addition, it was recently featured in a White Paper on leadership development (Dugan and O'Shea, 2014) published jointly by the Society for Human Resource Management (SHRM) and the Society for Industrial and Organisational Psychology (SIOP).

The *BluePrint* is based on the idea that future leadership (often called high-) potential is a multidimensional construct consisting of a mixture of traits, specific capabilities, knowledge, and skills that contribute individually and collectively to long-term leadership success in organisations. The attributes reflect three dimensions ranging from more stable traits to skills and capabilities that people can develop. The three dimensions are: "foundational" (that is, cognitive capabilities, and personality dispositions consistent with the Big Five Factors); "growth" (that is, learning orientation/agility, and individual motivation/drive); and "career" (that is, leadership competencies, functional knowledge and skills).

In terms of our risk-optimisation framework, these three dimensions clarify the definition of "potential", as it reflects hedging risk against future strategic or environmental changes. "Foundational" dimensions are generic investments, applicable to virtually all future situations, unlikely to be specifically suited to any one future situation, that tend to hold their general value. They do not change with time or emerging opportunities, and they provide necessary conditions for the other two dimensions to produce value. "Growth" dimensions are also somewhat generic in that they reflect traits that generally lead to increased individual value across many situations, but additionally reflect the generic likelihood of adaptation to new situations. "Career" dimensions reflect more specific "bets" on a particular future leadership role or technical skills set, and carry the risk of obsolescence if the particular role or skill challenge does not occur. Seen in this way, it is possible for leaders to articulate more clearly the sorts of risk hedging they are trying to achieve, and to identify an appropriate definition of the concept of "potential".

The *BluePrint* process consists of a review of existing tools, OD processes, learning programmes, and interventions (Church, 2014) to determine which of the three dimensions they measure or develop, to examine if the "portfolio" of dimensions best reflects the talent and succession questions. Is the right approach more "generic" to reflect uncertainty about the eventual contributions of a certain talent pool in a certain future position, or is the right approach more "specific" because there is likely to be a very high payoff to readiness for a particular position? In some cases, an application of the *BluePrint* may even lead an organisation to reevaluate its selection methods. Table 4.2 provides a brief overview of the elements of the model and how these can be applied to talent management (TM) succession-planning efforts.

Table 4.2   Overview of model elements

Elements of the *BluePrint*	TM Succession-Planning Emphasis
Foundational:	Talent Identification & Confirmation
– Cognitive capabilities	● External selection efforts
– Personality characteristics	● Early indicators of "raw" potential
Growth:	Pipeline and Bench Building
– Learning ability/agility	● Development through critical experiences
– Motivation and drive	● Formal assessment, feedback, and coaching
Career:	Slating and Succession Planning
– Leadership competencies	● Targeted development and gap closure
– Functional skills	● Building breadth and enhancing fungibility

The *BluePrint* represents a significant shift in the paradigm of how organisations think about and measure potential. It provides a common framework that allows an organisation to answer the question of potential for what? and to have the appropriate planning conversations at different levels in the talent-management process. For example, at junior levels (for example, entry-level MBAs in marketing) the focus is on raw potential; hence foundational dimensions such as cognitive skills and personality become more important to measure and review than, say, leadership capability. At higher levels in the organisation, discussions regarding succession to top Marketing VP roles may require a focus on growth dimensions, such as learning, openness to experiences, and the drive to get there. This type of review parallels the work on development of breadth through different types of critical experiences in the organisation (for example, McCauley and McCall, 2014), such as start-ups, turn-arounds following share loss, or assignments in emerging markets or in corporate HQ.

As the leadership demands and the destination of the individuals in the succession plan become clearer (for example, CMO North America, CFO China), the focus becomes more on the "career" dimensions, that represent more specific "bets" that a particular future will evolve for that individual. The developmental emphasis at this point is more targeted and nuanced. It focuses on potential in the context of a destination role, not only raw horsepower or personality.

Thus senior-talent reviews (such as GE's Session C or PepsiCo's People Planning Process – Church and Waclawski, 2010) can focus more effectively on comparing leaders/successors across a consistent set of dimensions and assess readiness and fit, versus the typical "he's a good guy" approach. The emphasis can still be fluid. There is no hard and fast set of rules that requires assessment of potential to reflect traits that are more generic (apply across many future situations but not deeply suited to any one) versus more specific (apply to only one future situation but likely to provide a very high payoff if that situation arises). However, organising talent-management and succession-system processes and discussions along these three dimensions provides a consistent framework that explicitly requires leaders to articulate their assumptions regarding the likelihood of future scenarios and their approach to selecting talent for those scenarios.

The *BluePrint* is grounded in theory and research in related areas, and organisations are adopting the model, but this approach is the subject of no empirical research. Church et al. (2015) in their survey work with 100 top development companies, found that the dimensions in the model accounted for 50–75 per cent of the content being assessed today. This is a good start, but other elements are still question marks. For example where do the popular concepts of resilience or character fall in the *BluePrint*? What role do cultural values play? Are they moderators of the framework or part of the model itself? Further, even if we consider the *BluePrint* to be relatively comprehensive, additional research questions remain, such as, are there universal indicators/ predictors of potential across organisations or is the model entirely fluid within the dimensions? What are the best psychometric measures to use in each factor and why? Can we confirm the hypotheses that some elements (for example, foundational) are more predictive of success at early career stages and play more gatekeeper roles at higher levels? These are all areas where more research is needed.

Despite these questions, it is clear that organisations need to move beyond the simplistic and individually based models of potential. They need to move to the next generation of how to conceptualise potential and a structure for organisations. Doing so will enable them to: (a) assess their current-state, TM high-potential segmentation and development programmes; and (b) develop new ones if they have not begun the process as yet. The *BluePrint* is one such approach that is providing insight in that direction.

4.6   Risk-optimisation-based talent "ownership" across organisation units

In a world of accelerated change, talent risks and returns will vary significantly across business units, regions and other organisational divisions. While it is an attractive idea to believe that every organisation unit should have the best and most-prepared talent possible, the fact is that the *existing* as well as the *needed* level of talent quality, readiness and resilience in the face of uncertainty and risk will and *should* vary across units. Not every organisation unit will produce or require the very best talent, the most ready talent, nor require maximum preparedness for future uncertainty. The relative needs and levels of these talent attributes across units will also change over time, as strategic challenges change. Finally, because strategic and economic worlds are increasingly interconnected, often the only feasible way to optimise risk-return trade-offs across an organisation is to coordinate talent and

Table 4.3   Risk optimisation today and in the future

Today	Future
• Talent is "owned" by individual units, functions or roles and succession occurs only in siloed units • Rudimentary rules for when talent is a shared organisation resource (e.g., the top 100, 300 or 500) • Conflict between unit-level and organisational talent goals is resolved politically or by ignoring the conflict • Idiosyncratic and inconsistent talent-decision rules in different units ("person like me", "person like the CEO", "emphasise unit goals")	• Talent is "owned" collectively across organisation units and succession occurs across units • Optimised rules regarding when talent is a shared organisation resource (e.g., strategic cost–return balance) • Collaboration across units through collective accountability for optimising unit versus organisation goals • Clear governance concepts identify unit and organisation-level rules that balance strategic priorities within and across units

succession decisions across global, hierarchical, and business units. Unfortunately, such risk-optimised systems are rare. Table 4.3 shows the contrast between today and the necessary future.

When strategic challenges arise within one organisation unit or region that does not have the pipeline of talent to address them, the best way to address those challenges is often for another unit to sacrifice its best talent. This is optimal when the sacrificing unit can afford to absorb risk by relying on a lower-quality replacement for the talent it sacrifices. Yet, how many leaders perceive that their unit can afford to give up its best talent, and how many talent systems (or executive compensation programmes) reward leaders who make such sacrifices? Few organisations can see their talent portfolios comprehensively and clearly enough to identify such opportunities. Even when organisations can identify the value of such cross-unit talent trades, few talent systems provide the tools to implement them. Nor do organisational cultures typically recognise and reward both the unit that receives the talent and the unit that makes the sacrifice.

Yet, in a world of rapidly changing strategic challenges that are increasingly interconnected across organisational units, the typical myopia regarding cross-unit talent optimisation is much like designing a supply chain in which different organisation units can neither perceive nor act upon cross-unit synergies in sourcing, purchasing, and transport.

Organisations differ widely, some with fully centralised functions that manage the entire identification, development, movement, and tracking of all high-potential or top-echelon talent, to others where talent authority is assigned to individual business functions with little central oversight. A recent study of top talent-development companies (that is, large organisations that have been recognised in the marketplace for having robust TM processes), reported that more than 60 per cent manage some elements of their "corporate assets" from the global centre (Church and Rotolo, 2013), and only 15–20 per cent leave it to local business units, but this is not the case in the majority of organisations today. Instead, one often observes talent-hoarding behaviour within units (Church and Waclawski, 2010), sometimes known as "pass the trash", to signify that units hold their best talent and release only their lower-quality talent.

Counter-arguments from the field are often direct and quite passionate. They generally address two key points:

(1)   why should a unit invest time and money to develop good talent, only to lose it to other parts of the business?; and
(2)   centrally determined rules cannot manage the entire organisation's talent optimally.

The first point may simply reflect a somewhat myopic (and/or selfish) perspective, and may be remedied with tactics that promote a cultural shift, such as modeling through senior-leader behaviours, or reward systems that tangibly and publicly reward units that make key sacrifices. The second point is more fundamental, because it is true that most organisational talent-management systems lack the comprehensive perspective and nuanced decision rules to claim to optimise talent across units. In that case, units might be forgiven for suggesting that although unit-level decisions may be myopic and suboptimal, they are no worse than the rudimentary rules often used by centralised talent-management systems (for example, arbitrary numbers of cross-unit movements, politics, expediency or "looks like me"). Smaller organisations may be better able to construct talent-management processes that encompass all operating units because talent visibility is easier when the talent pool is small. The paradox is that larger organisations have more opportunity for cross-unit optimisation, but also a much greater challenge. This is why clear, logical and optimised talent "ownership rights" are vital.

Our literature review of more than 300 articles on talent management that appeared since 1990 revealed a surprising and notable lack of research on this issue. We simply know very little about the antecedents, moderators, and consequences of cross-unit talent optimisation. For many decades, scholars (for example, Boudreau and Berger, 1985; Cascio and Boudreau, 2011) have observed that inter-unit talent movement bears striking similarities to a combination of talent "turnover" from the supplying unit, and talent "acquisition" into the receiving unit. They have suggested that many of the same theories, frameworks and measurement systems used to predict and evaluate turnover and selection might be applied in concert to examine the consequences of internal movement. Yet, we see no studies addressing such questions. Moreover, we know even less about the thorny issues of creating a culture and reward system where unit leaders understand and embrace their roles as talent suppliers and talent receivers, particularly when that means sacrificing their best talent in service of the greater good. Next, we describe some prominent examples of typical approaches to cross-unit talent optimisation.

The first and most typical approach is simply to assign talent ownership to the organisation for all talent above a certain hierarchy or role level. Many organisations take a global focus only on the top 10 (C-suite) or 100 critical roles. Or they might emphasise individual levels, such as the top 300 executives, top 500, all VPs and above, depending on size, resources, and their depth of strategy (for example, Conaty and Charan, 2010). While this is easy to understand and implement, it is not always the most strategic. As strategic challenges change, certain roles or capabilities will have differentially pivotal contributions to business goals, and certain roles will become more pivotal as developmental opportunities to hedge risk or build capability for emerging future challenges. In addition, not all talent demonstrates equivalent potential at the same level. In the context of risk-optimisation, different roles at different times may exponentially add "talent" value to the corporation by accelerating the development, and therefore, leadership potential, of the incumbents. Thus, if an organisation places a high-potential manager in a key role, that experience can accelerate his or her development. If it places a peer high-potential manager in a mission-critical, but not developmental, role – and leaves him or her there too long – his or her potential to achieve more senior-level positions is damaged, even if the business need is met.

A second approach is to align around talent-classification groups. Most typically, this means organisation-level talent ownership is provided for all high-potentials (however defined) throughout the organisation. Unlike the first option, this one can allow the organisation to prioritise its decision rights over individual units when it is vital to develop junior high-potential talent over other, more senior, but not high-potential talent. In addition, some senior roles may be left to the discretion of business units rather than the organisation level, if they are not vital destinations or developmental opportunities for high-potential talent. In addition to focusing on high-potential talent, some organisations use different segmentation models, such as those based on critical experiences gained, or other types of individual attributes (for example, stated mobility, career aspirations), or even demographics (for example, ethnicity, gender). The latter can be risky if it results in disparate impact on certain protected demographic groups. Whatever the approach taken, it is one based on talent differentiation, not hierarchical level or key roles. This more nuanced approach to segmenting talent-decision rights has the potential to allow greater cross-unit optimisation, if the decision rules can reflect appropriate strategic challenges, risk assessments, and trade-offs that hedge risk and opportunity. However, it is more complex to govern, and creates transparency challenges to communicate clearly and fairly with the organisation and the talent being managed. Rumours will abound, and this can result in increased pressure for transparency of classification methods (Church et al., 2015). For example, "You must be a high-potential if Corporate is managing your development, and not local leadership."

Some companies take a multi-factor approach by combining elements of these (level, role, and individual), which again offers great potential to shape the system to strategic challenges and risk trade-offs, but also results in very complex decision rules. Little research is available that identifies which approach is best, or what "best" even represents. It does appear, however, based on our collective experience, that the pendulum between centralisation and decentralisation swings back and forth in the talent-ownership domain, just as it does in the HR functional space.

PepsiCo's approach to this challenge offers an interesting twist. Several years ago the organisation comingled the concept of mobility with the definition of potential. In order to effectively distinguish these, and to drive greater organisational clarity around talent ownership, a new 3x3 grid was created using the dimensions of talent call or category (for example, high-potential, key contributor, or critical professional) and talent-mobility pool. Unlike the traditional nine-box, this was purely focused on talent ownership. One side of the grid represented the talent-call categories of high-potential, key contributor and critical professional (see Church and Waclawski, 2010 for detailed definitions). On the other side was the organisation's determination of whether the individual was local, regional, or global talent. Local talent described those employees who were able to take on new assignments within their current location only (which may or may not include progression). Regional talent included those employees who had the willingness to move within specific geographic regions or parts of the world, but there were clear limitations noted. Global talent included those who were open to new assignments anywhere the company operated. Interestingly, while this designation was based, in large part, on each individual's self-reported mobility and preferences, including locations of interest (and non-interest) and timing constraints (for example, mobile in two years when kids are out of the house), it also included a judgment on the leadership's part regarding the company's willingness to support a move for that individual. There was clear recognition that talent-mobility pools could change based on employees' life stages; hence the composition of the pools was reviewed and updated regularly.

This process resulted a grid (see Table 4.4) that allowed the clear segmentation of talent ownership. Specifically, it facilitated a clear delineation of enterprise ownership for all high-potential talent that was also global in nature. The bottom-line was that if the talent was fully open and supported for movement across the organisation it should be centrally managed. For those high-potentials who were constrained for movement within a region, however, the ownership was shared jointly between the enterprise and the sector/business. Part of the reason for this is the recognition that circumstances might change for the individual, and part was the fact that if left on their own, sectors might fill all their key roles with regional high-potential talent, which could eventually block them all from the global talent pool headed to C-suite roles in the future. Local high-potentials, however, were left to business Sectors and Divisions.

A similar logic of shared accountability was applied to the Key Contributors (strong performers, some of whom could be promoted,

Table 4.4   Segmentation of ownership of talent

	Local	Regional	Global
High Potential	Sector & Division	Enterprise & Sector	Enterprise
Key Contributor	Sector & Division	Sector & Division	Enterprise & Sector
Critical Professional	Sector & Division	Sector & Division	Enterprise & Sector

but just not identified as being high potential) and Critical Professionals (highly specialised individuals who are difficult to replace).

4.7   Conclusion and future directions

We have suggested that the level of uncertainty and change facing most future organisations will often make obsolete the assumptions underlying typical talent-management and succession-planning systems. Specifically, we propose that talent-management and succession systems should evolve to a focus on optimising agility and embracing uncertainty rather than trying to reduce it or ignore it. The goal is to optimise the balance between risk and opportunity, not to prepare talent for a particular future forecast (Cascio and Boudreau, 2014). We have tried to show that this is a far cry from the traditional approach to leadership succession and talent management, using illustrations reflecting the way that "potential" is defined and used, and illustrations of how talent "ownership" across organisation units is defined.

However, these are not the only arenas with striking contrasts between today's typical approaches and the necessary approaches for a risk-optimised future. A full treatment of others is beyond the scope of this chapter, but Table 4.5 summarises our observations about other key talent-management arenas.

Our literature review suggests that the vast majority of literature has focused mostly on the question of whether to "make or buy" talent, including the issue of whether external or internal CEO succession leads to better outcomes. This research is informative and important, but there is much work to be accomplished to build the evidence-based research agenda that will inform and support the evolution to a risk-optimised approach to talent management and succession. Research is needed to describe best practices, evaluate antecedents, consequences,

Table 4.5 Observations on old and new talent management arenas

Traditional (Old)	Evolved (New)
Goals as fixed and predictable	Goals as uncertain (but not random) and adapting
Success defined as fitting a replacement to a fixed requirement	Success defined as hedging against uncertain and changing requirements
Applying a linear mindset, optimising a few ultimate job outcomes	Applying a systems mindset, while optimising component parts
Goal of "fully ready" candidates	Goal of "close enough" talent solutions
Candidate failure to complete the career plan is a sign of system malfunction	Candidates changing paths or failing to succeed is a natural and desired part of hedging risk
Talent is seen as separate pools aligned on different fixed paths	Talent is seen as a portfolio of capabilities that span units, aligned against uncertain future options
Assumption that internal candidates are best and that external sourcing is a sign of system failure	Optimising "build" versus "buy" options based on situational analysis and balancing costs and benefits and risk and return
Talent development and sourcing limited to employees within the organisation	Talent development and sourcing spans multiple organisations and work arrangements (contractor, supplier, freelancer, etc.)
Relationship with BoD and top leadership is defined by formal reports and processes, with the goal of approval	Relationship with BoD and top leadership is defined by optimisation, organic and ongoing decisions, and a goal of top leaders as continuous talent-portfolio builders and investors

and mediators/moderators. In addition, there is almost no research examining the mental models of leaders when it comes to these important processes, and the sorts of data, communication, training, and experience needed to change mindsets. Those mindsets appear often to reflect a tradition that incorrectly assumes talent can be prepared for a predicted future that will resemble the past. Yet, all indications are that such a mindset is obsolete and that risk-optimised talent is increasingly vital.

NOTE
1. The authors would like to thank Brooke Z. Graham for her valuable assistance in conducting this review.

References

Aon-Hewitt (2013). Building the right high-potential pool: How organizations define, assess and calibrate their critical talent. Consulting performance, rewards and talent paper: Aon plc: http://www.aon.com/attachments/human-capital-consulting/2013_Building_the_Right_High_Potential_Pool_white_paper.pdf (accessed 27 April 2017).

Boudreau, J.W. and Berger, C.J. (1985). Decision-theoretic utility analysis applied to employee separations and acquisitions. *Journal of Applied Psychology*, 70: 581–612.

Cappelli, P. (2008). *Talent on Demand: Managing Talent in an Age of Uncertainty.* Boston, MA: Harvard Business Press.

Cappelli, P. (2011). Succession planning. In S. Zedeck (ed.), *APA Handbook of Industrial and Organizational Psychology* (vol. 3). Washington, DC: American Psychological Association, 673–690.

Cascio, W.F. (2015). Environmental scanning: A pivotal competency for all HR executives. In I. Ziskin (ed.), *Three: The Human Resources Emerging Executive.* Hoboken, NJ: Wiley, 191–195.

Cascio, W.F. and Boudreau, J.W. (2011). *Investing in People: Financial Impact of Human Resource Initiatives* (2nd edition). Upper Saddle River, NJ: Pearson Education.

Cascio, W.F. and Boudreau, J.W. (2012). *Short Introduction to Strategic Human Resource Management.* Cambridge: Cambridge University Press.

Cascio, W.F. and Boudreau, J.W. (2014). HR strategy: Optimizing risks, optimizing rewards. *Journal of Organizational Effectiveness: People and Performance*, 1(1): 77–97.

Church, A.H. (2014). What do we know about developing leadership potential? The role of OD in strategic talent management. *OD Practitioner*, 46(3): 52–61.

Church, A.H. and Rotolo, C.T. (2013). How are top companies assessing their high-potentials and senior executives? A talent management benchmark study. *Consulting Psychology Journal: Practice and Research*, 65(3): 199–223.

Church, A.H., Rotolo, C.T., Ginther, N.M. and Levine, R. (2015). How are top companies designing and managing their high-potential programs? A follow-up talent management benchmark study. *Consulting Psychology Journal: Practice and Research*, 67(1): 17–47.

Church, A.H. and Silzer, R. (2014). Going behind the corporate curtain with a blueprint for leadership potential: An integrated framework for identifying high-potential talent. *People & Strategy*, 36: 51–58.

Church, A.H. and Waclawski, J. (2010). Take the Pepsi Challenge: Talent development at PepsiCo. In R. Silzer and B.E. Dowell (eds), *Strategy-Driven Talent Management: A Leadership Imperative.* San Francisco, CA: Jossey-Bass, 617–640.

Clark, D. and Stynes, T. (2016). Intel to put more focus on cloud. *The Wall Street Journal*, 20 April, pp. B1, B4.

Conaty, B. and Charan, R. (2010). *The Talent Masters: Why Smart Leaders Put People Before Numbers.* New York: Crown Business.

Dobbs, R., Ramaswamy, S., Stephenson, E. and Viguerie, S.P. (2014). *McKinsey Quarterly* (September). www.mckinsey.com/insights/strategy/management_intuition_for_the_next-50_years (accessed 27 April 2017).

Dugan, B.A. and O'Shea, P.G. (2014). *Leadership development: Growing talent strategically*. Society for Human Resource Management (SHRM) and Society for Industrial and Organizational Psychology (SIOP). Science of HR White Paper Series.

Ernst & Young (2008). *2008 Global HR risk: From the Danger Zone to the Value Zone: Accelerating Business Improvement by Navigating HR Risk*. London: Ernst & Young.

Johansen, B. (2007). *Get There Early: Sensing the Future to Compete in the Present*. San Francisco, CA: Berrett-Kohler.

Lei, D. and Slocum, J.W. (2014). *Demystifying Your Business Strategy*. New York: Routledge.

MacRae, I. and Furnham, A. (2014). *High Potential: How to Spot, Manage and Develop Talented People at Work*. London: Bloomsbury.

McCauley C.D. and McCall Jr., M.W. (eds) (2014). *Using Experience to Develop Leadership Talent: How Organizations Leverage On-The-Job Development*. San Francisco, CA: Jossey-Bass.

Piip, J. and Harris, R. (2014). Leadership talent identification and management. In R. Harris and T. Short (eds), *Workforce Development: Perspectives and Issues*. Dordrecht, Netherlands: Springer, 213–231.

Silzer, R.F. and Borman, W.C. (2017). The potential for leadership. In D.G. Collings, K. Mellahi and W.F. Cascio (eds), *Oxford Handbook of Talent Management*. Oxford, UK: Oxford University Press, 87–114.

Silzer, R. and Church, A.H. (2009). The pearls and perils of identifying potential. *Industrial and Organizational Psychology: Perspectives on Science and Practice*, 2: 377–412.

Silzer, R.F. and Church, A.H. (2010). Identifying and assessing high-potential talent: Current organizational practices. In R. Silzer and E. Dowell (eds), *Strategy-driven Talent Management: A Leadership Imperative*. San Francisco, CA: Jossey Bass, 213–281.

Thornton, G.C., Johnson, S.K. and Church, A.H. (2017). Selecting leaders: High potentials and executives. In N. Tippins and J. Farr (eds), *Handbook of Employee Selection*. London: Routledge, 833–852.

Young, M.B. and Hexter, E.S. (2011), Managing human capital risk (Research Report No. 1477-11-RR). New York: The Conference Board.

5 Managing the selection and retention of human capital resources

Robert E. Ployhart and Jason Kautz

5.1 Introduction

All firms are challenged with attracting and retaining the talent needed to achieve operational excellence and competitive advantage. As noted in Chapter 2, *Selection* involves the identification of the desired knowledge, skills, abilities, and other characteristics (KSAOs) needed to effectively fit within the demands of the job and organisation (Ployhart, Schneider and Schmitt, 2006). *Retention* involves ensuring that the desired talent does not leave the firm, either voluntarily or involuntarily through terminations (Holtom et al., 2008; March and Simon, 1958). Selection and retention therefore represent different, but highly interdependent, processes and practices. Implementing the practices of selection and retention has always been challenging, but has taken on even greater importance in the modern economy due to a variety of economic, global, demographic, and technological forces. As the previous two chapters have explained:

1. Talent has become the primary driver of firm performance in many industries and firms. As competition and growth are increasingly shaped by innovation, knowledge, and information, talent becomes the catalyst for stimulating change.
2. The global economy is characterised as being VUCA: volatile, uncertain, complex, and ambiguous. The global economy is rapidly changing and diversifying.
3. The demographics of geopolitical regions are changing. The populations of developing countries are exploding, yet most of this population growth does not have the advanced education and skills needed by firms in developed countries. Thus, selection and retention are being strongly shaped by a variety of modern challenges.

Given that talent is a critical resource for competitive advantage in a VUCA-world, high-performing organisations have realised that the strategic management of human resources is critical for achieving a competitive advantage. Competition requires more nimble strategy, and the talent needed to implement those strategies has likewise needed to become nimble. Such changes have led organisations to downplay a focus on HR practices, and give greater attention to strategically managing their human capital resources, which:

> ... are individual or unit-level capacities based on individual KSAOs that are accessible for unit-relevant purposes. (Ployhart et al., 2014: 374)

A focus on human capital resources is necessary because it is human capital resources, and not practices, that explains firm differences in performance and contributes to competitive advantage (Crook et al., 2011; Ployhart and Hale, 2014). That is, HR practices can be copied and often are copied, but the talent that resides in human capital resources is not easily copied, imitated, or acquired. Further, human capital resources can be reshaped or rebundled with other resources for different strategic purposes, making human capital a resource that can be used flexibly for a variety of organisational goals.

The purpose of this chapter is to provide a concise review of contemporary research on selection and retention. We first summarise the current research literature, and then consider the challenges of selection and retention for modern organisations. We conclude by discussing how future research should be connected to practice.

5.2 Review of current research

There have been several recent large-scale reviews of the selection and retention literatures. Most research focuses on turnover rather than retention. However, in practice, firms try to increase retention and reduce turnover, and from our perspective it makes more sense to consider the selection and retention of talent. Thus, when we use the term retention, it is important to note that we are in effect reviewing what is usually described as the "turnover" literature.

5.2.1   Selection

In terms of selection, there is now over a century of scholarly research devoted to understanding how to make the most accurate hiring decisions (Ployhart, Schmitt and Tippins, 2017; Ryan and Ployhart, 2014; Schmitt, 2014). In these reviews, one of the most striking conclusions is that the basic questions studied by selection scholars have remained highly consistent over time. For the last 100 years, researchers have sought to identify the most effective ways to identify talent and make accurate hiring decisions. However, the forces that shape the nature, practice, and consequences of the hiring decision have evolved over time in response to a changing world. For example, research on the demographic consequences of selection did not appear until the 1960s, research on attraction and recruitment did not become widespread until the 1970s, and research on personality did not occur until the 1990s.

Overall, the field of selection has made considerable progress, and there is now reasonably shared consensus around a number of key points (see Schmitt, 2014; Ryan and Ployhart, 2014):

1. It is well-established that validity resides with scores obtained from different predictor methods, and it is critical to establish the validity of those scores.
2. The validity for many types of scores is generalisable across different contexts and cultures.
3. The distinction between KSAO scores and the predictor methods used to obtain those scores is an important one.
4. Cognitive ability is highly related to job performance across contexts and cultures, and the relationship is stronger as the complexity of the job increases.
5. Cognitive ability is rarely itself a sufficient KSAO for job performance, so other KSAO constructs based on personality or dispositions are also important.
6. Scores based on different predictor methods differ in their validity. Predictor methods that assess multiple job-related KSAOs, such as assessment centres, work samples, and situational judgment tests (SJTs), tend to predict performance better than homogenous KSAO predictor methods.
7. Predictor scores differ with respect to their sex or racioethnic subgroup differences, and the subgroup differences are greater the more the assessment captures cognitive ability.

8. Uncorrected validities still generally fall under a 0.30 ceiling, and
    the validities that break this ceiling are corrected for a variety of
    artifacts such as sampling variability, range restriction, and unre-
    liability.

Despite the broadening of the topics studied by selection scholars, the
core focus of current selection research remains fixated on identifying selection practices and techniques that produce scores with high
validity, low subgroup differences, are cost-effective, and are acceptable to candidates. For example, research has examined different ways
of scoring SJTs that vary the nature of the situations (Krumm et al.,
2014). Other research has examined characteristics of the interview
(Barrick et al., 2012) or considered different frameworks for assessment centre validity (Hoffman et al., 2011). In this sense, the basic
question being pursued by selection scholars has remained strikingly
consistent over the last decades – and strikingly linked to the basic
practice of selection.

Other research topics are new to the selection literature, even if the
problems they address are not new. For example, Bidwell (2011) has
examined the benefits and costs associated with internal versus external hiring. The basic finding is that hiring talent from the outside costs
more money and delivers worse performance, until a sufficient amount
of time has passed for performance to improve. Other research has
attempted to link either selection practices or the KSAOs assessed
by those practices to firm-level outcomes. Van Iddekinge et al. (2009)
found selection and training practices contributed to strategic-busi-
ness unit (SBU) level financial performance. Ployhart, Van Iddekinge
and MacKenzie (2011) demonstrated that improving the quality of
selection contributes to more effective training, which in turn contributes to better customer service delivery and ultimately financial performance. Kim and Ployhart (2014) found that firms that were more
selective demonstrated higher profit growth than less selective firms,
and this advantage was even greater following the Great Recession.

5.2.2   Retention

Retention and turnover are two sides of the same coin; each looking at the same phenomena, but asking slightly different questions.
Turnover concerns itself with the effects as employees leave the
organisation, whereas retention questions what organisations can do
to keep employees. Most research has focused on turnover. March and

Simon defined turnover as an employee's departure from the "formally defined organisation" (March and Simon, 1958: 99) and visualised it as a composition of pushing (desirability) and pulling (ease) forces. An employee is drawn to job opportunities outside the organisation if there is dissatisfaction with their current position and a large number of alternative positions available in the job market. The employee performs a cost–benefit type analysis of their options and will leave if the alternative is found to be better (Mobley, 1982).

Turnover has been conceptualised in terms of voluntary and involuntary turnover. Involuntary turnover (termination) involves the removal of low performers and employees that lack fit with the organisation (Dalton, Todor and Krackhardt, 1982; O'Reilly, Chatman and Caldwell, 1991; Campion, 1991). Voluntary turnover, on the other hand, deals with the employee's decision to leave and is highly determined by such factors as job satisfaction and embeddedness – the extent to which an individual is enmeshed in his/her community and organisation (Mitchell et al., 2001).

There is a long history of research on turnover, and reviews (for example, Holtom et al., 2008) and three major meta-analyses (Hancock et al., 2011; Heavey, Holwerda and Hausknecht, 2013; Park and Shaw, 2013) have summarised a great deal of this literature:

1. The majority of evidence finds negative consequences of turnover on nearly all performance indicators (productivity, financial performance, customer outcomes, and safety/quality outcomes; Hancock et al., 2011).
2. It is thought that low to moderate levels of turnover may be beneficial to an organisation in removing low-performers (Abelson and Baysinger, 1984).
3. There is a potential for a curvilinear relationship; by balancing the cost of human and social capital, the organisation may reach an optimal level of turnover (Abelson and Baysinger, 1984; Hancock et al., 2011; Hausknecht and Trevor, 2011).
4. While voluntary turnover may have empirical evidence to suggest a stronger negative relationship to organisational performance (McElroy, Morrow and Rude, 2001), this conclusion does not hold in light of meta-analytic analysis (Hancock et al., 2011).
5. Collective turnover has been shown to affect areas such as customer satisfaction and service quality, safety and quality metrics

(such as accident rates and waste), and productivity (Hancock et al., 2011).

6. There appear to be empirical differences in the consequences of individual versus collective turnover (Hausknecht and Trevor, 2011).

7. Embeddedness has been shown to predict the turnover intentions of individuals. The stronger employees are intertwined with their environment (inside and outside work) the less likely the employee is to leave (Mitchell et al., 2001).

8. Factors that enhance retention include HR practices that contribute to motivation and empowerment (Wright and Boswell, 2002), whereas factors that contribute to turnover include job (dis)satisfaction and unemployment rates (Heavey, Holwerda and Hausknecht, 2013).

There are a variety of theoretical arguments made to explain the relationship between turnover and performance.

First, the human capital argument describes turnover as a potential source of loss for valuable KSAOs (Osterman, 1987; Becker, 1993; Shaw, Gupta and Delery, 2005). Second, the operational disruption argument looks at turnover's role in the disruption of information flow and coordination (Staw, 1980; Leana and Van Buren, 1999; Summers, Humphrey and Ferris, 2012). Third, the cost argument looks at the financial costs associated with replacing an employee (Cascio, 2006; Dalton and Todor, 1979). The use of a meta-analysis has suggested that these categories may be more important than previously thought because there may be different types of mediators that explain turnover-performance relationships (Hancock et al., 2011). Researchers have also proposed several moderating factors that can attenuate the negative effects of turnover, such as level of skills required for performance (for example, Shaw et al., 2005), the organisation's industry (for example, Baron, Hannan and Burton, 2001), and HR practices (for example, Guthrie, 2000; Trevor and Nyberg, 2008).

A long-held assumption in turnover research was that the individual-level theory and findings are indicative of the unit level. Chapter 2 signalled that we need to conduct more research at the unit level, and this can be seen in the fields of selection and turnover. More recent research is challenging this assumption and testing this question directly (Hausknecht and Trevor, 2011). Nyberg and Ployhart (2013) utilised a multi-level framework to propose Context-Emergent

Turnover (CET) Theory as a resource-based theory explaining why collective turnover leads to different consequences than what is predicted at the individual level. They argue collective turnover represents the "depletion of employee knowledge, skills, abilities and other characteristics (KSAOs) from the unit" (Nyberg and Ployhart, 2013: 109); that is, the quality and quantity of human capital resources lost. The consequences of collective turnover take into account the KSAOs of employees, the social relationships, and the employee roles in the unit (Shaw, 2011). The antecedents of collective turnover can be divided into three major categories: HR systems and practices, collective attitudes and perceptions, and collective characteristics such as time dispersion and positional distribution (Hausknecht and Trevor, 2011; Hausknecht and Holwerda, 2013).

Newer approaches are starting to give more attention to retention and emphasise the role of embeddedness. This area of research focuses more on predictors and what can be done to mitigate detrimental turnover. Organisational embeddedness is comprised of three components: the fit between the employee and the organisation, the social links created through the job, and the sacrifice associated with leaving (Mitchell et al., 2001). While most researchers have chosen to focus on organisational embeddedness, Ng and Feldman (2012) have argued the need to include a focus on community when dealing with embeddedness research, providing evidence of the positive association between community embeddedness and changes in job motivation, social networking behaviour, and organisational identification (Ng and Feldman, 2013).

5.3   Modern challenges and research needs

Despite impressive progress, there are signs that selection and retention research have not kept pace with changes in business over the last 15 or so years – changes that relate to globalisation, business, and competition.

5.3.1   Globalisation

Chapter 12 examines the research agenda for Globalisation and HRM, and we would concur that there is insufficient research devoted to understanding the influence of globalisation, culture, political environments, and related factors on the science and practice of selection and retention. Research on cultural issues in HR has existed for some time, but it is usually focused on cultural influences on talent management practices and systems (Rabl et al., 2014). The research more specific to selection has focused on establishing the validity of KSAOs across contexts, and generally finds that professionally-developed assessments of cognitive ability and personality scores demonstrate generalisable validity (see Ryan and Ployhart, 2014). However, the effect of cultural influences on most predictor methods is largely unknown. Ryan et al. (1999) provide one of the few comparative studies; they found considerable variability in selection practice usage across countries, but cultural values provided only a modest explanation of the differences.

On the surface, the research on culture and selection offers an interesting paradox: selection practices differ considerably across cultures, but the KSAOs assessed in many selection practices are equivalent. This may be taken to suggest cultural differences in practice do not translate into cultural differences in selection effectiveness because validity is invariant. However, we caution such an interpretation. The research on generalisability of KSAOs has been limited to primarily paper/self-report assessments of cognitive ability and personality. What we don't know is whether different predictor methods, such as interviews or SJTs, produce scores with similar validity across cultures. Indeed, in our consulting work we have observed that scores on SJTs and assessment centres can differ dramatically across cultures even when the items are the same, because what is considered an appropriate response is more culturally sensitive. The next evolution of this research must directly compare the predictor methods and the corresponding scores from those methods, across cultures, to definitely know the role of culture on selection practice and outcomes.

Even less is known about cultural differences in retention practices and outcomes. The research cited above finds cultural variability in employment laws and thus there will be cultural variability in employee mobility. The antecedents and consequences of voluntary and involuntary turnover are likely to be strongly shaped by laws that enhance or inhibit employee mobility. Does this mean the consequences of collective turnover on firm performance are influenced by culture? Do firms that have operations in multiple cultures manage retention differently? We know almost nothing about whether or how culture may shape retention. This is obviously an area that is ripe for research.

5.3.2   Technology

Technology has created incredible opportunities and pressures on staffing and retention. Selection practice, in particular, has been heavily influenced by technology. Technology has enabled the use of high-fidelity simulations and gaming principles in assessment, unproctored assessments via mobile devices, and instant scoring and feedback (for example, Tippins et al., 2006). Technology offers the opportunity to include greater realism, lower costs, and delivery efficiencies. However, there is little research that directly examines the efficacy of different technological platforms, leaving organisations with little evidence-based guidance. The review by Ployhart, Schmitt and Tippins (2017) concluded that there is about a 10-year lag between the introduction of a major technology and research published on that technology. Most of the empirical research that has been conducted focuses on either comparing different assessment methods (for example, Internet versus paper) or examines the use of the Internet for recruitment (see Ployhart, Schmitt and Tippins, 2017). We are just starting to see research on social media in selection contexts (Van Iddekinge et al., 2013), but most of this work is theoretical and conceptual (Roth et al., 2013).

There is even less research linking technology to retention. Technology plays a role in understanding turnover because the platforms that record data (for example, social media usage or postings) can be used to predict behaviour. For example, Robinson, Sinar and Winter (2014) demonstrated that it is possible to review work experience and prior job mobility on LinkedIn profiles to predict turnover intentions and engagement. Practice is much further along in using technology for the prediction of turnover. In our experience, we have observed some organisations mining employee social media postings to make inferences about their likelihood to quit. For example, if an employee is posting such terms as "frustrated", "upset", and so on, they get identified as a potential flight risk. Other firms closely monitor reputational sites like Glassdoor to infer their workforce's engagement and turnover potential.

The scientific examination of technology for selection and retention is a missed opportunity for science to inform practice. One problem is that organisations are experimenting with technology so quickly that it is difficult for research to keep pace. For example, a research study conducted on a social media platform that is popular today could be gone by the time the study is published. McFarland and Ployhart (2015) developed a theoretical framework that seeks to provide a deeper explanation of technology and its role in HR and organisations. They argue that the digital context (for example, email, Internet, social networking) creates a fundamentally different type of environment from the physical, tangible world. Their framework enables researchers to study the core elements that make a particular type of technology unique, rather than simply conducting research on one platform versus another.

Ultimately, researchers must begin to study the role of technology in selection and retention. The number of interesting questions that have not been explored is staggering. To move this agenda forward, we believe it will be critical for academics to partner with organisations. First, organisations are able to capture large amounts of data quickly and efficiently. Second, many organisations are employing methodologies, analytics and digital platforms very different from those familiar to academics (for example, "big data" modelling). Third, the nature of the questions and challenges does not follow traditional theoretical trajectories. Yet, as do others (for example, Roth et al., 2013), we believe this is what makes this type of research so exciting. We are in a rare time in history for academic research to make a profound impact on organisational practice.

5.3.3 Strategy in a VUCA world

Due in part to globalisation and technology, the pace of competition is fast and organisations are challenged to remain nimble to survive. As was argued in the previous chapter on risk optimisation and talent management, an agile organisational strategy becomes particularly critical in such environments because it is impossible to predict the future. Cappelli (2015) notes how in the past, organisations would have highly detailed workforce plans. Today such plans do not make sense because the future is so uncertain, and, as a consequence, less attention has been given to long-term HR activities like development and succession planning.

Such rapid change puts incredible pressure on selection and retention because it means firms must be able to quickly hire or divest of their talent. In terms of selection, it moves the practice of selection to one that focuses on speed and efficiency. It also keeps the focus on hiring more generic KSAOs because such competencies can be redeployed for a number of purposes (Wright and Snell, 1998). In this manner, selection keeps the organisation nimble and responsive. Kim and Ployhart (2014) provided preliminary evidence to support such claims. They examined the impact of selection and training on firm productivity and profit, before, during, and shortly after the Great Recession. Selection became even more important after the Great Recession, and firms that used more stringent selection practices recovered more quickly. More research is needed that links selection practices to business strategy and the broader economic conditions in which firms operate (see Snow and Snell, 1993).

The effects of economic conditions on retention and turnover have been understood for a long time (March and Simon, 1958). The effects of unemployment rate, for example, are understood to have a negative impact on turnover (Hausknecht and Trevor, 2011). There is also research on HR practices that suggests commitment-focused practices should reduce turnover (Jiang et al., 2012). And yet, it's less clear how firms develop strategy that recognises challenges resulting from high and chronic turnover (for example, retail). It is also fairly unclear how firms manage turnover and retention strategically as a means to divest of talent no longer relevant to a change in company strategy (Sirmon, Hitt and Ireland, 2007).

The challenge of environmental VUCA for selection and retention research is to recognise that strategies change quickly, and so selection and retention must be nimble if they are to effectively implement strategy. This presents a major shift in focus because most selection and retention research have been conducted at the individual level. Therefore, future research will have to build on recent advancements that study selection and retention at the unit or firm levels, and this research will have to incorporate theory and research from organisational strategy (Ployhart, 2012). This research will need to sample across firms, and will need business metrics that are tracked longitudinally. Although daunting, such data exists in a number of sources and is increasingly collected within major industry groups and among human capital vendors.

5.3.4   Human capital resource pipelines

The forces noted above lead to a conclusion that selection and retention research need to make some dramatic shifts to better align with the realities facing modern organisations. But there is a latent theme that undercuts all of these observations, and this theme is that selection and turnover research must start to study human capital resource pipelines (a phenomenon picked up in Chapters 3 and 4 on talent management). As noted above, most prior research has focused on the selection and retention of individuals. In contrast, research in the last decade has emphasised that it is collective human capital resources that give firms the ability to perform, pivot, and achieve competitive advantage (see Wright, Coff and Moliterno, 2014). Collective human capital resources exist at the firm level (or unit levels) and emerge from individual KSAOs that are combined via organisational structures, HR practices, and task environments (Ployhart and Moliterno, 2011). Because collective human capital resources are based on collections of people, they are inherently firm-specific (Ployhart et al., 2014), and thus manifest the characteristics needed to generate competitive advantage (that is, valuable, rare, inimitable, and difficult to substitute; Barney and Wright, 1998).

With a focus on collective human capital resources, selection becomes the mechanism through which such resources are built and acquired (Ployhart, 2006), and turnover represents the erosion of such resources (Nyberg and Ployhart, 2013). Thus, research must examine the flow of collective human capital resources over time – that is, the human capital resource pipeline. There is some research that examines selection and retention simultaneously. For example, Reilly et al. (2014) modelled selection and turnover simultaneously and over time to show how they shaped patient satisfaction in a hospital setting. Call et al. (2015) examined changes in the quality and quantity of turnover and replacement hires longitudinally, to again show evidence of a dynamic system influencing unit financial performance. But studies like this are the exception, and most prior research usually gives a focus to selection *or* retention, while controlling for the other. Talent acquisition and retention are inherently linked in practice, and this connection needs greater recognition in research.

5.4   Conclusions

We believe that research examining how HR practices shape the flow of human capital resources within the context of firm strategy and competitive environments will lead to significant new insights that modify (and likely contradict) much of what we "know" about talent and human resources. Such insight, in turn, will more directly align

HR scholarship with contemporary practice. First, the research will become more relevant and actionable because it will reflect the contextualised dynamic system that managers operate within. Second, it will show how changes in one part of the system impact other parts of the system. Third, it will speak to questions about time, timing, and duration, and allow prescriptive guidance (for example, changing the selectivity of talent by X leads to a gain in Y, for a period of Z). Finally, the focus on pipelines and flows is flexible and responsive to broader environmental changes. This is all to say, researchers will be studying talent similar to how leaders manage talent, and thus achieving the promise of applied management research.

References

Abelson, M.A. and Baysinger, B.D. 1984. Optimal and dysfunctional turnover: Toward an organisational level model. *Academy of Management Review*, 9(2): 331–341.

Barney, J. and Wright, P. 1998. On becoming a strategic partner: The role of human resources in gaining competitive advantage. *Human Resource Management*, 37(1): 31–46.

Baron, J., Hannan, M. and Burton, M.D. 2001. Labor pains: Change in organizational models and employee turnover in young, high-tech firms. *American Journal of Sociology*, 106(4): 960–1012.

Barrick, M.R., Dustin, S.L., Giluk, T.L., Stewart, G.L., Shaffer, J.A. et al. 2012. Candidate characteristics driving initial impressions during rapport building: Implications for employment interview validity. *Journal of Occupational and Organizational Psychology*, 85(2): 330–352.

Becker, G.S. 1993. *Human Capital: A Theoretical and Empirical Analysis, with Special Reference to Education*. Chicago, IL: Chicago University Press.

Bidwell, M. 2011. Paying more to get less: The effects of external hiring versus internal mobility. *Administrative Science Quarterly*, 56(3): 369–407.

Call, M.L., Nyberg, A.J., Ployhart, R.E. and Weekley, J. 2015. The dynamic nature of turnover and unit performance: The impact of time, quality, and replacements. *Academy of Management Journal*, 58(4): 1208–1232.

Campion, M.A. 1991. Meaning and measurement of turnover: Comparison of alternative measures and recommendations for research. *Journal of Applied Psychology*, 76(2): 199–212.

Cappelli, P. 2015. Why we love to hate HR . . . and what HR can do about it. *Harvard Business Review*, 93(7): 56–61.

Cascio, W.F. 2006. The economic impact of employee behaviors on organizational performance. *California Management Review*, 48(4): 41–59.

Crook, T.R., Combs, J.G., Todd, S.Y., Woehr, D.J. and Ketchen, D.J. 2011. Does human capital matter? A meta-analysis of the relationship between human capital and firm performance. *The Journal of Applied Psychology*, 96(3): 443–456.

Dalton, D.R. and Todor, W.D. 1979. Manifest needs of stewards: propensity to file a grievance. *Journal of Applied Psychology*, 64(6): 654–659.

Dalton, D.R., Todor, W.D. and Krackhardt, D.M. 1982. Turnover overstated: The functional taxonomy. *Academy of Management Review*, 7(1): 117–123.

Guthrie, J.P. 2000. Alternative pay practices and employee turnover: An organization economics perspective. *Group & Organization Management*, 25(4): 419–439.

Hancock, J.I., Allen, D.G., Bosco, F.A., McDaniel, K.R. and Pierce, C.A. 2011. Meta-analytic review of employee turnover as a predictor of firm performance. *Journal of Management*, 39(3): 573–603.

Hausknecht, J.P. and Holwerda, J.A. 2013. When does employee turnover matter? Dynamic member configurations, productive capacity, and collective performance. *Organization Science*, 24(1): 210–225.

Hausknecht, J.P. and Trevor, C.O. 2011. Collective turnover at the group, unit, and organizational levels: Evidence, issues, and implications. *Journal of Management*, 37(1): 352–388.

Heavey, A.L., Holwerda, J.A. and Hausknecht, J.P. 2013. Causes and consequences of collective turnover: A meta-analytic review. *Journal of Applied Psychology*, 98(3): 412–453.

Hoffman, B.J., Melchers, K.G., Blair, C.A., Kleinmann, M. and Ladd, R.T. 2011. Exercises and dimensions are the currency of assessment centers. *Personnel Psychology*, 64(2): 351–395.

Holtom, B.C., Mitchell, T.R., Lee, T.W. and Eberly, M.B. 2008. Turnover and retention research: A glance at the past, a closer review of the present, and a venture into the future. *The Academy of Management Annals*, 2(1): 231–274.

Jiang, K., Lepak, D.P., Hu, J. and Baer, J.C. 2012. How does human resource management influence organizational outcomes? A meta-analytic investigation of mediating mechanisms. *Academy of Management Journal*, 55(6): 1264–1294.

Kim, Y. and Ployhart, R.E. 2014. The effects of staffing and training on firm productivity and profit growth before, during, and after the Great Recession. *The Journal of Applied Psychology*, 99(3): 361–389.

Krumm, S., Lievens, F., Hüffmeier, J., Lipnevich, A., Bendels, H. et al. 2014. How "situational" is judgment in situational judgment tests? *The Journal of Applied Psychology*, 100(2): 399–416.

Leana, C.R. and Van Buren, H.J.I. 1999. Organizational social capital and employment practices. *Academy of Management Review*, 24(3): 538–555.

March, J.G. and Simon, H.A. 1958. *Organizations*. New York: Wiley.

McElroy, J.C., Morrow, P.C. and Rude, S.N. 2001. Turnover and organizational performance: A comparative analysis of the effects of voluntary, involuntary, and reduction-in-force turnover. *Journal of Applied Psychology*, 86(6): 1294–1299.

McFarland, L.A. and Ployhart, R.E. 2015. Social media: A contextual framework to guide research and practice. *Journal of Applied Psychology*, 100(6): 1653–1677.

Mitchell, T.R., Holtom, B.C., Lee, T.W., Sablynski, C.J. and Erez, M. 2001. Why people stay: Using job embeddedness to predict voluntary turnover. *The Academy of Management Journal*, 44(6): 1102–1121.

Mobley, W.H. 1982. *Employee Turnover in Organizations*. Reading, MA: Addison-Wesley.

Ng, T.W.H. and Feldman, D.C. 2012. Breaches of past promises, current job alternatives, and promises of future idiosyncratic deals: Three-way interaction effects on organizational commitment. *Human Relations*, 65(11): 1463–1486.

Ng, T.W.H. and Feldman, D.C. 2013. Community embeddedness and work outcomes: The mediating role of organizational embeddedness. *Human Relations*, 67(1): 71–103.

Nyberg, A.J. and Ployhart, R.E. 2013. Context-emergent turnover (CET) theory: A theory of collective turnover. *Academy of Management Review*, 38(1): 109–131.

O'Reilly, C.A., Chatman, J. and Caldwell, D.F. 1991. People and organizational culture: A profile comparison approach to assessing person–organization fit. *Academy of Management Journal*, 34(3): 487–516.

Osterman, P. 1987. Turnover, employment security, and the performance of the firm. In M. Kleiner (ed.), *Human Resources and the Performance of the Firm*. Madison, WI: Industrial Relations Research Association, 275–317.

Park, T.-Y. and Shaw, J.D. 2013. Turnover rates and organizational performance: A meta-analysis. *Journal of Applied Psychology*, 98(2): 268–309.

Ployhart, R.E. 2006. Staffing in the 21st century: New challenges and strategic opportunities. *Journal of Management*, 32(6): 868–897.

Ployhart, R.E. 2012. The psychology of competitive advantage: An adjacent possibility. *Industrial and Organizational Psychology*, 5(1): 62–81.

Ployhart, R.E. and Hale, D. 2014. The fascinating psychological microfoundations of strategy and competitive advantage. *Annual Review of Organizational Psychology and Organizational Behavior*, 1: 145–172.

Ployhart, R.E. and Moliterno, T.P. 2011. Emergence of the human capital resource: A multilevel model. *Academy of Management Review*, 36(1): 127–150.

Ployhart, R.E., Nyberg, A.J., Reilly, G. and Maltarich, M.A. 2014. Human capital is dead: Long live human capital resources! *Journal of Management*, 40(2): 371–398.

Ployhart, R.E., Schmitt, N. and Tippins, N.T. 2017. Solving the supreme problem: 100 years of recruitment and selection research at the *Journal of Applied Psychology*. *Journal of Applied Psychology*, 102(3): 291–304.

Ployhart, R.E., Schneider, B. and Schmitt, N. 2006. *Staffing Organizations: Contemporary Practice and Theory*. Lawrence Erlbaum Associates Publishers.

Ployhart, R.E., Van Iddekinge, C.H. and MacKenzie, W.I. 2011. Acquiring and developing human capital in service context: The interconnectedness of human capital resources. *Academy of Management Journal*, 54(2): 353–368.

Rabl, T., Jayasinghe, M., Gerhart, B. and Kühlmann, T.M. 2014. A meta-analysis of country differences in the high-performance work system–business performance relationship: The roles of national culture and managerial discretion. *Journal of Applied Psychology*, 99(6): 1011–1041.

Reilly, G., Nyberg, A.J., Maltarich, M. and Weller, I. 2014. Human capital flows: Using context-emergent turnover (CET) theory to explore the process by which turnover, hiring, and job demands affect patient satisfaction. *Academy of Management Journal*, 57(3): 766–790.

Robinson, S.D., Sinar, E. and Winter, J. 2014. Social media as a tool for research: A turnover application using linkedIn. *TIP: The Industrial-Organizational Psychologist*, 52(1): 133–141.

Roth, P.L., Bobko, P., Van Iddekinge, C.H. and Thatcher, J.B. 2013. Social media in employee-selection-related decisions: A research agenda for uncharted territory. *Journal of Management.* http://doi.org/10.1177/0149206313503018.

Ryan, A.M., McFarland, L.A., Baron, H. and Page, R. 1999. An international look at selection practices: Nation and culture as explanations for variability in practice. *Personnel Psychology*, 52: 359–391.

Ryan, A.M. and Ployhart, R.E. 2014. A century of selection. *Annual Review of Psychology*, 65: 693–717.

Schmitt, N. 2014. Personality and cognitive ability as predictors of effective performance at work. *Annual Review of Organizational Psychology and Organizational Behavior*, 1: 45–65.

Shaw, J.D. 2011. Turnover rates and organizational performance. *Organizational Psychology Review*, 1(3): 187–213.

Shaw, J.D., Duffy, M.K., Johnson, J.L. and Lockhart, D.E. 2005. Turnover, social capital losses, and performance. *Academy of Management*, 48(4): 594–606.

Shaw, J.D., Gupta, N. and Delery, J.E. 2005. Alternative conceptualizations of the relationship between voluntary turnover and organizational performance. *Academy of Management*, 48(1): 50–68.

Sirmon, D.G., Hitt, M.A. and Ireland, R.D. 2007. Managing firm resources in dynamic environments to create value: Looking inside the black box. *Academy of Management Review*, 32(1): 273–292.

Snow, C.C. and Snell, S.A. 1993. Staffing as strategy. In M. Schmitt and W.C. Borman (eds), *Personnel Selection in Organizations*. San Francisco: Jossey-Bass, 448–478.

Staw, B.M. 1980. The consequences of turnover. *Journal of Occupational Behaviour*, 1: 253–273.

Summers, J.K., Humphrey, S.E. and Ferris, G.R. 2012. Team member change, flux in coordination, and performance: Effects of strategic core roles, information transfer, and cognitive ability. *Academy of Management Journal*, 55(2): 314–338.

Tippins, N.T., Beaty, J., Drasgow, F., Gibson, W.M., Pearlman, K. et al. 2006. Unproctored internet testing in employment settings. *Personnel Psychology*, 59(1): 189–225.

Trevor, C.O. and Nyberg, A.J. 2008. Keeping your headcount when all about you are losing theirs: Downsizing, voluntary turnover rates, and the moderating role of HR practices. *Academy of Management Journal*, 51(2): 259–276.

Van Iddekinge, C.H., Ferris, G.R., Perrewé, P.L., Perryman, A.A., Blass, F.R. et al. 2009. Effects of selection and training on unit-level performance over time: A latent growth modeling approach. *Journal of Applied Psychology*, 94(4): 829–843.

Van Iddekinge, C.H., Lanivich, S.E., Roth, P.L. and Junco, E. 2013. Social media for selection? Validity and adverse impact potential of a Facebook-based assessment. *Journal of Management.* http://doi.org/10.1177/0149206313515524.

Wright, P.M. and Boswell, W.R. 2002. Desegregating HRM: A review and synthesis of micro and macro human resource management research. *Journal of Management*, 28(3): 247–276.

Wright, P.M., Coff, R. and Moliterno, T.P. 2014. Strategic human capital: Crossing the great divide. *Journal of Management*, 40(2): 353–370.

Wright, P.M. and Snell, S.A. 1998. Toward a unifying framework for exploring fit and flexibility in strategic human resource management. *The Academy of Management Review*, 23(4): 756–772.

6 Human resource management and employee engagement

Alan M. Saks and Jamie A. Gruman

6.1 Introduction

During the last decade, a great deal has been learned about employee engagement. Research has identified various antecedents and consequences of engagement and shown how engagement mediates relationships between various antecedents and outcomes (Saks and Gruman, 2014). However, most research on employee engagement is based on the job demands-resources (JD-R) model. According to the JD-R model, job resources such as autonomy, participation in decision-making, task variety, performance feedback, and social support are positively related to engagement while job demands such as work overload, job insecurity, role ambiguity, and role conflict are negatively related to engagement (Crawford, LePine and Rich, 2010). Far less research has focused on human resource management (HRM) practices and employee engagement. This has resulted in a gap in both the research and practitioner literature when it comes to understanding how human resource management practices and systems can be configured to enhance employee engagement. This is a serious shortcoming given that employee engagement can provide organisations with a competitive advantage (Albrecht et al., 2015). Thus, there is a pressing need to develop a strategic human resource management approach to employee engagement (Sparrow, 2014).

The purpose of this chapter is to address the HRM gap in the engagement literature by focusing on the relationship between human resource management and employee engagement. First, we briefly review research on HRM and employee engagement using the ability–motivation–opportunity or AMO model of human resource management as a framework. Second, we develop an integrative model of the mechanisms or process variables that mediate the relationship between HRM and three levels of engagement (employee, team, and organisational). In the final section of this chapter, we offer a research agenda for future research on HRM and engagement.

6.2   Human resource management and employee engagement research

As indicated above, the primary theoretical model used to study employee engagement is the job demands-resources (JD-R) model, which focuses on various job resources and job demands that predict employee engagement. However, we believe that an alternative model better suited to human resource management is one that describes distinct human resource management practices such as the ability-motivation-opportunity or AMO model of human resource management (Jiang et al., 2012b). The AMO model suggests that HRM systems are comprised of policies and practices that focus on three areas of HRM:

(1)   skill-enhancing HRM practices;
(2)   motivation-enhancing HRM practices; and
(3)   opportunity-enhancing HRM practices.

Skill-enhancing HRM practices focus on ensuring that employees have the necessary knowledge, skills, and abilities (using the KSAO model) to perform their job, and include activities such as recruitment, selection, socialisation, and training. Motivation-enhancing HRM practices focus on ensuring adequate employee motivation and include activities such as performance management, compensation, incentives and rewards, promotion and career development, and job security. Opportunity-enhancing HRM practices focus on ensuring that employees are empowered to use their skills and motivation to achieve organisational objectives and includes practices such as job design, work teams, information sharing, and employee involvement (Jiang et al., 2012b; Lepak et al., 2006). Jiang et al. (2012b) found that the three HRM dimensions were differentially related to human capital and employee motivation, which partially mediated the relationships between the HRM dimensions and voluntary turnover, operational outcomes, and financial outcomes.

In the following sections, we briefly review research on HRM and employee engagement within each of the three HRM dimensions of the AMO model.

6.3   Skill-enhancing HRM practices

A number of studies have examined the role of various skill-enhancing HRM practices and employee engagement. For example, Albrecht et al. (2015) suggested that selection practices could be used to predict which job applicants are most likely to become engaged. They argued that both broad and narrow personality dimensions could be tested in the selection process using structured interviews and assessment centres. In addition to selecting for specific personality characteristics, practices that ensure a high degree of fit between employees and their roles and organisations can also lead to more engaged employees. For example, Saks and Gruman (2011) found that person–job fit and person–organisation fit perceptions were positively related to engagement. Similarly, May, Gilson and Harter (2004) found that the degree of perceived fit between employees' self-concepts and their jobs was positively related to engagement. Rich, LePine and Crawford (2010) found that the degree of congruence between employee values and organisational values was positively related to engagement.

Training and opportunities for learning have also been linked to employee engagement. Fletcher (2016) found that employees' satisfaction with training was positively related to engagement and engagement mediated the relationship between satisfaction with training and employees' self-rated work role behaviours. Sarti (2014) found that having job-related learning opportunities was the strongest predictor of engagement among the job resources included in her study. Similarly, Bal, Kooij and De Jong (2013) demonstrated that developmental HRM practices (that is, retraining) foster engagement through the mediating effect of psychological contracts. It has also been suggested that job rotation may promote engagement because it fosters learning and stimulates professional development (Salanova et al., 2010).

Socialisation is another skill-enhancing HRM practice that allows employees to learn the behaviours, attitudes and skills required to adjust to new jobs and roles. Saks and Gruman (2011) found that institutionalised socialisation tactics were indirectly related to engagement through a number of process variables including person–job fit perceptions, positive emotions, and self-efficacy. Saks and Gruman (2010) suggested that engagement could be promoted by exposing new hires to a set of socialisation resources. They reported positive relationships between various socialisation resources and employee engagement with correlations ranging from 0.29 to 0.52. Similarly, Ellis et al. (2015)

present a model of the socialisation process in which they argue that socialisation tactics might moderate the effect of job demands on newcomer engagement as a result of their impact on newcomers' perception of the availability of resources and ability to cope.

6.4   Motivation-enhancing HRM practices

Relative to skill-enhancing HRM practices, less research has investigated motivation-enhancing HRM practices and employee engagement. Barrick et al. (2015) found that a measure of HRM investments and expectation-enhancing practices, including job security, pay equity, pay-for-performance, and performance feedback, were positively correlated with collective organisational engagement. Sarti (2014) also found that financial rewards and performance feedback were positively associated with engagement. In a study of pay satisfaction among hospitality employees, Jung and Yoon (2015) found that benefits, pay level, and pay structure positively predicted engagement. Saks (2006) found positive correlations between receiving rewards and recognition for good performance and job and organisation engagement.

Performance management is another motivation-enhancing HRM practice that can influence employee engagement (Mone et al., 2011). Mone et al. (2011) suggest that engagement can be enhanced through the performance management activities of goal setting, feedback and recognition, employee development, regular appraisals, and a climate of trust and empowerment. Gruman and Saks (2011) developed an engagement management model, which builds on traditional performance management models to foster the engagement of employees. The model begins with a performance agreement stage that consists of goal setting and a review and agreement of the psychological contract. This is followed by engagement facilitation which involves providing employees with resources they need to become engaged (for example, job design, coaching, social support, leadership, training), and then performance and engagement appraisal and feedback which should lead to employee engagement and then improved performance.

It is worth noting, however, that performance management systems that are top-down and impose performance standards on employees can have a negative effect on employee engagement (see Conway et al., 2016). Thus, performance management systems need to focus on engagement and be supported by other HRM practices (for example, job design, training) that will facilitate and promote employee engagement.

6.5   Opportunity-enhancing HR practices

Among opportunity-enhancing HRM practices, job enrichment or job characteristics have received the most attention and repeatedly have been found to be strongly related to employee engagement. For example, May, Gilson and Harter (2004) found that job enrichment was positively related to engagement, and Saks (2006) found that job characteristics predict job engagement. Using meta-analytic path modeling, Christian, Garza and Slaughter (2011) found that autonomy, task variety, task significance, problem solving, feedback, and job complexity are positively related to engagement, while physical demands are negatively related. Barrick et al. (2015) found that enriched jobs are positively related to collective engagement among entry-level employees.

A number of studies have also found that engagement is enhanced when employees directly or indirectly enrich their jobs themselves. For example, Tims, Bakker and Derks (2012) found that job crafting is positively associated with engagement. Similarly, Breevaart, Bakker and Demerouti (2014) found that the positive relationship between daily self-management and daily engagement was mediated by the availability of daily resources including skill variety, feedback, and developmental opportunities.

Beugré (2010) suggests that employees who are given the opportunity to voice their opinions are more likely to be engaged. Rees, Alfes and Gatenby (2013) found that employee voice is positively associated with engagement, and this relationship is mediated by trust in senior management and the employee–supervisor relationship. Similarly, Conway et al. (2016) found that employee experiences of voice were positively related to employee engagement, and Allen and Rogelberg (2013) found that the degree to which employees felt they had voice during meetings was positively associated with engagement. Participation, a conceptually similar construct, has comparable effects. For example, Yoerger, Crowe and Allen (2015) found that participation in decision-making during meetings was positively associated with engagement. Empowerment has also been found to be positively related to engagement (Wang and Liu, 2015).

6.6   HRM systems

In recent years, scholars in the HRM field have emphasised the importance of HRM systems, as opposed to individual HRM practices (Subramony, 2009; Jiang et al., 2012a). As a result, a number of studies have taken a systems approach to HRM and engagement and examined bundles of HRM practices and particular types of HRM systems. For example, Alfes et al. (2013a) found that perceptions of a set of HRM practices were positively related to engagement, and engagement mediated the relationship between perceived HRM practices and organisational citizenship behaviours and turnover intentions. Alfes et al. (2013b) found that perceptions of a set of six high-performance HRM practices were positively related to engagement, and engagement mediated the relationships between perceived HRM practices and self-report task performance and innovative work behaviour. Cooke et al. (in press) found that high-performance work systems (HPWS) (rewards, training and development, performance appraisal, and employee participation) were positively related to employee engagement and resilience mediated the relationship between HPWS and engagement.

Several studies have investigated particular types of HRM systems. For example, Bal and DeLange (2015) found that the availability of flexibility HRM, which allows employees to choose when, where, and how to work, was positively related to engagement, and engagement mediated the relationship between availability of flexibility HRM and self-rated job performance. Boon and Kalshoven (2014) investigated high-commitment HRM practices which involve high job security, promotion from within, continuous training, extensive benefits, and career development. They argued that high-commitment HRM provides employees with organisational resources that will enhance their engagement and commitment. Indeed, they found that high-commitment HRM was related to employee engagement, and engagement mediated the relationship between high-commitment HRM and organisational commitment.

Barrick et al. (2015) investigated the relationship between HRM practices that focus on the firms' expectations of employees and enhance employees' expected rewards and outcomes and collective organisational engagement (that is, shared perceptions of organisational members that members of the organisation are, as a whole, physically, cognitively, and emotionally invested in their work) and firm performance. As expected, the HRM practices were positively related to collective organisational engagement which mediated the relationship between HRM practices and firm performance.

In summary, a handful of studies have shown that HRM systems are important for fostering employee engagement and therefore call attention to the need to focus on HRM systems that are most likely to facilitate engagement rather than just HRM practices.

6.7 An integrative process model of human resource management and engagement

Although research on HRM and employee engagement has been increasing in recent years, much of it is fragmented as each study examines different HRM practices and systems as well as different processes that link HRM to engagement. This issue is not limited to research on employee engagement. As noted by Jiang et al. (2012a), the configuration of the systems, in addition to the number and type of practices included, varies substantially from study to study in research on HRM systems. While we have tried to integrate the literature by categorising previous research using the three dimensions of the AMO model, it is difficult at this time to identify which HRM practices and dimensions are more or less strongly related to employee engagement.

Therefore, there is a need for an integrative model that includes HRM dimensions as well as the mechanisms through which HRM will lead to employee engagement. Albrecht et al. (2015) have developed a model of how four key HRM practices (selection, socialisation, performance management, and training and development) influence employee engagement through organisational climate, job resources and demands, and psychological meaningfulness, safety, and availability. However, this model includes only four specific HRM practices and leaves out a number of process variables that might link HRM to engagement. Furthermore, its focus is strictly on employee engagement rather than engagement at other levels such as the team and organisation.

In this section, we develop a more integrative process model of HRM and employee engagement that includes:

(1) the three HRM dimensions of the AOM model as well as HRM systems;

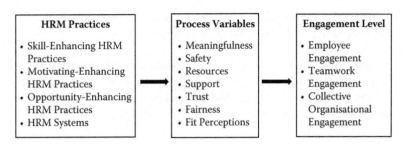

Figure 6.1   An integrative process model of HRM and engagement

(2)   a number of process variables that link HRM to engagement; and
(3)   employee engagement, team engagement, and collective organisational engagement.

Although several studies have begun to study team engagement and collective organisational engagement, most research on HRM and engagement has focused on employee engagement. A complete and integrated model of HRM and engagement should include all three levels of engagement.

As shown in Figure 6.1, we propose that each dimension of HRM as well as HRM systems will lead to each level of engagement (employee, team, organisation) through a number of process variables. Including the process variables is important for a number of reasons. First, previous research has largely treated engagement as a mediating variable that links HRM practices to various outcomes such as organisational citizenship behaviours, performance, and turnover intentions (for example, Alfes et al., 2013a, 2013b). As a result, less attention has been given to the process variables that link HRM to engagement. Understanding these linkages is fundamental for the development of a theory of HRM and engagement and for knowing how best to influence engagement. Furthermore, several studies have shown that process variables such as fit perceptions are related to engagement (Saks and Gruman, 2011).

The process variables included in our model are based on Kahn's (1990) work as well as previous research on engagement. First, Kahn (1990) found that an individual's degree of engagement was a function of the experience of three psychological conditions: psychological meaningfulness, psychological safety, and psychological availability. Employees who experience a greater amount of psychological meangingfulness, safety, and availability will engage themselves to a greater extent in their work role. May, Gilson and Harter (2004) found that meaningfulness, safety, and availability were significantly related to engagement.

Psychological meaningfulness involves the extent to which people derive meaning from their work and feel that they are receiving a return on investments of self in the performance of a role. People experience meaningfulness when they feel worthwhile, useful, and valuable and when they are not taken for granted. Psychological safety involves being able to employ and express one's true self without fear of negative consequences to one's self-image, status, or career. Social systems that are predictable, consistent, and non-threatening provide a greater sense of psychological safety. Psychological availability involves the belief that one has the physical, emotional, and psychological resources required to invest one's self in the performance of a role. Employees will be more engaged in workplaces that provide them with physical, emotional, and psychological resources necessary for role performances (Kahn, 1990).

Research on employee engagement has identified a number of other process variables that are important for engagement and might also be influenced by HRM practices. For example, many studies have found that social support is strongly related to engagement. Engagement is positively associated with social support in general (Christian, Garza and Slaughter, 2011; Halbesleben, 2010) and supervisor support in particular (Bakker et al., 2007; May, Gilson and Harter, 2004). Saks (2006) found that perceived organisational support predicted both job engagement and organisation engagement. Rich, LePine and Crawford (2010) suggest that performance management may directly impact engagement levels by increasing employees' perceived organisational support.

Other process variables in the model are trust, perceptions of fairness, and fit perceptions. Macey and Schneider (2008) argued that trust plays a central role in the engagement process and for increasing the likelihood of engagement behaviour. As indicated earlier, Rees, Alfes and Gatenby (2013) found that trust mediated the relationship between employee voice and engagement. Several studies have found that fairness is positively related to engagement (Maslach and Leiter, 2008; Saks, 2006). For example, Moliner, Martinez-Tur, Ramos, Peiro, and Cropanzano (2008) found that procedural and interactional justice were positively related to work engagement, and work engagement mediated the relationship between organisational justice and extra-role customer service (customer-focused organisational citizenship behaviours). Fit perceptions have also been recognised as important for engagement. Work–role and person–job fit perceptions as well as perceived value congruence have been found to be positively related to employee engagement (May, Gilson and Harter, 2004; Rich, LePine and Crawford, 2010; Saks and Gruman, 2011).

The final component of our model is engagement level. While most research on HRM and engagement has focused on individual or employee engagement, several studies have begun to investigate teamwork engagement and collective organisational engagement. Costa, Passos and Bakker (2014) define teamwork engagement as a shared, positive, fulfilling, motivational emergent state of work-related well-being. In one of the first studies on teamwork engagement, Torrente et al. (2012) found that teamwork engagement mediates the relationship between team social resources (for example, supportive team climate) and team performance.

Barrick et al. (2015) introduced the notion of collective organisational engagement, which as indicated earlier refers to shared perceptions of organisational members that members of the organisation are, as a whole, physically, cognitively, and emotionally invested in their work. They found that organisational resources (HRM practices, enriched entry-level jobs, and CEO transformational leadership) were positively related to collective organisational engagement, which mediated the relationship between organisational resources and firm performance.

In summary, the model of HRM and engagement indicates that each of the HRM dimensions as well as HRM systems will be related to each level of engagement through the various process variables and the process variables mediate the relationships between HRM and each level of engagement. As discussed in the next section, research is required to determine which HRM dimensions and systems best predict each process variable and level of engagement.

6.8   An agenda for future research on HRM and engagement

The model of HRM and engagement provides a foundation for future research. There are three key areas that form the basis for an agenda for future research:

(1)   the relationship between HRM dimensions and the process variables;
(2)   the relationship between HRM dimensions and each level of engagement; and
(3)   the mediating effects of the process variables.

In the remainder of this section, we briefly discuss each of these research topics and then summarise them with a research question.

6.8.1   The relationship between HRM dimensions and the process variables

As indicated earlier, there is some evidence that HRM practices are related to the process variables. However, much less is known about which HRM dimensions are most strongly related to each of the process variables. Given that the HRM dimensions have differential effects on human capital and employee motivation (Jiang et al., 2012b), they are also likely to have differential effects on the process variables. For example, because skill-enhancing HRM practices are designed to provide employees with the necessary knowledge, skills, and abilities to perform their role, they are likely to be most strongly related to resource availability and fit perceptions. Motivating-enhancing HRM practices are designed to enhance employee motivation and should be most strongly related to meaningfulness and fairness. Opportunity-enhancing HRM practices are designed to empower employees to use their skills and motivation and should be most strongly related to safety, support, and trust. However, future research is required to determine the extent to which each HRM dimension is related to each process variable and the strength of these relationships. Therefore, our first research question is the following:

Research Question #1: *What is the relationship between each HRM dimension and each process variable?*

As discussed earlier, a number of HRM systems (for example, high commitment, high-performance) have been linked to engagement although less attention has been given to the process through which different HRM systems might operate. Therefore, a second related research question is the following:

Research Question #2: *What is the relationship between different HRM systems and each process variable?*

In addition to the direct effects of each dimension and HR systems, the practices that make up an HRM system can have additive effects that complement each other, synergistic effects that strengthen each other, or can be redundant with each other (Delery, 1998; Jiang et al., 2012a). Thus, a better understanding of the dynamics and interrelationships among HRM dimensions and practices in fostering each process variable is also required. This leads to the following research question:

Research Question #3: *What are the additive, synergistic and redundant effects of HRM dimensions and practices with each process variable?*

6.8.2   The relationship between HRM dimensions and levels of engagement

There is now evidence that HRM practices are related to employee engagement, however, much less is known about what practices are more or less strongly related to engagement and each level of engagement. Only a few studies have investigated teamwork engagement and organisational collective engagement and even fewer have linked HRM practices to each level of engagement. Furthermore, previous research has not linked the three HRM dimensions to each level of engagement. As with the process variables, it is likely that the HRM dimensions will be differentially related to each level of engagement. For example, skill-enhancing HRM practices might be most important for employee engagement and teamwork engagement, while opportunity-enhancing HRM practices might be most important for collective organisational engagement, and motivating-enhancing HRM practices might be equally important for all three levels of engagement. Therefore, a fourth research question is:

Research Question #4: *What is the relationship between each HRM dimension and each level of engagement?*

Given that engagement research has focused on employee engagement, it is difficult to speculate on the relationships between different HRM systems and each level of engagement. It is possible that some HRM systems might be especially important for a particular level of engagement. Therefore, future research is needed to investigate the relationship between different HRM systems and each level of engagement. This leads to the following research question:

<u>Research Question #5</u>: *What is the relationship between different HRM systems and each level of engagement?*

As noted earlier, the practices that comprise an HRM system can have additive, synergistic, or redundant effects with each other. Understanding the interrelationships among HRM practices and dimensions in fostering the various levels of engagement is important for ensuing that HRM systems are designed to maximise levels of engagement. This suggests the following research question:

<u>Research Question #6</u>: *What are the additive, synergistic and redundant effects among HRM dimensions and practices with each level of engagement?*

6.8.3   The mediating effects of the process variables

The core of our model is that the HRM dimensions and systems are related to each level of engagement through a number of process variables. Thus, we are suggesting a mediating model in which the process variables mediate the relationships between the HRM dimensions and systems and each level of engagement. As indicated previously, there is some evidence that HRM practices are related to the process variables. In addition, previous research has shown that the process variables are related to employee engagement. However, much less is known about the relationship between each process variable and teamwork engagement and collective organisational engagement. Thus, it is possible that the process variables will be differentially related to each level of engagement. For example, meaningfulness, safety, resource availability, and fit perceptions might be especially important for employee engagement while support, trust, and fairness might be most important for teamwork engagement and collective organisational engagement.

Figure 6.1 is actually a simplistic model of the possible relationships between the variables. This is because each process variable might mediate one or more of the HRM dimensions for one or more of the three levels of engagement. In other words, each HRM dimension might operate through different process variables to influence each level of engagement. Thus, there are many possible mediation effects for the relationships between the HRM dimensions and the levels of engagement as well as between HRM systems and engagement levels. This leads to the final two research questions:

<u>Research Question #7</u>: *To what extent does each process variable mediate the relationship between each HRM dimension and each level of engagement?*

<u>Research Question #8</u>: *To what extent does each process variable mediate the relationship between HRM systems and each level of engagement?*

In summary, our model and accompanying research questions should lead to a more complete and integrated theory of HRM and engagement by helping to identify what HRM practices, dimensions, and systems are most likely to lead to high levels of employee engagement, work team engagement, and collective organisational engagement, and which process variables explain and mediate these relationships. This will require the use of a variety of research methodologies including longitudinal designs that can test the causal sequence of the variables in the model. In addition, experimental designs will also be useful to test the causal effects of various HRM interventions. In addition, because our model includes different levels of engagement, future research should consider collecting data at multiple levels (for example, individual, group, organisation).

6.9   Conclusion

Employee engagement has become one of the most important topics in recent years for management and HRM. However, research has focused primarily on the JD-R model and the importance of various job resources for employee engagement. Much less attention has been given to HRM practices that are important for employee engagement. This is a serious shortcoming because HRM provides the most systematic way for organisations to create a coherent and coordinated set of practices that are designed to create an engaged workforce. In addition, although research has begun to link HRM practices to employee engagement, the extant literature is disparate and fragmented. As a result, at this time it is difficult to provide organisations with guidelines as to what HRM practices are most likely to improve employee engagement.

In this chapter, we have developed an integrated process model that links three HRM dimensions and HRM systems to seven process variables that have the potential to mediate relationships between the HRM dimensions and systems and three levels of engagement. This model not only provides a means to integrate research on HRM and engagement, but it also helps to set an agenda for future research on HRM and engagement.

In addition to contributing to research on HRM and engagement, our model also extends existing research on strategic HRM and the AMO model. In particular, by including engagement within the AMO model, engagement becomes a new HRM outcome along with others such as human capital and employee motivation. Jiang et al. (2012b) found that human capital and employee motivation mediated the relationship between the three HRM dimensions and voluntary turnover, operational outcomes, and financial outcomes and called for future research to consider additional mediators. Thus, as shown in Figure 6.2, the three levels of engagement can be considered additional mediators for the relationships between HRM and organisational outcomes. Therefore, future research on strategic HRM might consider the extent to which the three levels of engagement mediate relationships between HRM and operational and financial organisational outcomes.

Our model also provides some guidance to practitioners and organisations as it provides a means to organise HRM practices and consider them in relation to particular processes and levels of engagement. Thus, organisations can use the model as a diagnostic tool to determine what level of engagement they want to enhance, what process variables to consider for improvement, and what HRM dimensions or systems should be developed to improve the process variables and increase engagement. For now, this is just a starting point as future research is required to provide more concrete guidelines regarding what HRM dimensions and systems are most likely to improve each process variable and lead to higher levels of employee, team, and organisational engagement.

In conclusion, although a great deal has been learned about employee engagement over the last decade, much less is known about HRM and engagement. In this chapter, we have attempted to provide a greater understanding of how HRM might lead to three levels of engagement. We hope that this helps to set the agenda for the next decade of research and contributes to the emerging theory and science of human resource management and engagement.

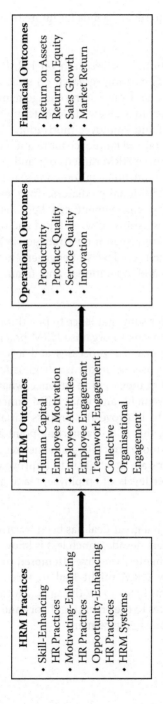

Figure 6.2 HRM practices and organisational outcomes

HRM Practices
• Skill-Enhancing HR Practices
• Motivating-Enhancing HR Practices
• Opportunity-Enhancing HR Practices
• HRM Systems

HRM Outcomes
• Human Capital
• Employee Motivation
• Employee Attitudes
• Employee Engagement
• Teamwork Engagement
• Collective Organisational Engagement

Operational Outcomes
• Productivity
• Product Quality
• Service Quality
• Innovation

Financial Outcomes
• Return on Assets
• Return on Equity
• Sales Growth
• Market Return

References

Albrecht, S.L., Bakker, A.B., Gruman, J.A., Macey, W.H. and Saks, A.M. (2015). Employee engagement, human resource management practices and competitive advantage: An integrated approach. *Journal of Organizational Effectiveness: People and Performance*, 2: 7–35.

Alfes, K., Shantz, A.D., Truss, C. and Soane, E.C. (2013a). The link between perceived human resource management practices, engagement and employee behaviour: A moderated mediation model. *The International Journal of Human Resource Management*, 24: 330–351.

Alfes, K., Truss, C., Soane, E.C., Rees, C. and Gatenby, M. (2013b). The relationship between line manager behavior, perceived HRM practices, and individual performance: Examining the mediating role of engagement. *Human Resource Management*, 52: 839–859.

Allen, J.A. and Rogelberg, S.G. (2013). Manager-led group meetings: A context for promoting employee engagement. *Group & Organization Management*, 38: 543–569.

Bakker, A.B., Hakanen, J.J., Demerouti, E. and Xanthopoulou, D. (2007). Job resources boost work engagement, particularly when job demands are high. *Journal of Educational Psychology*, 99: 274–284.

Bal, P.M. and DeLange, A.H. (2015). From flexibility human resource management to employee engagement and perceived job performance across the lifespan: A multisample study. *Journal of Occupational and Organizational Psychology*, 88: 126–154.

Bal, P.M., Kooij, D.T.A.M. and De Jong, S.B. (2013). How do developmental and accommodative HRM enhance employee engagement and commitment? The role of psychological contract and SOC strategies. *Journal of Management Studies*, 50: 545–572

Barrick, M.R., Thurgood, G.R., Smith, T.A. and Courtright, S.H. (2015). Collective organizational engagement: Linking motivational antecedents, strategic implementation, and firm performance. *Academy of Management Journal*, 58: 111–135.

Beugré, C.D. (2010). Organizational conditions fostering employee engagement: The role of "voice". In S.L. Albrecht (ed.), *Handbook of Employee Engagement: Perspectives, Issues, Research, and Practice*. Cheltenham, UK and Northampton, MA, USA: Edward Elgar Publishing, 174–181.

Boon, C. and Kalshoven, K. (2014). How high-commitment HRM relates to engagement and commitment: The moderating role of task proficiency. *Human Resource Management*, 53: 403–420.

Breevaart, K., Bakker, A.B. and Demerouti, E. (2014). Daily self-management and employee work engagement. *Journal of Vocational Behavior*, 84: 31–38.

Christian, M.S., Garza, A.S. and Slaughter, J.E. (2011). Work engagement: A quantitative review and test of its relations with task and contextual performance. *Personnel Psychology*, 64: 89–136.

Conway, E., Fu, N., Monks, K., Alfes, K. and Bailey, C. (2016). Demands or resources? The relationship between HR practices, employee engagement, and emotional exhaustion within a hybrid model of employment relations. *Human Resource Management*, 55: 901–917.

Cooke, F.L., Cooper, B., Bartram, T., Wang, J. and Mei, H. (in press). Mapping the relationships between high-performance work systems, employee resilience and engagement: A study of the banking industry in China. *The International Journal of Human Resource Management*.

Costa, P.L., Passos, A.M. and Bakker, A. (2014). Empirical validation of the team work engagement construct. *Journal of Personnel Psychology*, 13: 34–45.

Crawford, E.R., LePine, J.A. and Rich, B.L. (2010). Linking job demands and resources to employee engagement and burnout: A theoretical extension and meta-analytic test. *Journal of Applied Psychology*, 95: 834–848.

Delery, J.E. (1998). Issues of fit in strategic human resource management: Implications for research. *Human Resource Management Review*, 8: 289–309.

Ellis, A.M., Bauer, T.N., Mansfield, L.R., Erdogan, B., Truxillo, D.M. and Simon, L.S. (2015). Navigating uncharted waters: Newcomer socialization through the lens of stress theory. *Journal of Management*, 41: 203–235.

Fletcher, L. (2016). Training perceptions, engagement, and performance: Comparing work engagement and personal role engagement. *Human Resource Development International*, 19: 4–26.

Gruman, J.A. and Saks, A.M. (2011). Performance management and employee engagement. *Human Resource Management Review*, 21: 123–136.

Halbesleben, J.R.B. (2010). A meta-analysis of work engagement: Relationships with burnout, demands, resources, and consequences. In A.B. Bakker and M.P. Leiter (eds), *Work Engagement: A Handbook of Essential Theory and Research*. New York: Psychology Press, 102–117.

Jiang, K., Lepak, D.P., Han, K., Hong, Y., Kim., A. and Winkler, A. (2012a). Clarifying the construct of human resource systems: Relating human resource management to employee performance. *Human Resource Management Review*, 22: 73–85.

Jiang, K., Lepak, D.P., Hu, J. and Baer, J.C. (2012b). How does human resource management influence organizational outcomes? A meta-analytic investigation of mediating mechanisms. *Academy of Management Journal*, 55: 1264–1294.

Jung, H.S. and Yoon, H.H. (2015). Understanding pay satisfaction: The impacts of pay satisfaction on employees' job engagement and withdrawal in a deluxe hotel. *International Journal of Hospitality Management*, 48: 22–26.

Kahn, W.A. (1990). Psychological conditions of personal engagement and disengagement at work. *Academy of Management Journal*, 33: 692–724.

Lepak, D.P., Liao, H., Chung, Y. and Harden, E.E. (2006). A conceptual review of human resource management systems in strategic human resource management research. In J.J. Martocchio (ed.). *Research in Personnel and Human Resources Management* (vol. 25). New York: Elsevier, 217–271.

Macey, W.H. and Schneider, B. (2008). The meaning of employee engagement. *Industrial and Organizational Psychology*, 1: 3–30.

Maslach, C. and Leiter, M.P. (2008). Early predictors of job burnout and engagement. *Journal of Applied Psychology*, 93: 498–512.

May, D.R., Gilson, R.L. and Harter, L.M. (2004). The psychological conditions of meaningfulness, safety, and availability and the engagement of the human spirit at work. *Journal of Occupational and Organizational Psychology*, 77: 11–37.

Moliner, C., Martinez-Tur, V., Ramos, J., Peiro, J.M. and Cropanzano, R. (2008). Organizational justice and extrarole customer service: The mediating role of well-being at work. *European Journal of Work and Organizational Psychology*, 17: 327-348.

Mone, E., Eisinger, C., Guggenheim, K., Price, B. and Stine, C. (2011). Performance management at the wheel: Driving employee engagement in organizations. *Journal of Business and Psychology*, 26: 205-212.

Rees, C., Alfes, K. and Gatenby, M. (2013). Employee voice and engagement: Connections and consequences. *The International Journal of Human Resource Management*, 24: 2780-2798.

Rich, B.L., LePine, J.A. and Crawford, E.R. (2010). Job engagement: Antecedents and effects on job performance. *Academy of Management Journal*, 53: 617-635.

Saks, A.M. (2006). Antecedents and consequences of employee engagement. *Journal of Managerial Psychology*, 21: 600-619.

Saks, A.M. and Gruman, J.A. (2010). Organizational socialization and newcomer engagement. In S.L. Albrecht (ed.), *Handbook of Employee Engagement: Perspectives, Issues, Research and Practice*. Cheltenham, UK and Northampton, MA, USA: Edward Elgar Publishing, 297-308.

Saks, A.M. and Gruman, J.A. (2011). Getting newcomers engaged: The role of socialization tactics. *Journal of Managerial Psychology*, 26: 383-402.

Saks, A.M. and Gruman, J.A. (2014). What do we really know about employee engagement? *Human Resource Development Quarterly*, 25: 155-182.

Salanova, M., Schaufeli, W.B., Xanthopoulou, D. and Bakker, A.B. (2010). The gain spiral of resources and work engagement: Sustaining a positive worklife. In A.B. Bakker and M.P. Leiter (eds), *Work Engagement: A Handbook of Essential Theory and Research*. New York: Psychology Press, 118-131.

Sarti, D. (2014). Job resources as antecedents of engagement at work: Evidence from a long-term care setting. *Human Resource Development Quarterly*, 25: 213-237.

Sparrow, P. (2014). Strategic HRM and employee engagement. In C. Truss, K. Alfes, A. Shantz and E. Soane (eds), *Employee Engagement in Theory and Practice*. Oxon: Routledge, 99-115.

Subramony, M. (2009). A meta-analytic investigation of the relationship between HRM bundles and firm performance. *Human Resource Management*, 48: 745-768.

Tims, M., Bakker, A.B. and Derks, D. (2012). Development and validation of the job crafting scale. *Journal of Vocational Behavior*, 80: 173-186.

Torrente, P., Salanova, M., Llorens, S. and Schaufeli, W. (2012). Teams make it work: How team work engagement mediates between social resources and performance in teams. *Psicothema*, 24: 106-112.

Wang, S. and Liu, Y. (2015). Impact of professional nursing practice environment and psychological empowerment on nurses' work engagement: Test of structural equation modelling. *Journal of Nursing Management*, 23: 287-296.

Yoerger, M., Crowe, J. and Allen, J.A. (2015). Participate or else!: The effect of participation in decision making in meetings on employee engagement. *Consulting Psychology Journal: Practice and Research*, 67: 65-80.

7 Workplace well-being: responsibilities, challenges and future directions

Susan Cartwright

7.1 Introduction

In recent years, the issue of workplace health and well-being has received increasing attention from researchers, employers and policy makers throughout the developed economies (Cartwright and Cooper, 2009; Cooper et al., 2015). In the main, this has occurred in response to the rising costs of sickness absence and premature withdrawal of labour from the workforce due to ill health and the increasing requirement for individuals to extend their working lives due to changes in state pension arrangements. As a result, underpinned by the substantial growth in the science supporting the value of health interventions, the workplace has increasingly become the focus for health promotion programmes and health improvement related activities (Bertera, 1990; O'Donnell, 2002; Black, 2008; Foresight, 2008). Furthermore, a growing number of organisations have extended or created new job roles related to workplace health and well-being. In the USA, many organisations are increasingly moving to incorporate non-negotiable values relating to health and well-being and develop a core group of measures to support these values by which managers are held accountable (O'Donnell 2002).

According to recent estimates (ONS, 2014), 131 million working days were lost due to sickness absence in the UK in 2013. Whilst the average number of days lost per employee in the UK has fallen from 6.5 days in 2010 to 5.3 days in 2012, the annual direct costs of sickness absence still amount to around £14 billion (CBI/Pfizer, 2013). Sickness absence rates continue to vary across occupations, industry sector, geographical region and organisational size. Absenteeism rates are highest in the public sector and are three times higher than in the industry sector with the lowest rates, that is, technology. Similarly, larger organisations tend to experience higher rates of absenteeism than smaller organisations (that is, less than 250 employees) and absence is more prevalent amongst manual workers than non-manual workers (ONS, 2014). Although recent trends suggest that the gap in absence behaviour between manual and non-manual workers is steadily closing (CBI/Pfizer, 2013). Whilst musculoskeletal disorders still account for the most lost working time, stress, anxiety and depression consistently remain a leading cause of both long- and short-term absence and result in 15.2 million lost days (CIPD, 2014). However, caring for family members has recently been cited by employers as a growing factor behind absence (CBI/Pfizer, 2013). Therefore, it is both encouraging, and not surprising, that 92 per cent of UK employers report that they have in place some type of stress and anxiety management policies to support employees and 82 per cent offer flexible working arrangements (CBI/Pfizer, 2013).

Whilst the recent trend towards falling sickness absence appears to be encouraging, this should be considered alongside the reported rise in sickness presenteeism (Hemp, 2004; Collins and Cartwright, 2012) – the phenomenon of individuals attending work when they are not fit to do so – said to amount to £15.1 billion in terms of reduced productivity each year (NEF, 2014). At the same time, the tightening of absence management policies cited by over 80 per cent of employers as effective in reducing their sickness absence rates (CIPD, 2014), work overload and uncertain labour markets are also likely to have impacted on employee attendance behaviours (Collins and Cartwright, 2012).

7.2   Health and well-being – what does it mean?

As long ago as 1948, the World Health Organization defined health "as a state of complete physical, mental and social well-being and not merely the absence of disease or infirmity" (WHO, 1948). Yet, traditional measures of health status have for the most part continued to adopt a medical perspective and focus on the negative aspect of (ill) health whereby health is taken as the normative baseline and ill health is a measured (negative) deviation from the baseline. Indeed, this "medical" perspective is enshrined in the legislative obligations of employers in the UK and most of Europe which require them to act to ensure that employees are not made ill or harmed by their work. According to Gable and Haidt (2005: 104) within this paradigm the predominant emphasis has been placed on "learning how to bring people up from negative 8 to zero but not at understanding how people rise from zero to positive 8". Within this paradigm, healthy workplaces are those in which stress and harm are absent.

Well-being is a subjective concept and much more problematic to define than health status. However, it is widely associated with the experience of pleasant emotions such as self-evaluated happiness (Warr, 2008), the engagement in interesting and fulfilling activities (Ryff and Singer, 1998) and generalised satisfaction with life (Kahneman, Diener and Schwarz, 2003). Subjective well-being (SWB) at work is influenced by personal characteristics including gender (Warr, 2007), age (Plagnol, 2010), personality and ability (Lucas and Diener, 2009) as well as aspects of the job and workplace (Judge and Klinger, 2007). Features of the job which contribute to well-being include job demands, control, role clarity, security, pay and equity in addition to wider factors such as co-workers, HR practices, and aspects of the workplace environment more generally.

The relationship between human resource management (HRM) and employee well-being is complex. On the one hand HRM practices can work to positively enhance employee well-being and at the same time result in gains in organisational performance, but on the other hand, HRM can work to the benefit of corporate performance, largely through work intensification and so adversely impact on employee well-being (Wall and Wood, 2005; Van de Voorde, Paauwe and Van Veldhoven, 2012).

In this respect the concept of Flexible Working and current focus of policies to promote it present an interesting paradox. Since the 1970s when the participation of women in the workforce began to increase, there has been a steadily increasing demand for employers to give employees a degree of choice over their working arrangements to help them achieve a satisfactory work–life balance. Flexible Working is a broad term covering initiatives which facilitate choices that workers can make as to how much, when and where they work including reduced hours, compressed working time and remote working. Currently, around 80 per cent of UK employers offer some form of flexible working.

A recent systematic review of 148 studies on Flexible Working Arrangements (FWAs) by De Menezes and Kelliher (2011) found that overall FWAs had the greatest impact on reducing absenteeism and increasing job satisfaction suggesting that they resulted in both individual and organisational gains. However, the discourse on who benefits from FWAs has been called into question. In a study of professionals engaged in knowledge based work, Kelliher and Anderson (2010) compared the experiences of those working flexibly, that is, either working reduced hours or remotely, with those with non-flexible work arrangements. On the positive side, the findings showed that those working flexibly reported higher levels of job satisfaction and organisational commitment than those not working flexibly. However, the study found considerable evidence that flexible workers experience high levels of work intensification. Importantly those working reduced hours found that whilst their work hours had reduced no adjustments had been made to their workloads, consequently they were doing a full time job in fewer paid hours, which meant that they were often taking calls and answering emails at times when they were not supposed to be working. Those who worked remotely also reported greater work intensification, greater extensive effort and general difficulties in switching off from work both literally and metaphorically. Kelliher and Anderson (2010) conclude that work intensification is potentially imposed and enabled by FWAs. Furthermore, drawing on social exchange theory (Blau, 1964), they argue that workers do not necessarily experience the negative health outcomes usually associated with work intensification in circumstances where they feel obliged to exercise additional discretionary effort as an act of reciprocation or exchange out of gratitude for concessions in working patterns. However, further evidence concerning the long-term impact of work intensification amongst flexible workers is needed.

7.3 Approaches to the improvement of workplace health and well-being

Organisations and governments continue to look for evidence-based ways to prevent and address the occurrence of ill health and to promote health, well-being and performance in organisational contexts. Whilst over time there has been a substantial growth in the science supporting health promotion (O'Donnell, 2002), the research evidence informing practice and innovation in the field is still a limited but emerging area of research (Giga, Cooper and Faragher, 2003; Sui, Cooper and Phillips, 2014), particularly as concerns the conditions which facilitate well-being and positive mental health and enable individuals "to thrive" at work.

To date, most organisations have been concerned with doing whatever is reasonably practicable to prevent work related ill health (rather than the positive promotion of well-being) usually in a way which causes as little disruption to the organisation as possible. This means that the strategic focus of organisational attention has traditionally been on activities intended to reduce the incidence of ill health, and to manage and support employees who have developed medical conditions or been injured at work.

Worksite Health Promotion (WHP) or Organisational Wellness Programmes (OWP) traditionally incorporate a combination of diagnostic, educational and behavioural modification activities which are initiated, endorsed and supported by the employing organisations (Sauter, Lim and Murphy, 1996). According to the World Health Organization (WHO, 1986), health promotion is defined as "the process of enabling people to exert control over the determinants of health and thereby improve health".

Results of a meta-analysis conducted by Parks and Steelman (2008) confirmed that employees who participated in an OWP were less likely to take time off than non-participants and were generally healthier. However, most programmes focus on modifiable lifestyle factors such as smoking, sedentary lifestyle, poor nutrition with an increasing focus on providing training designed to build resilience. Whilst such programmes can form a valuable part of an organisation's health and well-being strategy, there is a great deal of evidence to suggest that programmes focused on changing unhealthy behaviours have a limited impact in the longer term (O'Donnell, 2002; Murphy, 1996) and fail to attract the participation of those higher risk employee groups, that is, poorer, less educated and most stressed employees (Thompson, Smith and Bybee, 2005). Other meta-analytical studies specifically focused on the evaluation of stress management interventions to improve the way in which individuals manage and cope with stress have been encouraging (Van der Klink et al., 2001; Richardson and Rothstein, 2008) and have shown significant medium to large effects in relation to the benefits of cognitive behavioural techniques.

There is also moderate (McLeod, 2010) to strong (Arthur, 2000) evidence to suggest that counselling is effective in reducing anxiety and depression and enabling the return to work of employees. However, counselling has been shown to be unlikely to have any positive impact on work attitudes such as job satisfaction and engagement (Arthur, 2001: McLeod and McLeod, 2001).

Additionally, organisations have been increasingly encouraged to monitor the stress levels of employees (Johnson, 2009) and to take steps to reduce exposure to workplace stressors which are outside the control of individual workers. Despite strong theoretical and methodological support for this type of organisational action, most interventions continue to be focused on at the individual (worker) level. A meta-analysis conducted by Bond and Loivette (2006) found that organisational interventions focused on improving job control were the most effective in terms of improved worker performance, reduced absenteeism and turnover. A more recent series of systematic reviews found consistent and positive evidence as to the effectiveness of organisational interventions to increase employee participation (Hillage et al., 2014). However, the results of other systematic reviews and meta-analytic studies on organisational level interventions have generally presented inconsistent and less convincing evidence as to their effectiveness (for example, Parkes and Sparkes 1988; Van der Klink et al., 2001). However, it has been argued that this is in large part due to the paucity and poor quality of many intervention evaluation studies (for example, lack of control groups), coupled with the lack of attention paid to process issues (Biron, Karamika-Murray and Cooper, 2012) which can adversely affect the success of an intervention programme even though the underlying theoretical assumptions on which it is based are sound.

7.4   Improving well-being: a positive enjoyment of life

In recent years there has been a notable step change in the conceptualisation of what constitutes healthy work. Segliman and Powelski (2003) leading proponents of the "positive psychology" movement consider that traditional research perspectives have overwhelmingly focused on the study of negative aspects of human behaviour and have persuasively argued that this should be counterbalanced by the investigation of what is good and positive about human experience. In extending this philosophy into the workplace, Luthans and Youssef (2007) developed the concept of Positive Organisational Behaviour (POS), as encompassing the study of aspects of work and the work environment which engender positive emotional states and have the capability of improving employee well-being.

Many suggestions have been made as to what constitutes a psychological and emotionally healthy workplace (Gibbs and Burnett, 2011; Cooper et al., 2015; Quick et al., 2010; Quick, McFayden and Nelson, 2014) which have consistently emphasised the importance of work–life balance, employee growth and development, health and safety, recognition and reward and employee involvement.

Indeed, recent guidelines issued by NICE (2015) on the promotion of well-being at work emphasise the need for organisational initiatives directed at helping individuals to feel happy, competent and satisfied in their roles and are consistent with the recommendations and models of well-being proposed by the Foresight report to the UK government (2008). The guidelines highlight the importance for organisational action in addressing the following issues:

- Getting work–life balance right;
- Re-evaluating salaries and pay related structures to ensure they are fair;
- Job security;
- Working with employees to ensure that they have a sense that their job is achievable;
- Recognising the importance of management behaviours on employee well-being;
- Creating a safe environment;
- Taking steps to improve relationships at work;
- Helping employees to take greater control; and
- Ensuring good levels of job fit and skill use.

Whilst some critics have observed that this positive perspective is not new and has already been embedded in research areas such as pro-social and citizenship behaviour for some time (Wright, 2003), there is little doubt that it has refreshed the dialogue and debate about work and health in a way which is more engaging and appealing to managers.

Increasingly researchers are now investigating and measuring positive emotional states and traits, their antecedents and outcomes. The concepts and indicators of these positive "strengths" are many and various and include hope, confidence, resiliency, motivation, purpose, meaning, engagement, and flourishing (Cartwright and Holmes, 2006; Warr, 2007; Fullagar and Kelloway, 2009; Avey et al., 2010). However, many of these constructs are still poorly defined and the evidence base informing practice regarding organisational interventions which might improve the positive psychological capital and health of employees is, as yet, in its infancy.

In a recent systematic review of 14 studies into resilience training, Robertson et al. (2015) concluded that there was strong evidence that resilience training increased personal resilience, mental health and subjective well-being. However they found the link between resilience training and performance to be tentative based on the available evidence. In summarising their findings Robertson et al. (2015) reinforced the view that evaluation studies needed to be methodologically stronger and more robust in demonstrating the value of well-being interventions.

7.5 Responsibilities and process issues

Whilst the fundamental responsibility for health lies within the individual as concerns the lifestyle choices they make, organisations can provide advice, support and encouragement to help employees adopt healthier behaviours. However, organisations also need to proactively accept that it is their responsibility and best interests to take steps to monitor, address and modify workplace policies, practices and job characteristics that may adversely impact on health and which employees are powerless in their ability to change or control.

Importantly, organisations need to recognise the significant role played by supervisors and line managers in influencing the health and well-being of those they manage. There is consistent and significant research evidence to indicate a clear link between supervisor/line manager behaviour and job satisfaction, psychological strain, sickness absence, presenteeism and intention to leave from studies in a variety of occupations internationally (Gilbreath and Benson, 2004; Nyberg et al., 2008: Skakon et al., 2010). For example, studies have shown that positive supervisor intervention can enhance employee satisfaction during organisational change (Nielsen, Randall and Christensen 2010), that supervisory support can reduce work/family conflicts (Hammer et al., 2011) and that a range of positive leadership behaviours can improve both employee well-being and workplace safety (Mor Borak et al., 2009). Conversely, there is strong evidence to demonstrate that pressure from managers and an aggressive management style are predictive of poor health and increased absence (Hershcovis and Barling, 2009). Hillage et al. (2014) summarise the positive leadership behaviours associated with health and well-being as characterised by the following:

- Regular consultation about workplace decisions;
- Treating employees fairly;
- High visibility and accessibility;
- Giving information;
- Creating an emotionally supportive environment;
- Giving praise and recognition; and
- Providing employees with a degree of challenge (and autonomy).

Two Japanese studies (Takeo et al., 2006; Tsutsumi et al., 2005) have shown that face-to-face training of supervisors in mental health issues can have a large positive effect on the levels of psychological distress experienced by the people they manage. However, this impact was reduced when the training was delivered via the Internet (Kawakami et al., 2005).

A continuing theme throughout the current literature is that even well intended interventions often fail to demonstrate improvements in employee health and well-being due to poor implementation and/ or flawed evaluation. Indeed, there is growing evidence to show that poorly implemented interventions can actually have a negative impact on employee outcomes (Aust et al., 2010).

The framework proposed by Noblet and LaMontagne (2009) emphasises that health interventions are similar to planned organisational change programmes in that they are dynamic and are influenced by contextual factors (for example, management support, quality of programme delivery, competing projects). Their framework is composed of seven broad interdependent steps: (1) gaining managerial support; (2) forming a coordinating group; (3) conducting a needs/risk assessment and analysis of issues; (4) identifying priority issues and setting intervention goals; (5) designing interventions and an action plan; (6) implementing interventions; and (7) evaluating implementation processes and intervention effectiveness.

The needs assessment/analysis stage of the process is particularly important in determining the most appropriate form and target of the intervention. This stage can also be useful in providing baseline measures against which the subsequent effectiveness of the intervention can be assessed.

Many organisations have pre-existing data, such as annual employee surveys, sickness absence records, staff turnover rates, safety/accident records, customer feedback and performance data which can be analysed to identify geographical regions, departments, job roles and age groups where employee health and well-being may be suboptimal and would benefit for some form of tailored intervention. For example, a high incidence of absence due to back and neck injuries in a call centre may be indicative of a need to re-examine work station design. Dependent on the existing expertise in house, organisations may benefit from input from specialised external advice, particularly in relation to evaluation. Given the dynamic nature of organisations, regular monitoring to re-assess and identify the future needs of employees.

7.6   Conclusions

In conclusion, what are the future challenges to health and well-being? As Chapter 9 reminds us, the Human Resource function is likely to come under increasing future pressure to develop and comply with Human Capital reporting standards and to account for the value of their employees and their collective knowledge, skills, abilities and capacity to develop and innovate (Hesketh, 2014). In demonstrating the value of human capital the issue of health, well-being and engagement can be expected to assume greater prominence.

Recent international surveys suggest that countries like the UK need to optimise their health and well-being activities to drive employee productivity and employee value. The results of a recent Gallup World Poll (Gallup, 2013) found that only 14 per cent of employees in Western Europe are psychologically engaged with their job. Furthermore, this problem is more acute amongst long serving and experiences employees, with almost 50 per cent reporting a lack of engagement. The 2012 UK Skills and Employment Survey of 3,000 British workers compiled by Felstead et al. (2014) found that employees were feeling more job insecure and under pressure at work than at any time in the previous 20 years. Concerns about the political, economic and structural changes in Europe, following the UK's decision in 2016 to leave the EU are likely to further increase job uncertainty and anxiety over the following years.

Despite increasing work pressures and growing work intensification, the UK continues to perform poorly against its G7 competitors and ranks variously between 16th (out of 162 countries) and 21st (out of 158 countries) in terms of overall well-being (Boston Consulting Group, 2016) and happiness (Helliwell, Layard and Sachs, 2015). In terms of well-being and happiness levels the UK significantly lags behind its Northern European neighbours such as Norway, Denmark, Sweden and Iceland where traditionally health and well-being issues have assumed a high priority both nationally and organisationally.

Apart from the challenge of managing an uncertain workforce and increasing productivity in a changing environment, there are other pressing future challenges, namely changing worker profiles and the nature of work.

It is predicted that the average age of the UK workforce will rise to 43 by 2030. At the same time more workers will be caring for older people with an estimated 2.3 workers to every pensioner by 2032.

Increases in life expectancy within the developed economies have provided a strong economic and social imperative for governments to extend the working lives of individuals beyond previous expectations of "normal" retirement age. Although work is generally regarded as good for physical and mental health as compared with worklessness (Black, 2008). However, organisations will have to place a high priority on ensuring that older workers remain physically and psychologically healthy and that appropriate work adjustments are made to accommodate their needs. This means that organisations will need to ensure that ageing workers have the same access to training, are treated as fairly as younger workers and experience work as meaningful, purposeful and motivating and to take place in a workplace environment conducive to maintaining self-esteem and providing job satisfaction.

The continued growth in technology is likely to be accompanied by a growth in remote working and further erode the boundaries between work and home life. This is likely to lead to greater work intensification and the need for more support from organisations to help their employees to achieve a satisfactory work–life balance and to ensure they do not feel isolated by their work arrangements. The inevitable increase in cross border/virtual teams presents a special challenge in potentially extending working hours and the difficulties of communicating and building work and social relationships remotely through technological media.

At the same time the future is likely to see a further increase in sedentary jobs. Recent banner headlines in the press have loudly proclaimed "Sitting is the new smoking" (Daily Mail, 2016) in response to strong and mounting evidence that independent from exercise, sitting is associated with an increased risk of heart disease, obesity, diabetes, cancer, back and posture problems as well as mental health problems such as stress, anxiety, depression and sleep disorders.(Thorp et al., 2011). As well as continuing to promote the benefits of exercise, organisations will also need to consider ways in which jobs and workplaces can be designed to prevent employees sitting for long periods of time.

Finally, given the paucity of robust and consistent evidence on the effectiveness of work place interventions, in the design and evaluation of future workplace health interventions, there are benefits to be gained by organisations partnering with academic researchers in the co-production of knowledge.

References

Arthur, A. (2000) Employee assistance programmes: The emperor's new clothes of stress management. *British Journal of Guidance and Counselling*, 28(4): 549–559.

Arthur, A. (2001) Mental health problems and British workers: A survey of mental health problems in employees receiving counselling from employee assistance programmes. *Stress and Health*, 18(2): 69–75.

Aust, B., Rugulies, R., Finken, A. and Jensen, C. (2010) When workplace interventions lead to negative effects: Learning from failures. *Scandinavian Journal of Public Health*, 38(3): 106–119.

Avey, J.B., Luthans, F., Smith, R.M. and Palmer, N.F (2010) The impact of positive psychological capital on employee well-being over time. *Journal of Occupational Health Psychology*, 15(1): 17–28.

Bertera, R.L. (1990) The effects of workplace health promotion on absenteeism and employment costs in a large industrial population. *American Journal of Public Health*, 80(9): 1101–1105.

Biron, C., Karamika-Murray, M. and Cooper, C. (2012) *Improving Organisational Interventions for Stress and Well-being: Addressing Process and Context*. London: Routledge.

Black, C. (2008) *Working for a Healthier Tomorrow*. London: Department for Work and Pensions.

Blau, P. (1964) *Exchange and Power in Social Life*. New York: John Wiley & Sons.

Bond, F.W. and Loivette, S. (2006) A business case for the management standards for stress (No RR 431). Norwich: Health and Safety Executive.

Boston Consulting Group (2016) Sustainable economic development assessment report. Boston: Boston Consulting Group.

Cartwright, S. and Cooper, C.L. (2009) *The Oxford Handbook of Organisational Well-being*. Oxford: Oxford University Press.

Cartwright, S. and Holmes, N. (2006) The challenge of regaining employee engagement and reducing cynicism. *Human Resource Management Review*, 16: 199–208.

CBI/Pfizer (2013) Workplace health and absence survey. London: Confederation of British Industry.

CIPD (2014) Absence management survey. London: Chartered Institute for Personnel and Development.

Collins, A. and Cartwright, S. (2012) Why come to work ill? Individual and organizational factors underlying presenteeism. *Employee Relations*, 34(4): 429–442.

Cooper, C.L., Campbell Quick, J. and Schabracq, M.J. (2015) *International Handbook of Work and Health Psychology*. Chichester: Wiley-Blackwell.

Daily Mail (2016) Sitting is the new smoking! 9 August.

De Menezes, L.M. and Kelliher, C. (2011) Flexible working and performance: A systematic review of evidence for a business case. *International Journal of Management Reviews*, 13(4): 452–474.

Felstead, A., Gallie, D., Green, F. and Inanc, H. (2014) 2012 Skills and Employment Survey available at http://cardiff.ac.uk/research/explore/find-a-project/view/117804-skills-and-employment-survey-2012 (accessed 15 May 2017).

Foresight (2008) *Mental Capital and Well Being*. London: Government Office for Science.

Fullagar, C. and Kelloway, E.K. (2009) "Flow" at work: An experience sampling approach. *Journal of Occupational and Organizational Psychology*, 82(3): 595–615.

Gable, S. and Haidt, J. (2005) What (and why) is positive psychology? *Review of General Psychology*, 9(2): 103–110.

Gallup (2013) *State of the Global Workplace*. Washington, DC: Gallup Organization.

Gibbs, P.C. and Burnett, S. (2011) Well-being at work, a new way of doing things? A journey through yesterday, today and tomorrow, in A-S Antoniou and C. Cooper (eds), *New Directions in Organizational Psychology and Behavioral Medicine*. Farnham: Gower, 25–42.

Giga, S., Cooper, C. and Faragher, B (2003) The development of a framework for a comprehensive approach to stress management interventions at work. *International Journal of Stress Management*, 10(4): 280–296.

Gilbreath, B. and Benson, P.G. (2004) The contribution of supervisor behaviour to employee psychological well-being. *Work and Stress*, 18(3): 255–266.

Hammer, L.B., Kossek, E.E. Anger, W.K., Bodner, T. and Zimmerman, K.L. (2011) Clarifying work–family intervention processes: The roles of work family supportive supervisor behaviours. *Journal of Applied Psychology*, 96(1): 134–150.

Helliwell, J., Layard, R. and Sachs, J. (2015) World happiness report. New York: Sustainable Development Solutions Network.

Hemp, P. (2004) Presenteeism at work – burn out of it. *Harvard Business Review*, 82(10): 49–58.

Hershcovis, M.S. and Barling, J. (2009) Towards a multi-foci approach to workplace aggression: A meta-analytic review of outcomes from different perpetrators. *Journal of Organizational Behavior*, 31(1): 24–44.

Hesketh, A. (2014) *Managing the Value of your talent: A New Framework for Human Capital Measurement*. London: Chartered Institute for Personnel and Development.

Hillage, J., Holmes, J., Rickard, C., Marvel, R., Taskila, T., Bajorek, Z., Bevan, S. and Brine, J. (2014) Workplace policy and management practices to improve the health of employees – Evidence Reviews 1, 2 and 3. Brighton: Institute for Employment Studies.

Johnson, S. (2009) Organizational screening: The ASSET model, in S. Cartwright and C.L. Cooper (eds), *The Oxford Handbook of Organizational Well-Being*. Oxford: Oxford University Press, 133–158.

Judge, T.A. and Klinger, R. (2007) Job satisfaction: Subjective well-being at work, in M. Eid and R. Larsen (eds), *The Science of Subjective Well Being*. New York: Guilford Publications, 393–413.

Kahneman, D., Diener, E. and Schwarz, N. (eds) (2003) *Well Being: The Foundation of Hedonic Psychology*. New York: Russell Sage Foundation.

Kawakami, N., Kobayashi, Y., Takao, S. and Tsutsumi, A. (2005) Effects of web-based supervisory training on supervisor support and psychological distress among workers: A randomized control trial. *Preventative Medicine*, 41(1): 471–478.

Kelliher, C. and Anderson, D. (2010) Doing more with less? Flexible working practices and the intensification of work. *Human Relations*, 63(1): 83–106.

Lucas, R.E. and Diener, E. (2009) Personality and subjective well-being, in E. Diener (ed.), *The Science of Well Being, Social Indicators Research Series* (vol. 37). London: Springer, 75–102.

Luthans, F. and Youssef, C.M. (2007) Emerging positive organizational behaviour. *Journal of Management*, 33(3): 321–349.

McLeod, J. (2010) The effectiveness of workplace counselling: A systematic evidence. *Counselling and Psychotherapy Research*, 10(4): 238–248.

McLeod, J. and McLeod, J. (2001) How effective is workplace counselling? A review of the research literature. *Counselling and Psychotherapy Research*, 1(3): 184–190.

Mor Borak, M.E., Travis, D.J., Pyun, H. and Xie, B. (2009) The impact of supervision of work outcomes: A meta-analysis. *Social Service Review*, 83(1): 3–32.

Murphy, L.R. (1996) Stress management in work settings: A critical review of the health effects. *American Journal of Health Promotion*, 11(2): 112–135.

New Economics Foundation (NEF) (2014) *Well-Being at Work: A Review of the Literature*. London: New Economics Foundation.

NICE (2015) Workplace health: Management practices, Guideline NG13 London: National Institute for Health and Care Excellence, June.

Nielsen, K., Randall, R. and Christensen, K.B. (2010) Does training managers enhance the effects of implementing team-working? A longitudinal mixed methods field study. *Human Relations*, 63(11): 1719–1741.

Noblet, A. and LaMontagne, A.D (2009) The challenges of developing, implementing and evaluating interventions, in S. Cartwright and C.L. Cooper (eds), *The Oxford Handbook of Organizational Well-being*. Oxford: Oxford University Press, 466–496.

Nyberg, A., Westerlund, H., Magnusson Hanson, L.L. and Theorell, T. (2008) Managerial leadership is associated with self-reported sickness absence and sickness presenteeism among Swedish men and women. *Scandinavian Journal of Public Health*, 36(8): 803–811.

O'Donnell, M.P. (2002) *Health Promotion in the Workplace* (3rd edition). Albany, NY: Delmar.

ONS (2014) Sickness absence in the labour market. London: Office for National Statistics, February.

Parkes, K.P. and Sparkes T. (1988) Organizational interventions to reduce work stress: Are they effective? Contract Research Report 193/198 Norwich UK: Health and Safety Executive Books.

Parks, K.M and Steelman, A.A. (2008) Organizational wellness programs: A meta-analysis. *Journal of Occupational Health Psychology*, 13(1): 58–68.

Plagnol, A. (2010) Subjective well-being over the life course: conceptualizations and evaluations. *Social Research: An International Quarterly*, 77(2): 749–768.

Quick, J.C., Cooper, C.L., Gibbs, P.C., Little, L.M. and Nelson, D. (2010) Positive organizational behaviour at work, in G.P. Hodgkinson and J.K. Ford (eds), *International Review of Industrial and Organizational Psychology* (vol. 25). Chichester: Wiley-Blackwell, 187–216.

Quick, J.C., McFayden, A. and Nelson, D.L. (2014) No accident: Health, well-being and performance at work. *Journal of Organizational Effectiveness: People and Performance*, 1(1): 98–119.

Richardson, K.M. and Rothstein, H.R. (2008) Effects of occupational stress management interventions programs: A meta-analysis. *Journal of Occupational Health Psychology*, 13(1): 69–93.

Robertson, I.T., Cooper, C.L., Sarkar, M. and Curran, T. (2015) Resilience training in the workplace from 2003 to 2014. *Journal of Occupational and Organizational Psychology*, 88(3): 533–562.

Ryff, C.D. and Singer, B. (1998) The contours of positive human health. *Psychological Inquiry*, 9(1): 1–28.

Sauter, S., Lim, S.Y. and Murphy, L.R. (1996) Organizational health: A new paradigm for occupational stress research at NIOSH. *Japanese Journal of Occupational Mental Health*, 4: 248–254.

Segliman, M.E.P. and Powelski, J.O. (2003) Positive psychology: FAQs. *Psychological Inquiry*, 14: 159–169.

Skakon, J., Nielsen, K., Borg, V. and Guzman, J. (2010) Are leaders' well-being, behaviours and style associated with the affective well-being of their employees? A systematic review of three decades of research. *Work and Stress*, 24(2): 107–139.

Sui, O.L., Cooper, C.L. and Phillips, D.R. (2014) Interventions studies on enhancing work and well-being, reducing burnout and improving recovery experiences among Hong Kong healthcare workers and teachers. *International Journal of Stress Management*, 10(4): 280–296.

Takeo, S., Tsutsumi, A., Nishiuchi, K., Mineyama, S. and Kawakami, N. (2006) Effects of stress education for supervisors on psychological distress and job performance among their immediate subordinates: A supervisor-based randomized control trial. *Journal of Occupational Health*, 48: 494–503.

Thompson, S.E., Smith, B.A. and Bybee, R.F. (2005) Factors influencing participation in worksite wellness programs among minority and underserved populations. *Family and Community Health*, 28(3): 267–273.

Thorp, A.A., Owen, N., Neuhaus, M. and Dunstan, D.W. (2011) Sedentary behaviours and subsequent health outcomes in adults: A systematic review of longitudinal studies 1996-2011. *American Journal of Preventative Medicine*, 41(2): 207-215.

Tsutsumi, A., Takao, S., Mineyama, S., Nistiuchi, K., Komatsu, H. and Kawakami, N. (2005) Effects of supervisory education for positive mental health in the workplace: A quasi experimental study. *Journal of Occupational Health*, 47(3): 226-235.

Van der Klink, J.J., Blonk, R.W., Schene, A.H. and van Dijk, F.J. (2001) The benefits of interventions for work related stress. *American Journal of Public Health*, 91(2): 270-276.

Van de Voorde, K., Paauwe, J. and Van Veldhoven, M. (2012) Employee well-being and the HRM–organizational performance relationship: A review of quantitative studies. *International Journal of Management Reviews*, 14(4): 391-407.

Wall, T. and Wood, S. (2005) The romance of human performance management, and the case for big science. *Human Relations*, 58(4): 429-462.

Warr, P. (2007) *Work, Happiness and Unhappiness*. New York: Routledge.

Warr, P. (2008) Work values: Some demographic and cultural correlates. *Journal of Occupational and Organizational Psychology*, 81(4): 751-775.

WHO (World Health Organization) (1948) Preamble to the Constitution of the World Health Organization as adopted by the International Health Conference New York 19-22 June 1946; signed on 22 July 1946 by the representatives of 61 states and entered into force on 7 April 1948.

WHO (1986) The Ottawa Charter for Health Promotion. World Health Organization First International Conference on Health Promotion, Ottawa, 21 November.

Wright, A. (2003) Positive organizational behaviour: An idea whose time has truly come. *Journal of Organizational Behaviour*, 24(4): 427-442.

8 Leadership models: the future research agenda for HRM

Johan Coetsee and Patrick C. Flood

8.1 Introduction

Leadership research has increased exponentially over the past 10 years, resulting in the development of a range of leadership theories and approaches (see Table 8.1). Different conceptualisations and definitions of leadership have led to a number of ways in which leadership is investigated and measured (Hernandez et al., 2011). In Chapter 4 questions were raised about our definitions of leadership potential and the nature of succession programmes. We argue that there also remains a lack of understanding about the importance of underlying leadership models. Leader-centric approaches, traits and behaviours of leaders, relational approaches, follower-centric approaches, team leadership and identity-based approaches serve as examples in this regard. Despite the developments in leadership research and the development of new leadership theories, it seems:

> . . . we know much less about how leaders make organisations effective than how leaders are perceived. (Kaiser, Hogan and Craig, 2008: 96)

Putting it differently, we have a better understanding of leaders and their qualities than how leaders go about changing processes in individuals, groups, or organisations to achieve effectiveness. Furthermore, current research is characterised by the use of a leader-centric approach (the romance of leadership), retrospective and single time survey measures; single level approaches; a lack of longitudinal studies and the use of single method approaches. Uhl-Bien, Marion and McKelvey (2007: 298) argue further that current leadership models are:

> Products of top-down, bureaucratic paradigms. These models are eminently effective for an economy premised on physical production but are not well-suited for a more knowledge-oriented economy.

Table 8.1   Classification of leadership theories

Established theories	Emerging theories
Neo-charismatic theories (e.g., Transformational leadership)	*Strategic leadership* (e.g., Upper echelons theory)
Leadership and information processing theories (e.g., Implicit leadership)	*Team leadership* (Leadership in teams)
Social exchange/Relational leadership theories (e.g., LMX)	*Contextual, complexity and systems perspectives of leadership* (e.g., Social networks)
Dispositional/Trait theories (e.g., Leadership skills)	*Leader emergence and development* (e.g., Leadership development)
Leadership and diversity (e.g., Cross-cultural leadership)	*Ethical/moral leadership theories* (e.g., Authentic leadership)
Follower-centric leadership theories (e.g., Followership theories)	*Leading for creativity, innovation and change* (e.g., Change leadership)
Behavioural theories (e.g., Participative/shared leadership)	*Identity-based leadership theories* (e.g., Social identity theory)
Contingency theories (e.g., Situational leadership)	*Other nascent approaches* (e.g., Emotions; destructive; biological approaches; e-leadership; green-leadership; leader error and recovery; entrepreneurial leadership)
Power and influence of leadership (Political theory and influence tactics)	

Source: Adapted from Dinh et al. (2014).

What is now required are new paradigms of leadership and the use of methodologies that will enhance our understanding of a complex phenomenon. Further the implications of these trends for HRM implementation are poorly understood and the literatures bridging leadership and HRM execution are poorly defined. In this chapter based on leadership reviews (that is, theoretical trends and future research perspectives) as identified by Gardner et al. (2011); Hernandez et al. (2011) and Dinh et al. (2014), examples of contemporary leadership perspectives are explored and the implications for HRM research especially HRM execution are explored in detail.

8.2   Contemporary leadership perspectives

8.2.1   Neo-charismatic theory

Transformational leadership can be regarded as a multidimensional leadership style and includes the following dimensions: *idealised influence, inspirational motivation, intellectual stimulation,* and *individualised consideration.* These are known as the four 'I's of transformational leadership. *Idealised influence* denotes role modelling behaviour, *intellectual stimulation* motivates followers, allow them to challenge existing assumptions, and *individualised consideration* emphasises followers' development. Lastly, *inspirational motivation* refers to creating a vision to inspire followers (Avolio and Bass, 2004). Demonstrating these behaviours, leaders create trust, goal aliment and inspire employees to do more than what is expected. A comprehensive analysis and review by Wang, Courtright and Colbert (2011) demonstrate that there is a positive relationship between transformational leadership and performance. This means transformational leadership will positively influence aspects such as task-, contextual- and creative performance. It also influences performance at individual, team and organisational levels but may be less effective in environments characterised by low levels of interdependence where interpersonal cooperation is less important. In contrast, in contexts where task performance is the primary focus, transactional leadership may be more effective. It seems however that we need to have a better understanding of the mediators of transformational leadership at different levels of analysis.

8.2.2   Ethical/moral leadership theories

Authenticity, the idea of "being oneself" or being "true to oneself" has been described in many different ways and there is no agreed definition for authentic leadership. Kernis (2003: 13) describes authenticity as:

> The unobstructed operation of one's true, or core self in one's daily enterprise consisting of four components: awareness, unbiased processing, authentic action and relational authenticity.

Walumbwa et al. (2008: 94) building on this definition regard authentic leadership as:

> A pattern of leader behaviour that draws upon and promotes both psychological capacities and a positive ethical climate, to foster greater self-

awareness, an internalised moral perspective, balanced processing of information, relational transparency on the part of the leaders working with followers, fostering positive self-development.

Authenticity is to be informed by the "true" self, authentic leaders demonstrate high levels of self-awareness, have a clear understanding of their personal values and principles. Being a role-model, that is, demonstrating authentic behaviours, impacts followers work attitudes and behaviours and enables followers to identify with the leader. This increases followers' levels of hope, optimism, trust and self-efficacy (Gardner, Avolio and Walumbwa, 2005), also known also as "psychological capital".

In practice this means the leader acts transparently, ethically (that is, guided by moral compass), is open to ideas and encourages active participation from followers. Empirical evidence (Gardner et al., 2011) suggests that authentic leadership is positively related to identification with the leader. Leading authentically will positively influence variables such as leader and following well-being; trust; work engagement; follower job satisfaction; organisational commitment and follower job performance. However, work remains to provide convincing evidence of the long-term efficacy of this approach.

Ethical leadership can be regarded as:

> Demonstrating normatively appropriate conduct through personal actions and interpersonal relationships, and the promotion of such conduct to followers through two-way communication, reinforcement and decision-making. (Brown, Treviño and Harrison, 2005: 120)

By demonstrating behaviours such as honesty and trustworthiness, followers perceive the leader as an honourable (moral) person (Treviño, Brown and Hartman, 2003) and by acting as a role model demonstrate ethical behaviours to their followers. They not only communicate ethical standards and their beliefs, but also use rewards and punishment to align and support behaviour. Ethical leadership is related to follower's job satisfaction; willingness to do more than what is expected; voice behaviour and perceptions of a positive ethical climate (Toor and Ofori, 2009; Walumbwa and Schaubroeck, 2009).

8.2.3   Follower-centric leadership theories

The addition of followership in leadership studies is important as the majority of leadership studies omit the role of the follower in affecting or defining leader behaviours. Different lenses for example a follower-centric (Kean and Haycock-Stuart, 2011) or a processual perspective (Uhl-Bien et al., 2014) are used to describe followership. A follower-centric perspective, that is, how followers construct leadership, explore areas such as *how followers perceive their leaders* and *influence tactics* followers use to influence their leaders, serve as examples in this regard. This role-based view of followership helps us to understand how followers contribute to the development of the leadership relationship, how they empower or disempower the leader and exploring the consequences of the leadership relationship (Shamir, 2007). In contrast, a processual perspective (Uhl-Bien et al., 2014) explores followership as a social process and that followers and leaders co-develop leadership through interactions. This approach implies that in some instances the leader might be a follower and in other instances the follower might fulfil a leader role. Therefore, real leadership can only take place "through combined acts of leading and following" (Uhl-Bien et al., 2014: 99).

Putting it differently, understanding the interdependence of, as well as the relationship between leadership and followership (and how these processes are interdependent and interact), will increase our understanding of what constitutes leadership success or failure. The contingency approach of situational leadership theory has fallen out of grace although the need to understand contingent approaches grows apace.

8.2.4   Social exchange/relational leadership theories

Leader–member exchange (LMX) remains a popular and frequently studied leadership model (Dulebohn et al., 2012; Dinh et al., 2014). It is based on the premise that a leader forms different types of relationships with their followers over time that may influence or impact important outcomes. High-quality LMX relationships are characterised by mutual trust, respect, and obligation (Sparrowe and Liden, 1997). This leads to better levels of leader support and access to resources. In contrast, low LMX relationships can be regarded as transactional relationships, for example focusing on pay for performance. The quality of the leader–follower relationship has been found to predict various positive work-related outcomes, that is, higher levels of performance, including job satisfaction, demonstrating increased levels of organisational citizenship behaviours (Fisk and Friesen, 2012). Empirical evidence (Dulebohn et al., 2012) suggests that the quality of the relationship is determined by the leader demonstrating the following behaviours: *contingent reward, transformational leadership* and their *own expectations* of follower success. This means the leader needs to give feedback, recognition and provides followers with a compelling vision and implies that a high quality relationship is characterised by both transactional and transformational behaviours.

Relational leadership theory can be regarded as an:

> . . . overarching framework for the study of the relational dynamics that are involved in the generation and functioning of leadership. (Uhl-Bien, 2006: 667)

It moves away from the role leaders play in influencing followers to the ability of the leader to create positive relationships within the organisation. In this context, leadership can be viewed as a relational construct and is developed through interaction. It can therefore be regarded as co-constructed in social interaction processes (Fairhurst, 2007). This is an important distinction as relational leadership moves beyond traditional perspectives of leadership, that is, who is leading and who is following. Leadership is regarded as a shared influence process and is not related to a hierarchical position in an organisation. Despite the importance of relationships in new emerging leadership theories, we still need a more comprehensive understanding about (1) how relationships form and (2) develop in organisations (Uhl-Bien, 2006). It seems however that relational leadership lead to higher levels of job satisfaction; lower job turnover and stronger working relationships (Raelin, 2003).

As indicated in the previous discussion, leadership is embedded in a specific context and is shared, moving away from an individual perspective. The use of a social network approach is a further lens that can be used to understand leadership emergence and effectiveness (Balkundi, and Kilduff, 2006). The traditional approach to leadership views leadership as top-down and transactional. In contrast, a comprehensive review of research on social network approaches by Carter et al. (2015) argued that a network leadership approach views leadership as relational, context specific, it manifests as patterns of relationships and can be formal or informal. Collective engagement in leadership (that is, leadership through informal and formal relationships) can be regarded as a key leader competence to be able to lead in volatile environments. A social network approach to leadership is therefore concerned with the resources that exist between individuals. These connections or ties create a network structure that may support or constrain access to resources, power and influence in the network as well as demonstrating interpersonal helping behaviours. Carter et al. (2015) state in this regard that using a social network approach seeks answers to two fundamental questions, namely why do relationships come about and what outcomes developed from the pattern of relationships?

8.2.5   Leadership and diversity

Much of the research in the leadership field has been conducted by Western researchers working in Western contexts. However, it has been generally accepted that leadership is culturally bound and the cultural context (in which it operates) should be taken into account (Hernandez et al., 2011). Putting it differently, effective leadership is contextual and is embedded in the societal values and beliefs of the followers. For leaders to be effective in cross-cultural contexts, they need to understand their own preferred leadership style and how it is understood in different contexts. The Global Leadership and Organisational Behavioural Effectiveness (GLOBE) study identified six global leadership dimensions (Dorfman et al., 2012):

(a)   Autonomous (independent and individualistic);
(b)   Charismatic (inspirational, motivational and high performance expectations for followers);
(c)   Humane-oriented (supportive, compassionate, and generous behaviours);
(d)   Participative (followers involved in decision-making and implementation);
(e)   Self-protective (status and face-saving behaviours to reinforce group's sense of security); and
(f)   Team-oriented (team building behaviours and implementation of a common goal).

A key finding from the study is that the majority of leader behaviours were contingent on culture. Despite the contribution of the GLOBE study to our understanding of leadership in cross-cultural context, it can still be regarded as an under researched area. Yammarino (2013: 4) argues in this regard:

[T]he field still lacks a clear understanding of the universalistic as compared with the culture-specific and the emic as compared with the etic approaches to leadership.

8.3   Key research needs over the next five years

One of the most important concerns for research over the next few years concerns the question of study designs and methodological aspects. Leadership can be regarded as a socially constructed process, it is complex, takes place at multiple levels and this makes leadership difficult and challenging to study (Gardner et al., 2011). Reflecting on analysis by Yammarino et al. (2005), Gardner et al. (2011), Yammarino (2013) and Dinh et al. (2014), it seems that leadership researchers focus predominantly on:

(1)   the use of retrospective survey measures;
(2)   single studies versus increasing the number of studies in the same study; and
(3)   do not give sufficient attention to levels of analysis (Yammarino et al., 2005).

Specifying the level of analysis plays an important role in how theory is conceptualised and developed, how the phenomenon is measurement and how data is analysed and interpreted. Failing to do so leads to inadequate theory building and testing and may lead to flawed interpretations. Furthermore, leadership research relies heavily on the use of quantitative methods or the use of single-method studies in exploring leadership and while helpful, does not explain the leadership phenomenon in full. Also, it is generally accepted that leadership take place in a specific context and that contextual variables may influence how leadership is enacted and experienced by followers. Yammarino (2013: 4) states in this regard that:

> Most leadership research is still conducted as if it was context free rather than context dependent or context specific.

Finally, although we have a better understanding of the moderators, mediators and antecedents of leadership, we still do not understand the interaction patterns between them or how they develop over time. From the previous discussion it is clear that there is some scope in improving the way we design research studies and measure leadership, by focusing on aspects such as:

(1) the inclusion of real-time measurement and direct measurement of leadership;
(2) the use of qualitative and quantitative methods to broaden our understanding of leadership;
(3) clearly specifying the level of analysis;
(4) designing studies that are longitudinal in nature;
(5) exploring the interaction between moderators, mediators and antecedents; and
(6) specifying the level of analysis as well as taking the context into account, which may further develop and improve our understanding of leadership.

Gardner et al. (2011) highlight the importance of moving away from an over-reliance on the use of survey measures, cross-sectional designs and the use of single source data. Many authentic leadership studies rely predominantly on followers to rate the leader's behaviour and this can lead to common-method bias where correlations may be inflated. There are also some questions about the construct validity of (for example the ALQ) measuring instruments used as well as the nomological network of authentic leadership. We need not only a better understanding of the antecedents, mediators and moderators of authentic leadership but also how authentic leadership is viewed across cultures. Banks et al. (2016) argue that better conceptualisation of the constructs may lead to better operationalisation and measurement. A comprehensive review of transformational leadership theory by Van Knippenberg and Sitkin (2013) shares many of the concerns highlighted in the previous discussion. Problems with measurement, underdevelopment of the transformational leadership concept, and lack of criteria for the inclusion or exclusion of constructs, serve as examples in this regard (Van Knippenberg and Sitkin, 2013).

Bedi, Alpaslan and Green (2016) have provided a comprehensive review of ethical leadership. They argue that researchers should:

(1) use more longitudinal research designs in order to get a better understanding of the causal directions between ethical leadership and its consequences; and
(2) further explore the role of moral issues, moral intensity and moral identity on ethical leadership. It is further highlighted that

researchers should also use organisational as well as leader level data in order to get a better understanding of the consequences of ethical leadership.

Future researchers exploring leader–member exchange should give some attention to problems such as measurement (for example, development of validated scales); conceptualising the social context in which leaders and followers operate, the development and use of objective criteria when performance is operationalised and finally, get a better understanding of the impact of national culture on the development of high or low quality relationships (Avolio, Walumbwa and Weber, 2009). There is a need to move beyond the limited focus of manager–follower and include informal leadership that happens outside formal relationships.

Following is a complex process and leadership research need to explore the social construction of leadership, the interdependence between followership and leadership, how these processes interact and contribute to the success of leadership (Kean and Haycock-Stuart, 2011). This also includes the development of robust followership theories and the inclusion of a range of methodological approaches to enhance our understanding. Regarding a social network approach to leadership, Carter et al. (2015) argue that we need a better understanding of for example: how network leadership develops, what relational processes generate leadership and what are the boundaries that control the relationships between leadership structures and outcomes.

8.4   Building bridges from research on leadership models to HR practice

To summarise, in order to move leadership research forward, it is important to re-examine the current assumptions and paradigms we use in the study of leadership as well as the methodologies we use. But what are the implications of these research models and theories for the practice of HR and OD at organisational level? The HR and OD roles are now frequently fused together in large organisations in recognition of the fact that the implementation of HRM requires a proactive developmental orientation on the part of HR specialists. In this section, we focus especially on the OD oriented HR director charged with the task of executing change through senior and middle level managers. These levels are often very difficult to get "on board" in practice and middle managers often experience a disconnection between strategy intent and strategy in practice as a result. Beginning our analysis with the top team illustrates the point. At this level senior managers are often individualistic and rivalrous and indeed both the goal of eventually becoming CEO coupled with behavioural incentives which encourage inter-unit competition join together to create a difficult arena for collaboration. Teams are often fragmented at the top and there is often a yawning gap between the leadership espoused and the leadership enacted at the senior level. Despite this, collaboration is seen as the "new competitive" agenda according to a recent HBR article. Often a process of OD needs to take place to create and/or agree the vision and mission never mind create a collaborative climate for strategy implementation. This requires a lot of liaison work by HR to bring everyone together in a single forum and to achieve alignment through a series of team-building days usually led by an experienced facilitator. Such meetings are often fraught with tension and undisclosed agendas leading to an environment which does not promote openness and change. Catharsis often takes place in these events and the power of catharsis has to be managed very carefully. HR has a key role on follow-up to ascertain positions and resistance before during and between events and to smooth the way towards consensus. However, we know little about this process. So, one area that bridges HRM and leadership is understanding and diagnosing resistance and bargaining during the phases associated with top team strategy making and development. Another area of OD practice relates to the use of "live coaching" in the top team. This is a virtually un-researched area but one which would inform HR practice while adding to the knowledge base around group dynamics at the senior level. Similarly, the role of 360-degree feedback and coaching and its influence on senior team leadership decision-making is not well understood. Each of these areas would inform practice at the upper echelons in organisations.

8.5   Conclusion: collaboration and the role of HR director as coach

To conclude, as the chapter makes clear, collaboration has emerged as a "holy grail" of competitive advantage in recent literature. Strategic collaboration at the industry and firm level is predicated on a collaborative culture at the top of the organisation. Yet, we know from studies of teaming and psychological safety that these prerequisites to a collaborative competitive strategy are very difficult to achieve at the senior level. Authors such as Lencioni (2002) also argue that the five dysfunctions of team are pervasive at the senior team level. Nor has this topic gone unremarked in the OD literature. As far back as Beckhard (1967), one of the founding fathers of organisational development, who proposed a dynamic technique to flush out interest positions in an article entitled "The confrontation meeting". We believe that a real valued-added contribution of the HR director is to provide or arrange OD interventions at the top to unblock the stalemate and stagnation that is often found there.

From our review of research studies in leadership, it is also clear that the role of the HR director as coach is an important area of development. For example, if a decision is taken to develop transformational leadership through the 4Is at the top, what are we to make of the exhortations to be authentic. While the 4Is are teachable and coachable, would the organisation be better off with authentic but professional managers? For some authenticity and integrity perceptions are intertwined and employees quickly see when managers are adopting styles which are not natural and react accordingly. Another key area is that of middle managers and their role in executing strategy through leadership and change initiatives. Middle managers have a wide range of roles during change including synthesising information, championing, implementing strategy and facilitating adaptability (Zain, Richardson and Adam, 2002). Each of these has development implications and middle managers are often scathing about the expectations of senior managers who push huge responsibilities to implement change on their shoulders without any prior process involvement or leadership development in persuasive communication. Middle managers often feel like the proverbial meat in the sandwich. Again there is a key educational role for HR here to point out to senior leaders the process difficulties in implementing strategy and the need to support and resource middle managers.

Coaching leaders on how to build followership is another key challenge for HR managers flowing from our analysis of leadership development needs at senior levels in the organisation. Kotter (2014) has recently advocated a new change operating model whereby the power of the hierarchy is coupled with the volunteer power which resides in every organisational network in order to harness volunteerism in organisations in the strategy implementation process. Increasingly employees at all levels of the organisation are seeking purpose at work through the crafting of meaning in their jobs. Indeed are often cited as exerting pressure that their organisation has a purposeful "soul" which is dedicated to the development of the community, less developed countries and the avoidance of exploitation in the supply chain. "People, planet, profits" is now a key catchphrase that millennials expect to see expressed in corporate purpose and acted upon. The astute HR director recognises that these sentiments also influence top talent and their choice of organisation to work for.

Leadership models thus challenge us as to how we can implement their recommendations. We are sure that the development of a HR/OD perspective must be taken by the profession if these challenges are to be met. We envisage a strategic but process driven perspective whereby the HR function engages in important diagnostic work but also follows the process through to conclusion. If it does this then the statistics of successful change are much more likely to be on an upward trend for the future.

References

Avolio, B.J. and Bass, B.M. (2004). Multifactor leadership questionnaire (MLQ). http://www.mindgarden.com/16-multifactor-leadership-questionnaire (accessed 28 April 2017).

Avolio, B.J., Walumbwa, F.O. and Weber, T.J. (2009). Leadership: Current theories, research, and future directions. *Annual Review of Psychology*, 60: 421–449.

Balkundi, P. and Kilduff, M. (2006). The ties that lead: A social network approach to leadership. *The Leadership Quarterly*, 17(4): 419–439.

Banks, G.C., McCauley, K.D., Gardner, W.L. and Guler, C.E. (2016). A meta-analytic review of authentic and transformational leadership: A test for redundancy. *The Leadership Quarterly*, 27(4): 634–652.

Beckhard, R. (1967). The confrontation meeting. *Harvard Business Review*, 45(2): 149–156.

Bedi, A., Alpaslan, C.M. and Green, S. (2016). A meta-analytic review of ethical leadership outcomes and moderators. *Journal of Business Ethics*, 139(3): 517–536.

Brown, M.E., Treviño, L.K. and Harrison, D.A. (2005). Ethical leadership: A social learning perspective for construct development and testing. *Organizational Behavior and Human Decision Processes*, 97(2): 117–134.

Carter, D.R., DeChurch, L.A., Braun, M.T. and Contractor, N.S. (2015). Social network approaches to leadership: An integrative conceptual review. *Journal of Applied Psychology*, 100(3): 597.

Dinh, J.E., Lord, R.G., Gardner, W.L., Meuser, J.D., Liden, R.C. and Hu, J. (2014). Leadership theory and research in the new millennium: Current theoretical trends and changing perspectives. *The Leadership Quarterly*, 25(1): 36–62.

Dorfman, P., Javidan, M., Hanges, P., Dastmalchian, A. and House, R. (2012). GLOBE: A twenty-year journey into the intriguing world of culture and leadership. *Journal of World Business*, 47(4): 504–518.

Dulebohn, J.H., Bommer, W.H., Liden, R.C., Brouer, R.L. and Ferris, G.R. (2012). A meta-analysis of antecedents and consequences of leader–member exchange integrating the past with an eye toward the future. *Journal of Management*, 38(6): 1715–1759.

Fairhurst, G.T. (2007) *Discursive Leadership: In Conversation with Leadership Psychology*. Thousand Oaks, CA: Sage.

Fisk, G.M. and Friesen, J.P. (2012). Perceptions of leader emotion regulation and LMX as predictors of followers' job satisfaction and organizational citizenship behaviors. *The Leadership Quarterly*, 23(1): 1–12.

Gardner, W.L., Avolio, B.J. and Walumbwa, F.O. (2005). Authentic leadership development: Emergent trends and future directions. *Authentic Leadership Theory and Practice: Origins, Effects, and Development* (Monographs in Leadership and Management), 387–406.

Gardner, W.L., Cogliser, C.C., Davis, K.M. and Dickens, M.P. (2011). Authentic leadership: A review of the literature and research agenda. *The Leadership Quarterly*, 22(6): 1120–1145.

Hernandez, M., Eberly, M.B., Avolio, B.J. and Johnson, M.D. (2011). The loci and mechanisms of leadership: Exploring a more comprehensive view of leadership theory. *The Leadership Quarterly*, 22(6): 1165–1185.

Kaiser, R.B., Hogan, R. and Craig, S.B. (2008). Leadership and the fate of organizations. *American Psychologist*, 63(2): 96.

Kean, S. and Haycock-Stuart, E. (2011). Understanding the relationship between followers and leaders. *Nursing Management (Harrow)*, 18(8): 31–36.

Kernis, M.H. (2003) Toward a conceptualization of optimal self-esteem. *Psychological Inquiry*, 14(1): 1–26.

Kotter, J. (2014). *Accelerate: Building Strategic Agility for a Faster-Moving World*. Boston: HBS Press.

Lencioni, P. (2002). *The Dysfunctions of a Team*. San Francisco, CA: Jossey-Bass.

Raelin, J. (2003). *Creating Leaderful Organizations*. San Fransisco, CA: Berrett Koehler.

Shamir, B. (2007). From passive recipients to active co-producers: Followers' roles in the leadership process. In B. Shamir, R. Pillai, M. Bligh and M. Uhl-Bien (eds), *Follower-centered Perspectives on Leadership: A Tribute to the Memory of James R. Meindl* (pp. 9–39). Charlotte, NC: Information Age Publishers.

Sparrowe, R.T. and Liden, R.C. (1997). Process and structure in leader–member exchange. *Academy of Management Review*, 22(2): 522–552.

Toor, S. and Ofori, G. (2009). Ethical leadership: Examining the relationships with the Full Range Leadership Model, employee outcomes, and organizational culture. *Journal of Business Ethics*, 90(4): 533–547.

Treviño, L.K., Brown, M. and Hartman, L.P. (2003). A qualitative investigation of perceived executive ethical leadership: Perceptions from inside and outside the executive suite. *Human relations*, 56(1): 5–37.

Uhl-Bien, M. (2006). Relational leadership theory: Exploring the social processes of leadership and organizing. *The Leadership Quarterly*, 17(6): 654–676.

Uhl-Bien, M., Marion, R. and McKelvey, B. (2007). Complexity leadership theory: Shifting leadership from the industrial age to the knowledge era. *The Leadership Quarterly*, 18(4): 298–318.

Uhl-Bien, M., Riggio, R.E., Lowe, K.B. and Carsten, M.K. (2014). Followership theory: A review and research agenda. *The Leadership Quarterly*, 25(1): 83-104.

Van Knippenberg, D. and Sitkin, S.B. (2013). A critical assessment of charismatic–transformational leadership research: Back to the drawing board? *The Academy of Management Annals*, 7(1): 1-60.

Walumbwa, F.O., Avolio, B.J., Gardner, W.L., Wernsing, T.S. and Peterson, S.J. (2008). Authentic leadership: Development and validation of a theory-based measure. *Journal of Management*, 34(1): 89-126.

Walumbwa, F.O. and Schaubroeck, J. (2009). Leader personality traits and employee voice behavior: Mediating roles of ethical leadership and work group psychological safety. *Journal of Applied Psychology*, 94(5): 1275.

Wang, G., Oh, I., Courtright, S.H. and Colbert, A.E. (2011). Transformational leadership and performance across criteria and levels: A meta-analytic review of 25 years of research. *Group and Organisation Management*, 36(2): 223-270.

Yammarino, F. (2013). Leadership past, present, and future. *Journal of Leadership & Organizational Studies*, 20(2): 149-155.

Yammarino, F.J., Dionne, S.D., Chun, J.U. and Dansereau, F. (2005). Leadership and levels of analysis: A state-of-the-science review. *The Leadership Quarterly*, 16(6): 879-919.

Zain, M., Richardson, S. and Adam, M.N.K. (2002). The implementation of innovation by a multinational operating in two different environments: A comparative study. *Creativity and Innovation Management*, 11(2): 98-106.

9 Architectures of value: moving leaders beyond analytics and big data

Anthony Hesketh

9.1 Introduction

The starting point of this chapter is Aristotle's observation that in order to unravel an intellectual knot, one first needs to be aware of its existence. Drawing on previous work making this very point (Fleetwood and Hesketh, 2010), the chapter explores how, despite recent suggestions for the field to complicate itself and take the field further (for example, Paauwe, 2009; Janssens and Steyaert, 2009), most researchers continue to think the answer lies in using more of the same analytical techniques, as opposed to employing alternative, meta-theoretical approaches and their associated techniques. This, the second section of the chapter argues, is symptomatic of a wider malaise relating to what constitutes knowledge in general, and what counts as analytical evidence of *causality* in driving business outcomes, in particular. By way of an example, extant research in the field exploring the relationship between human resources management and performance (hereafter, the HRM-P link) will be presented as being captured by the discourse of quantification, conflating with the quantum form of the dependent variable – finance – an imbued quantification through the enumeration of the *qualitative* explanatory variables represented by different human resources *practices* and managerial interventions. This attempted *quantified materialisation* of what are largely intangible and complex social entities via analytical techniques is examined through the lens of Foucault's presentation of a *General Science of Order* (Foucault, 1966/2002), focusing in particular on his identification of how *mathesis* – a universal science of measurement and order represented by algebra – is in the final analysis another form of *taxinomia* – the ordering and representation of the signs which constitute our complex experience and constitution of knowledge. The final section, perhaps counter-intuitively to what has preceded above, points the way forward as not being the rejection of the quantum form offered by analytics, per se, but to a purer form of *analytical argumentation* via a new form of analysis with *financial ürtext*, on the one hand, and its more productive combination with more reflexive accounts of how human resource interventions both unlock and contribute to improved and *material* performance improvements, on the other. There is, however, no escaping from the fact that there are problems on both sides of the analytical equation, that both require attention, and even then this might not be enough to support the empirical claims made by the HRM research community in its present dominant metatheoretical guise. That this will be unwelcome news is hardly surprising. That the HRM research community has routinely failed to satisfactorily engage with such emerging critique, the chapter concludes, is.

9.2   The big data debate

"Figures often beguile me", wrote Mark Twain in 1906, "particularly when I have the arranging of them myself". It was at this point in his memoirs Twain attributes to the former British Prime Minister, Benjamin Disraeli, the phrase now ubiquitous in modern parlance, "there are three kinds of lies: lies, damned lies and statistics". There is no formal record in *Hansard* or elsewhere of Disraeli ever uttering this phrase but Twain was perhaps alluding to another point: why would we want to let evidence get in the way of a good story? And here in a nutshell we have the current fascination with all things analytics.

"Big data is everywhere" (George, Haas and Pentland, 2014: 321). It is easy to see why. According to one leading consulting house:

> [C]ompanies that adopt "data-driven decision-making" have productivity levels 5 to 6 per cent higher than can be explained by other factors, including investment in technology [and] the focus now needs to shift to quantifying the enterprise: capturing the actions, interactions, and attributes of the employees and processes that make the enterprise tick. (Accenture, 2013: 21)

Of course, what makes enterprises tick is a moot point. For some, analytics provide insights on which managers can make more effective and evidence-based decisions to better lead their organisations themselves (for example, Davenport and Harris, 2007). For others, the answers to organisational challenges lie in the analytics (for example, Edwards and Edwards, 2016). At first glance the "analytical turn" appears to have passed academic researchers by. Closer scrutiny, however, reveals how the techniques utilised in analytics are principally the same as those in conventional statistics. While Fitz-Enz and Mattox (2014: xvi) seek to describe analytics as being, "derived from the Greek word *analysis*, meaning a breaking up, from *ana-*, 'up, throughout', and *lysis*, 'a loosening'", they appear to overlook the previous statistical techniques used by scholars for nearly a century also represent:

> [I]n practice, analysis [as] the isolation and identification of the variables in a situation for the purpose of better understanding the phenomenon under consideration. (Fitz-Enz and Mattox, 2014: xvi)

Similarly, Edwards and Edwards (2016: 2) operate under a similar misconception defining predictive HR analytics as:

> [T]he systematic application of predictive modelling using inferential statistics to existing HR people-related data in order to inform judgements about possible causal factors driving key HR-related performance indicators.

But they too describe their approach as the taking of "sophisticated statistics and quantitative analyses techniques that scientists use to predict things (such as what may cause heart disease or what might help to cure cancer) and apply them to the information that we hold about people in our organisations" (Edwards and Edwards, 2016: 2). There is nothing new under the statistical sun.

You could be forgiven, however, for thinking the statistics used by analysts are not the same as those used by your father. Far from justifying the emergence of analytics as something resting on the deep foundations of existing statistical techniques there appears to be a desire to paint the analytics in new colours. Ultimately, predictive analytics, at least certainly those used in HR, rests on little more than regression and advanced modelling techniques with which generations of statisticians and operational research students are highly familiar. The increase in the volume of data is encouraging researchers to examine new statistical techniques to cope with the volumes of streaming data generated by digitalisation. The new statistical toolbox to cope with these new structures of data are now under construction but it will be some time yet until they feed their way into the application of human resources management or even, it seems, academic studies in the area. This was a point not lost on a recent editorial in the *Academy of Management Journal* which observed, "though 'big data' has now become commonplace as a business term, there is very little published management scholarship that tackles the challenges of using such tools – or, better yet, that explores the promise and opportunities for new theories and practices that big data might bring about" (George, Haas and Pentland, 2014: 321).

What is new, however, is the volume and speed at which such statistical techniques can be applied. There is even a view that it does not even need to get this far. Recent writers have been so bold as to suggest we know longer need to worry about the coefficients of determination as with the advent of so-called "big data" correlation coefficients can tell us everything we need to know. The typical statistical approach of resting on p values to establish significance makes little sense when data are so "big" everything is statistically "significant". On this reading at least, it appears correlation is indeed now causality. Cautioning against such statistical superficiality some academics have reached the dramatic conclusion that two possible ways to ameliorate such problems would be to recognise the central importance of theory and to test the theoretical arguments emerging from our new giant datasets in field experiments where, "a wider net can be cast, as a richer set of data about behaviours and beliefs can be collected, and over an extended period of time" (George, Haas and Pentland, 2014: 323). Big data? Big deal.

The visualisation, and consequently the possible insights offered by big data, is being transformed, however. Where once only the data analysts at leading consulting firms could command such compelling imagery for their analyses, new programmes and software have made the drawing of analytically underpinned insights more commonplace, offering insights to less statistically-inclined end-users in organisations and beyond. I have seen some impressive illustrations where hiring patterns across competitor firms can reveal underpinning strategies and business models through the skills competitor firms are hiring. Not all patterns are quite so revealing, however, and resemble more tasseography than analytics. This development is being fuelled by a greater demand from wider stakeholders for greater transparency regarding the inner-workings of capitalism's largest commercial structures (for example, Gleeson-White, 2014). For now, however, we remain in the foothills of analytical maturity, be it in terms of data capture or its analysis and application to strategy within a HR context (see Hesketh, 2014).

Ultimately, the key question regarding HR analytics turns on its capacity to provide insights to both human resources scholars and practitioners. As we shall see below, the *statistical* evidence is far from convincing, illustrating Twain's point regarding it is with statistical arranging where the problems start to emerge. For example, recent meta-analyses of the research output of the analytics exploring the relationship between human resources practices and organisational performance during the last two decades – arguably *the* central focus of emerging HR analytics – has concluded that the best science on the table to date demonstrates human resource interventions can explain less than 5 per cent of the variation in the *financial* performance between organisations (Combs et al., 2006; Guest, Paauwe and Wright, 2012. This sits uneasily with most chief executives who routinely make the observation that their people are "our most important asset". So uneasy, in fact, that many of them and their executive colleagues routinely reject the "people analytics" on offer from academics, consultants and think tanks. Despite such universal rejection from the C-suite, compounded by statistical methods of analysis which have remained largely unchanged since Huselid's (1995) pioneering work two decades ago, scholars routinely continue *The Hunting of the Snark* otherwise known as the statistical relationship between a particular human resource element of focus (the dependent variable) and its relationship with, and determination by, multiple influences (or independent variables) on the other side of the equation. The specific human resource management processes under analysis may vary – factors influencing successful recruitment; those shaping retention; others which drive engagement; or the development of effective leaders – but the method of analysis always remains the same: the relationship or correlation between the two sides of the equation at an initial level, with more complex analyses applied to determining or modelling the "causal" extent to which human resources can impact on other processes or outcomes, both within and (albeit rarely) without the human resources function.

It cannot go on like this, only, those working in the field refuse to acknowledge such. This refusal is surprising as the metatheoretical challenges and shortcomings of HR analytics are now well documented (Godard, 2004; Boselie, Dietz and Boon, 2005; Legge, 2005; Hesketh, 2014; Hesketh and Fleetwood, 2006; Fleetwood and Hesketh, 2006; 2008; 2010; Tourish, 2011; Gerhart, 2012). Research in the field, however, continues unabated in the same methodological vein and has almost universally ignored the challenges from other scholars, some of whom can hardly be dismissed as those operating outside mainstream business schools (for example, Pfeffer, 1997; Moss Kanter, 2003; Ghoshal, 2005). The reasons for this apparent oversight on the part of HR analytics scholars are complex but worthy of exploration if only to establish how future developments in the field are to best proceed. The potential application to human resources of analytics is vast and well beyond the scope offered by this chapter. Our focus then needs to be concentrated and, consequently, is on the field where most of the heat surrounding analytics has been at its warmest if not brightest: namely the research exploring the analytical or statistical link between human resources management and organisational performance.

9.3   Tied up in knots

The HRM analytics field appears to be seemingly unaware of the metatheoretical problems it faces. As Aristotle informs us in *The Metaphysics*, in order to be able to untie a knot we must first be aware of its existence. No such awareness of the field's metatheoretical short-comings is manifest in current HRM scholars' reflections on the pro-gress of their analytical work to date. For example, the latest collection of essays by dominant scholars in the HRM and performance field opens with the question, "is the HRM-performance relationship one that is strong, universal and causal, or is it potentially weak, contin-gent and even spurious" (Guest, Paauwe and Wright, 2012: 2)? Nearly two hundred pages later, and after observing that some scholars have, "convincingly outlined major problems of reliability and validity", the original questioning appears to be nothing more than rhetorical as the solution is still seen as one which will, "point to ways in which our *measurement* could be improved" (Guest, Paauwe and Wright, 2012: 199, emphasis added). Far from untying the metatheoretical knot, then, its grip appears to be tightening round the HRM analytics research community, as the prescription appears to be one of pulling the ends of both measurement and prediction via analytics tighter still.

A second oversight, and one very much contributing to the intractabil-ity of the overall analytical knot, lies in the trust placed in numbers by scholars in the HRM analytics field to ontologically reflect the mana-gerial and organisational realities they seek to better understand. The *explanans*, however, need not be wholly determined by the *explanan-dum*. For example, that we might be seeking to better understand what drives organisational performance, which is primarily described in the quantum form of finance, does not necessarily mean that we require all subsequent explanation and the enablement of such improved performance to be in correspondingly quantum form. Only statistical convention requires that it does: in order to pursue convention in a deductivistic mode of empirical research, the variables under analysis are required to be quantitative, dichotomous and linear in relationship. Even where linear relationships do not exist, researchers subject data to transformations (for example, in to logarithmic scales) enabling them to pursue the linear analysis their techniques require. This in itself might not be problematic. When such techniques are applied to social processes that have been enumerated, that is, complex social processes, understandings and actions turned into a Lickert Scale, both ontological and, especially, epistemological questions arise. I will pick up this problem in the second section. In so doing, scholars commit both the ontic and epistemic fallacies of first assuming that they can realistically convert into a unit of measurement the adequacy of an intangible human resource management practice, and then compound this by assuming they can quantitatively estimate the relative and differential impact of this reified measure on an organisation's financial performance (Bhaskar, 1978).

For example, I can safely deduce that the operating profit at Company A will be $100m if its revenues are $1bn and operating costs are $900m. We can also deduce that if at Company B, operating profits come in at $200m from $1bn revenues, Company B's operating costs are $100m lower than Company A's. We could even maintain the argument that Company B's performance – at least at the level of margin – is twice that of Company A's. Translating the same logic to, for example, high performance work systems and their *causal* relationship with an organisation's financial performance in the quantum form is highly problematic. Whilst researchers might want to suggest, "a one-standard deviation increase in High Performance Work Practices yields a $27,044 increase in sales and a $3,814 increase in profits" (Huselid, 1995: 662), it is not immediately apparent exactly what management intervention comprises a one standard deviation increase in high performance work practices. There is also the not insignificant factor, rarely explored by HR analytics scholars, that even if we could accurately quantify management intervention, let alone quantify its capacity to release additional sales and/or profits, the required level of financial investment to deliver a one standard deviation increase in high performance work practices may exceed the anticipated gains in additional sales and/or profits! This was precisely why Pfeffer warned at the onset of HRM–performance research in the late 1990s that the HR function was "entering a game where winning is unlikely and playing by the rules set by others exposes human resource professionals to the possibility of at best short-term victories and long-term problems" (Pfeffer, 1997: 357). The current analytical turn represents a second refusal by academic researchers in the field to acknowledge Pfeffer's warning shot.

A third problem, again symptomatic of this calculative and subsequently deductive logic and mode of statistical analysis at the heart of analytics, has been the art of data reduction or the "spinning" of variables on both sides of the (largely) linear equations deployed in statistical techniques. Publications in the field are replete with a multitude of dependent variables representing actual financial performance (for example, return on assets, Tobin's q, p/e ratios) or proxies of performance (for example, customer satisfaction levels, employee engagement), which are inserted in to regression equations in an attempt to *analytically* or, more accurately, *statistically*, establish the extent to which variance in the independent variables (almost without exception now represented by versions of the 13 high performance work practices) can "explain" differential performance between organisations. Different dependent variables of financial performance – be they return on assets, operating profits, share price, and so on, or alternative proxies of performance – are routinely inserted, tested and retained or rejected on the grounds of their correlation coefficients with different HRM interventions. Similarly, on the other side of the equation, academics move between groups of high performance work practices, discarding individual practices at a time in an attempt to better refine their modelling of the relationship between HR and organisational performance. Almost without exception scholars appear to overlook the reductionism of their "explanation" of variance to being a statistical estimate of the variation between the integers contained in their mathematical model as opposed to a corresponding variation in the understanding and explanation of the underlying managerial practices and routines which represent the object of researchers' analyses. The everyday world of management, in this case, human resources practices, is seen to be synonymous with the world of numbers represented in the spreadsheet of *Excel* or *SPSS*. This apparent fusion of the qualitative with the quantitative represents one of the attractions with analytics, eliding the reductionistic ontological divide that exists between the practice and understanding of the human resource technique and its apparent "causal" impact on performance.

Which brings us neatly to a fourth oversight, one which is partly a response to the reluctant and niggling acknowledgement if not full acceptance by analytics scholars that converting organisational complexity into the "black box" which lies between the dependent and independent variables in their linear equations may result in error. Statistical error represents the *leitmotif* of the analytics field's Achilles' heel. Like advocates of statistical techniques in other research communities such as those applying the highest abstractions of theoretical physics to financial analysis, HR analysts have chosen to represent this weakness as a strength: exposing the "error" contained in the (alleged) material actuality of organisational life recorded in their data as merely being another step along the way to the incremental refinement of their stochastic analysis in order to bring their insights closer to the higher, overarching immaterial "truth" they claim their increasingly sophisticated and consistently refined scientific techniques represent (Miller and Miller, 2005).

This "problem" with materiality brings us to the crux of the issue. For economists and financial traders, the "real" market is not that which is generated on a daily basis by traders but is constituted by a "reality" found in the pure world of analytical probability models (Miller and Miller, 2005). Indeed, new financial products and markets such as arbitrage have originated out of such differences between the "fiction of reality" and the (equal fiction of the) "purity" of economic models (see MacKenzie, 2006). That their analyses continually demonstrates human resource interventions in general, and high performance work systems in particular, to be of relatively small impact in accounting for differences in the outperformance of organisations, represents for researchers the need for further refinement of *existing* analytical techniques *within* the current positivistic paradigm, not the re-evaluation of the metatheoretical assumptions underpinning their approach.

This, then, raises two significant questions for the human resources and analytics research communities. First, at which point might researchers declare their investigations to have reached magnitude, or more formally stated, the optimal proportion of variance at which the performance of organisations can be analytically explained by human resource interventions? Clearly, given the continued replication of studies, the hitherto undeclared optimal level of explanation appears to lie beyond that of the less than 5 per cent estimated by meta-analyses of the research output to date (Combs et al., 2006). Why else would the HRM-P community continue with such studies? Second, and perhaps more important, given this continued failing of numerological investigation to move beyond a perfunctory proportion of explanation, why do scholars stubbornly persist in using the same techniques? As we shall see, more recent meta-analysis has claimed a large increase in the proportion of performance explained by human resources practices. This claim is somewhat odd as it draws on the same research as previous meta-analysis estimating the "effect" to be smaller. I pick this up in the next section.

9.4   Captured by the discourse?

The beginnings of an answer to these questions might lie in asking the extent to which HR analysts can be described as being captured by the discourse involved in the enumeration of human resource processes. Such a *critical performativity* "entails pragmatically, but critically, working with already accepted discourses", in order to, "move beyond a critique of contemporary practices [of HR analytics] that actually exist to create a sense of what could be" (Alvesson and Spicer, 2012: 377).

The apparent insecurity established in the discourse of human resources executives when faced with the prospect of engaging with senior members of the boardroom is well documented (for example, Ulrich, 1997; Legge, 2005; Fleetwood and Hesketh, 2010; Hesketh and Hird, 2010; Charan, Barton and Carey, 2015). Many see the reason for this lack of confidence lying in a failure on the part of the HR function to quite literally provide a causal, transparent and, above all else, *financial* account of the contribution to the performance of their host organisation. Interestingly, recent empirical research demonstrates such a lack of confidence can also be found among executives in other functions *outside* HR (Teece, 2012; Cleemann and Hesketh, 2013). Crucially, the pursuit of a causal link with financial performance in executive circles is not simply an intellectual exercise but a demonstration of commercial relevance: an attempt on the part of individual executives – and subsequently by the academics who study them – to quite literally measure the, in this case, HR function to credibility. That such activities might be shaped by other deeper and underlying social and discursive forces at work is rarely considered, let alone explored.

While the relatively disappointing results obtained from the now hundreds of studies by the HRM-P community means, "we are still in no position to assert with any confidence that good HRM has an impact on organisation performance" (Guest, Paauwe and Wright, 2012: xx), researchers continue in the same metatheoretical vein. One possible reason for this lies not in their anticipation of an empirical break-through of God particle-like magnitude, but because they see no viable alternative to the inflationary currency of analytical and financial discourses in which they are now engaged with fellow executives from across the wider host organisation. An examination of executives' affinity with the articulation of their practice via the discourse of financial and analytical causality not only reveals the underlying social dynamics at work in the circles in which organisational elites move (for example, Reed, 2012), but following Foucault, reveals how the discourse of these interactions itself, "is also the object of desire" and that the struggle for power does not simply take place *through* discourse: but the "discourse [itself] is the power which is to be seized" (Foucault, 1984/1996: 110, original emphasis).

To abandon the underlying discourse of the analytical pursuit of the financial contribution of HR would effectively constitute a step back away from the discursive struggle in the articulation of executive power. The discursive currency through which such power exchanges take place is strategy, which, in turn, invokes the interdiscursive realm of finance through which the eligible order of knowledge prescribes recourse to the quantum, hence analytical form. The analytics of big data, then, opens up a new pathway to the appliance of science to human resources management. For a methodological discussion of the discursive processes referred to see Fairclough (2005).

Critically, for our purposes, Foucault draws our attention here to the philosophical distinction between the ordering of "simple natures" or what philosophers refer to as the sensible, primary or real state of objects represented by a calculable order: *mathesis*, or algebra, on the one hand. This is in opposition to the ordering of complex natures, what philosophers refer to as the "substratum" or underlying system of complex signs of representations from our experiences, articulations and classifications or what Foucault labels *taxinomia*. So far so good, but then Foucault raises two caveats.

First, while, "empirical representations must be analysable into simple natures", represented by algebra and the analytical form, or what Foucault labels, "a science of equalities, and therefore of attributions and judgements", Foucault sensitises us to, "the perception of proofs

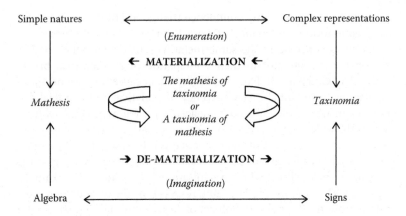

Source: Adapted from Foucault, 1966/2002: 80.

Figure 9.1   An analytical general science of order

[as being] only one particular case of representation in general [and that] one can equally well say that mathesis is only one particular case of *taxinomia*" (Foucault, 1966/2002: 80, original emphasis). The upshot of this is that the signs established by our thoughts can also be seen to constitute and can, consequently, be ordered in to an algebra of complex relations, or "qualitative mathesis". Just as there is a *mathesis of taxinomia*, there is, simultaneously, a *taxinomia* of *mathesis* (see Figure 9.1). Again, so far so good, but then comes a second caveat.

For Foucault, *taxinomia* also implies a certain continuum of things. More specifically, this continuum points to that which might exist in plenitude, or not. Again, this is hardly contentious but then comes the observation that this certain continuum of things is accompanied by a, "certain power of the imagination that renders apparent what is not, but makes possible by this very fact, the revelation of that continuity" (Foucault, 1966/2002: 80). It is in this "rendering apparent" the relationship between the two sides of the required analytical equation (financial performance and human resource processes) where the problems begin. This, too, comes in two forms, on each side of the equation.

First, "the power of the imagination" has to reveal the complex representations that are human resource practices on the independent side of the equation. This has to be achieved in such a way so as to render these complex representations through an ordering or valuing of the entities in question. These constituted facts require representation by non-interpretative numerical description (that is, uncontroversial values), which, in turn, are embedded in systematic claims about orders that are in some way derived from, and derivative of, those categories so allegedly unproblematically and uncontroversially valued (Poovey, 1998). This materialisation or *mathesis of taxinomia* is effectively the *enumeration* of entities representing, "the achievement of valuing – very often through practices of numbering – [and] attests the self-evident given-ness of the category valued" (Verran, 2011: 66). Reaching this point of being an enumerated entity requires what Poovey (1998) describes as a "three-step epistemic dance" in which categories are initially derived as parts of a vague whole (for example, individual "strategic high performance work systems" in HRM research). These categories are then "measured" and "valued" as parts of specific units or elements (for example, the rating scales used to evaluate the adequacy of specific elements comprising high performance work systems or "bundles" of practices). The categories derived in the initial step, and valued in the second, are then finally universalised into how things are (for example, the "contingency"; "configurational"; "universal" models established in HR performance analytics).

Second, on the opposite dependent side of the equation, similar epistemic dances are constantly taking place. Many practitioner consumers of HR analytics remain largely unaware that a shift in the *Delta* of performance does not equate to an actual shift in financial performance. Rather, this is also achieved by a Foucaultian rendering of that comprising the financial value under analysis. Returning to the example cited at the beginning of the chapter, whilst an influential piece of HR analytics has claimed the combined "meta effect" of all of the studies in the field revealed how a one standard deviation increase in the "value" attributed to human resource interventions could quite literally "account" for a corresponding 4.6 per cent increase in financial performance (Combs et al., 2006: 517–518), a second meta-analysis utilising many of the same studies could calculate several years later that this effect had at least doubled, or depending on the various measures used, nearly quadrupled (Jiang et al., 2012: 1278). However, closer analysis of the studies used in each of the meta-analyses (see Hesketh, 2016), reveals that the vast majority of individual studies did not use financial data to evaluate performance but a mixture of operational or other non-financial dependent variables including ordinal or "plastic" data where survey respondents were asked to rate their perceptions of the organisation's or their business unit's performance. Significantly, closer scrutiny of the later meta-analysis provided by Jiang and colleagues (2012) reveals how the significant increase in "financial" performance attributed to human resources owes more to the doubling of studies utilising plastic ordinal scales than an increase in the performance of the human resources under analysis.

While many in human resources might want to claim a significant increase in the performance of their function, such a course of action would in fact rest on nothing more than reification. A one standard deviation increase in an ordinal rating scale of performance does not, as claimed by meta-analyses authors, equate to a corresponding increase in financial performance. Unlike interval data, the difference between a score of 1 or 2 is not the same as the difference between 2 and 3, or that between 4 and 5. The mean return on assets might be calculated at $3.6 billion. But a mean subjective rating for performance of 3.6 is not the same thing. Only both the Combs and Jiang studies, like many others across different disciplines, treat them as synonymous. The calculated *statistic* is seen as the same as the calculated *financial* return. This ontological sleight of hand matters less when exploring the perceptions of the impact when reporting research subjects' *perceptions* of performance (for example, their perceived performance of a team, business unit or even organisation), but when the relationship between such ratings data are translated into interval-based financial terms (for example, a one standard deviation increase in the independent variable – in this case HR practices – translates into a standard deviation increase in the mean score of *perceived* performance – equates to a one standard deviation increase in return on assets), the assertion amounts to the reification of the financial impact claimed. Consequently, to claim an increase in subjective ratings can be translated into an increase in financial performance is misleading. The failure to point out this significant sidestep from a *financial* construct to a "plastic" one based on *subjectivity* is a subtle but nevertheless significantly distorting material one.

9.5   Conclusion: towards a solution (of sorts)

What has preceeded leaves HR analysts with a significant dilemma. While analytics offers an opportunity to measure the function to credibility, many of the measures on which the analytics rest are highly problematic. Recent research has highlighted how both the accounting profession and financial regulators reject the modelling on offer from academic research largely because of the perceived lack of veracity of the data involved (Hesketh, 2014). This leaves future research in the HR analytics field with two main challenges.

First, it is perhaps incumbent on journal editors in the field to be far more demanding as to what constitutes a worthwhile and new contribution to the field of HR analytics. Guest, Paauwe and Wright (2012) point to how there are now over 200 studies exploring the relationship between HR and organisational performance and yet still point to major weaknesses within the field. They are joined by a major scholar in the field who recognises:

> Few seem to believe that the "best practice" or "universal" model of HR is valid. Most of us find that unlikely and can make plenty of persuasive arguments for why HR practices must display (a) internal/horizontal fit among themselves, (b) external/vertical fit with strategy, and (c) fit with the institutional (including country) environment (Boxall, 2003; Dowling et al., 2008). The fact is, however, there is precious little (formal research) evidence that (a), (b) or (c) make much difference to business performance. (Gerhart, 2012: 167)

A second challenge represents a solution to the first. As we have seen above, much analytics masquerades as quantum data points when in fact they represent nothing more than subjective opinion translated into quasi-quantum form. Worse, "plastic" data used to operationalise financial performance misleads end users of research. Far from identifying those so-called leading indicators shaping superior performance, such attitudinal data serves no other purpose than to repeat people's preconceptions of what works as opposed to identifying what actually works. No amount of spurious *alpha* tests can replace real, independent data. A possible solution here, again raising the bar for journal editors and reviewers, relates to the levels of veracity they request in relation to the dependent variables used by researchers. If analytics are testing respondents' perceptions of performance, the title of their research should say as much. More importantly, reviewers must become hypersensitive to the spurious claims made on behalf of the relationship between subjective data on either side of the equation and their impact on the dependent variable under analysis. An increase of one standard deviation in the perception of the quality of hires does not cause a corresponding increase in the financial performance of the firm. There are simply too many other variables in play shaping such outcomes. Just because analysts may use a few thousand more data points when they invoke Monte Carlo methods, or claim to have rectified certain distortions by their use of Bayesian techniques, does not make their claims any more robust than other subjective analyses masquerading as quantitative analysis. If researchers want to make claims about the impact of HR variables on the financial performance of firms they should use financial data. A solution of sorts, then, lies in the adoption of *ürtext*, itself a technique used in the analysis of the performance of historical classical music. This involves stripping modern versions of pieces of music back to their original or "authentic" performance by referring to a printed version based on the original handwritten score – or *ürtext* version – of a composition as opposed to more modern versions which have evolved and subsequently changed over time, with significant distorting effects on what the composers would have originally wanted us to hear. The analytical methods of HR need to be purged of the distorting effects of subjective proxies for the performance, financial or otherwise, of HR-related outcomes. This represents a significant challenge to analytics in general and to a HR academic research community seeking impact in the real world of organisational life. But if we are as a community of scholars collectively responsible for ensuring analytics is to succeed where the statistics before it have failed, we must stop lying to ourselves and engage in a more robust approach to the veracity of our data to avoid the "garbage-in, garbage-out" trap.

References

Accenture 2013. *Accenture Technology Vision 2013: Every Business is a Digital Business.* Dublin: Accenture.

Alvesson, M. and Spicer, A. 2012. Critical leadership studies: The case for critical performativity. *Human Relations,* 65(3): 367–390.

Bhaskar, R. 1978. On the possibility of social scientific knowledge and the limits of naturalism. *Journal for the Theory of Social Behaviour,* 8(1): 1–28.

Boselie, P., Dietz, G. and Boon, C. 2005. Commonalities and contradictions in HRM and performance research. *Human Resource Management Journal,* 15(3): 67–94.

Boxall, P. 2003. HR strategy and competitive advantage in the service sector. *Human Resource Management Journal,* 13(3): 5–20.

Charan, R., Barton, D. and Carey, D. 2015. People before strategy. *Harvard Business Review,* 93(7/8): 62–71.

Cleemann, C.M. and Hesketh, A. 2013. Two's company, three's a crowd? The executive social life of the HR director. EIASM Conference on Strategic Management, Copenhagen Business School, Copenhagen, Denmark, 15–16 April.

Combs, J., Liu, Y., Hall, A. and Ketchen, D. 2006. How much do high-performance work practices matter? A meta-analysis of their effects on organizational performance. *Personnel Psychology,* 59(3): 501–528.

Davenport, T.H. and Harris, J.G. 2007. *Competing on Analytics: The New Science of Winning*. Boston, MA: Harvard Business School Press.

Edwards, M. and Edwards, K. 2016. *Predictive HR Analytics: Mastering the HR Metric*. London: Kogan Page.

Fairclough, N. 2005. Peripheral vision discourse analysis in organization studies: The case for critical realism. *Organization Studies*, 26(6): 915–939.

Fleetwood, S. and Hesketh, A. 2006. HRM–performance research: Under-theorized and lacking explanatory power. *The International Journal of Human Resource Management*, 17(12): 1977–1993.

Fleetwood, S. and Hesketh, A. 2008. Theorising under-theorisation in research on the HRM-performance link. *Personnel Review*, 37(2): 126–144.

Fleetwood, S. and Hesketh, A. 2010. *Explaining the Performance of Human Resource Management*. Cambridge: Cambridge University Press.

Foucault, M. 1966/2002. *The Order of Things: An Archaeology of the Human Sciences*. London: Psychology Press.

Foucault, M. 1984/1996. Foucault Live: Collected interviews, 1961–1984.

George, G., Haas, M.R. and Pentland, A. 2014. Big data and management. *Academy of Management Journal*, 57(2): 321–326.

Gerhart, B. 2012. Research on human resources and effectiveness: Some methodological challenges. In D. Guest, J. Pauuwe and P. Wright (eds), *HRM and Performance: Achievements and Challenges* (pp. 149–171). London: John Wiley & Sons.

Ghoshal, S. 2005. Bad management theories are destroying good management practices. *Academy of Management Learning & Education*, 4(1): 75–91.

Gleeson-White, J. 2014. *Six Capitals or Can Accountants Save the Planet? Rethinking Capitalism for the Twenty-First Century*. London: Norton.

Godard, J. 2004. A critical assessment of the high-performance paradigm. *British Journal of Industrial Relations*, 42(2): 349–378.

Guest, D.E., Paauwe, J. and Wright, P. (eds) 2012. *HRM and Performance: Achievements and Challenges*. London: John Wiley & Sons.

Hesketh, A. 2014. *Valuing Your Talent: A New Framework for Human Capital Management*. London: CIMA, CMI, CIPD, RSA.

Hesketh, A. 2016. Making a performance out of performance: Meta-analyses and the construction of HRM's *financial* contribution to business performance. Lancaster University Management School Working Paper.

Hesketh, A. and Fleetwood, S. 2006. Beyond measuring the human resources management–organizational performance link: Applying critical realist meta-theory. *Organization*, 13(5): 677–699.

Hesketh, A. and Hird, M. 2010. Using relationships between leaders to leverage more value from people: Building a golden triangle. In P. Sparrow, M. Hord, A. Hesketh and C. Cooper (eds), *Leading HR* (pp. 103–121). London: Palgrave Macmillan.

Huselid, M.A. 1995. The impact of human resource management practices on turnover, productivity, and corporate financial performance. *Academy of Management Journal*, 38(3): 635–672.

Janssens, M. and Steyaert, C. 2009. HRM and performance: A plea for reflexivity in HRM studies. *Journal of Management Studies*, 46(1): 143–155.

Jiang, K., Lepak, D.P., Hu, J. and Baer, J.C. 2012. How does human resource management influence organizational outcomes? A meta-analytic investigation of mediating mechanisms. *Academy of Management Journal*, 55(6): 1264-1294.

Legge, K. 2005. Preview/PostScript for the anniversary edition: Times they are a-changing: HRM rhetoric and realities ten years on. In K. Legge, *Human Resource Management: Rhetorics and Realities* (pp. 1-42). Basingstoke: Palgrave Macmillan.

MacKenzie, D. 2006. *An Engine, Not a Camera: Finance Theory and the Making of Markets*. Cambridge, MA: MIT Press.

Miller, D. and Miller, D. (eds) 2005. *Acknowledging Consumption*. London: Routledge.

Moss Kanter, R. 2003. Foreword. In M. Effron, R. Gandossy and M. Goldsmith (eds), *Human Resources in the 21st Century* (pp. vii–xii). New Jersey: Wiley.

Paauwe, J. 2009. HRM and performance: Achievements, methodological issues and prospects. *Journal of Management Studies*, 46(1): 129-142.

Pfeffer, J. 1997. Pitfalls on the road to measurement: The dangerous liaison of human resources with the ideas of accounting and finance. *Human Resource Management*, 36(3): 357–365.

Poovey, M. 1998. *A History of the Modern Fact: Problems of Knowledge in the Sciences of Wealth and Society*. Chicago, IL: University of Chicago Press.

Reed, M.I. 2012. Masters of the universe: Power and elites in organization studies. *Organization Studies*, 33(2): 203-221.

Teece, D.J. 2012. Dynamic capabilities: Routines versus entrepreneurial action. *Journal of Management Studies*, 49(8): 1395-1401.

Tourish, D. 2011. Performativity, metatheorising and journal rankings: What are the implications for emerging journals and academic freedom?. In S. Dameron and T. Durand (eds), *Redesigning Management Education and Research: Challenging Proposals from European Scholars* (pp. 183-196). Cheltenham, UK and Northampton, MA, USA: Edward Elgar Publishing.

Ulrich, D. 1997. *Human Resource Champions: The Next Agenda for Adding Value and Delivering Results*. Boston: Harvard Business School.

Verran, H. 2011. The changing lives of measures and values: From centre stage in the fading "disciplinary" society to pervasive background instrument in the emergent "control" society. *The Sociological Review*, 59(s2): 60-72.

10 HRM and productivity

Paul Sparrow and Lilian Otaye-Ebede

10.1 Introduction

Sparrow, Hird and Cooper (2015) have argued that in many areas of research – such as dealing with performance challenges including innovation, customer centricity, lean management – the demand-pattern for professional knowledge both inside organisations for practitioners, and for the academics studying these issues, is changing. In this chapter we deal with the issue of productivity (Chapters 11 and 12 will examine the challenge of innovation and globalisation). For HRM researchers the study of any of these performance drivers, or their enablers, presents both a "multi-level" and a "horizontal" problem. The phenomenon is multi-level because different interventions are needed at national (macro), organisational (meso), and task or business process (micro) level. It is horizontal, because even within an organisation, the solution often sits "above" and "across" the traditional management functions, such as HRM. The challenges can only be properly understood and solved by cross-functional action and focus inside the organisation, but also connections to, and coordination across, people beyond the organisation (partners, supply chain, governments). Solving the performance challenges also needs coordinated investments at national and institutional levels, coupled with changes inside organisations. They also require new combinations of technology, business models, organisation design, knowledge and people.

HRM researchers have only made limited inroads into the topic of productivity. Their focus, understandably, has come from a control perspective focused mainly on the effectiveness of individual level interventions, as seen in debates around workforce skills and productivity, and the impact of performance management, or performance-related pay. There have been challenges to the effectiveness of many traditional HRM functions or practices in terms of their contribution to productivity, and it is notoriously difficult to link them to strategic performance outcomes.

As a performance outcome, productivity may be thought of as one form of resilience. The chapter argues that HR directors will be tasked with contributing to fundamental workforce and business model transformations aimed at reversing what is now a serious productivity problem, and raises some important questions for them around productivity.

It begins by showing why there is now renewed concern about productivity, and argues that as organisations face multiple risk events, this is drawing attention to the economic health, productivity and resilience of organisations or nations. It outlines two challenges – developments in national and organisational level productivity. It explains some of the main factors involved in organisation level productivity and links the national and organisational agendas by drawing attention to areas such as the role of skills in improving productivity – which is mainly seen in terms of the intangible benefits it has on knowledge transfer and innovation – and the challenge that future skills scenarios might present for HR functions.

The chapter identifies three important contextual factors that HRM research has to take into account: the role of time in the HRM–productivity challenge; the relationship between productivity, HRM, and risk; and the importance of understanding the most appropriate level of analysis question in examining the relationship between HRM and productivity. It uses a range of different productivity challenges across several sectors to demonstrate this – such as supermarkets, fast food, oil and energy, aerospace, nuclear sector, healthcare, and on-demand business models. These examples reveal the highly idiosyncratic nature of productivity strategies that are typically needed.

Understanding the true drivers of productivity at the level of the organisation is a major challenge. Even with today's improvements in business analytics, often only a handful of internal managers can grasp productivity in its totality, and the idiosyncratic nature of each business model generally means that even within an industrial sector recipe, each organisation often finds bespoke ways of delivering improved productivity. It argues that we need much better use of human capital metrics and HR analytics so that organisations, and important stakeholders such as the financial community, can get a better fix on the true health and future value of an organisation.

10.2   A global concern

Chapter 4 raised the need to look at key areas of HRM through a risk optimisation lens. Regardless of eventual outcomes of these risk events, they bring the economic health and resilience of an organisation or a nation to the fore. Productivity can be analysed, thought about, and managed across very different levels: operations, departments, facilities, organisations, sectors and industries, business models or networks of actors and institutions, countries, and even economic regions or blocks. HR directors naturally focus on improving their organisation's internal productivity, but the ability of their organisation to improve its internal productivity is invariably dependent on external and institutional developments. We begin therefore by briefly outlining the national-level debate about productivity.

At a national level economic productivity is one of three key factors determining the trend growth rate of an economy, the other two being the pace at which a country can expand without pushing up prices, and population growth. It is seen in terms of measures such as output per hour, output per job and output per worker, for the whole economy.

Productivity problems have been seen in several countries. It is becoming a focus of attention again in part because of concern that the global economy remains extremely fragile and open to disruption. By 2014 Spain, the USA and France were at or above their pre-crisis productivity levels, but labour productivity in the UK, Germany, Italy and Norway still remained below its level at the beginning of the crisis. Financial crises are now associated with larger output losses, and slower recoveries, than more "conventional" recessions (Reinhart and Rogoff, 2009).

The Bank of England has classified events in three ways: world demand shocks, world supply or price shocks and world financial shocks (Chowla, Quaglietti and Rachel, 2014). Since the global financial crisis we have seen economic spasms over Grexit and the potential demise of the euro, the inability of US Federal Reserve to wean markets off free money, debt bubbles in China, and Brexit. Such shocks are now transmitted rapidly through trade linkages (demand for exports and import prices), financial linkages (tighter supply of credit and more volatile asset prices), and spillovers into general uncertainty.

The OECD's Compendium of Productivity Indicators provides a comprehensive overview of recent and long-term trends in productivity levels and growth in OECD and some G20 countries. Their analyses suggest that the decline in productivity is a global phenomenon, and began well before the 2008 financial crisis despite the increased participation of firms in value chains, rising education and technological innovations. Growth rates began declining in the early 2000s in Canada, the UK and the USA, and in the 1970s in France, Germany, Italy and Japan. This suggests a structural, rather than cyclical, slowdown caused by skill mismatches, sluggish investment and, particularly post-crisis, declining business dynamism.

Whilst there is a general fragility of economic markets, the relative positions of the EU economies and the USA on GDP per hour worked has not changed greatly between 1993 and 2013. However, in some countries productivity challenges have become particularly protracted (Hughes and Saleheen, 2012). For example, in the UK there has been much debate about what has been termed "the productivity puzzle". On international comparisons of productivity and employment, back in 2009, the UK was placed 10th out of 30 OECD countries for its employment and 11th for its level of productivity (Spilsbury and Campbell, 2009). The level of productivity in the UK is higher than in Japan given its continued deflation, but remains lower than in other major developed economies such as the USA, Germany, Sweden, Norway and the Netherlands.

However, UK productivity collapsed after the global financial crisis in 2008, broadly flat-lining from 2010 to 2015, and after a short respite, falling again in 2017, an event unprecedented in the post-war era. By 2014 output per worker was still 17 per cent below where it would have been had the pre-recession trend continued, with falls still occurring throughout 2015, resulting in a lost decade for living standards. Hours worked rose sharply, but output per hour did not keep pace.

Economists have been at a loss to fully explain this trend. Part of the problem lies in corporate and institutional behaviours (such as lower corporate and public investment, the unwillingness of banks to lend to new businesses after the financial crisis), and part in demographic factors (such as population and pensions changes resulting in higher numbers of people working beyond normal retirement age).

The structural slowdown caused by skill mismatches, sluggish investment and declining business dynamism has created three debates which HR directors are finding hard to avoid, and which HR researchers are now showing an interest in:

1. There are fears it may exacerbate already growing income and wealth inequalities, trapping many more workers in low-productivity activities with high job insecurity. In the UK, for example, the Bank of England has begun to question whether organisations are becoming more inclined to use labour-intensive forms of production rather than investing in new efficiency-enhancing technology, which has become relatively more expensive, or whether there is tendency over time for employment to be concentrated in sectors where productivity gains are difficult to secure or measure, such as care homes and nurseries.
2. Where fears grow that some national industrial structures are becoming based on permanent low skilled, low wage industries, HR directors will be tasked with contributing to fundamental workforce and business model transformations aimed at reversing what is now a serious problem. This has serious implications for the future HRM context such as: an inability of firms to retain staff because of low pay growth; an undesirable expansion of low-skill, low-productivity business models; and a continued weakening of labour bargaining power.
3. Poor international performance has led to institutional criticisms of the way in which organisations collaborate with host countries to build productivity and the way they behave within particular national business systems.

Although from a managerial and economic perspective, productivity is mainly seen as a function of three variables (technology, labour and organisation) it may be viewed more broadly. Organisational productivity began to receive serious attention by the 1980s, because it was seen as a concept that could tie together issues such as an organisation's international competitive position, the survival of specific organisations, the success of industries, and the quality of life of individuals.

The national level focus on tangible inputs to productivity, such as capital and labour, fails to account for important variations of intangible assets, such as organisation-level competences around things like brand, training and management, their research and development, and their IT capital. At the organisational level, productivity is interpreted as a measure of effectiveness (doing the right thing efficiently) and is an *outcome*-oriented rather than *output*-oriented way of looking at organisational performance.

HRM researchers struggle to think about organisational performance in such ways. They are not alone of course. Even with today's improvements in business analytics (see Chapter 9) often only a handful of internal managers can grasp productivity in its totality. Understanding the true drivers of productivity can be a major challenge at the level of the organisation. Managing productivity typically involves analytics that draw upon measures of the amount of output (the amount of goods and services) obtained from a certain amount of input (time, labour, materials, energy, and so on), or how well various resources or inputs in the organisation are used to achieve the planned or desired results (outputs) (Madrick, 1997). At the organisational level, productivity is usually expressed in one of three forms:

1. *partial factor productivity* (using single ratios such as labour, machine, materials, capital or energy productivity);
2. *multifactor productivity* (using combinations of such ratios); or
3. *total productivity* (combining the effects of all the resources used in the production of goods and services).

The latter might need to incorporate a wide range of factors such as capital investments in production, technology, equipment and facilities, technological changes, economies of scale, work methods, procedures and systems, quality of products, processes and management, the legislative and regulatory environment, workforce education, and workforce knowledge and skill resulting from training and experience.

10.3   The HRM–productivity research agenda: identifying the productivity recipes

Given the complexity of factors involved, HR directors, and their staff (and HRM researchers moving into this field of research) therefore have to quickly build their insight into the business challenge, and the relative contribution that might be made by solutions that are dependent upon people management and organisational behaviour.

For HRM researchers, often driven by the need for comparable performance measures so that they can engage in generic academic debates, there will be a need to adopt much more idiosyncratic measures. We need to unravel the HRM agendas that are triggered by productivity initiatives.

The idiosyncratic nature of each organisation's business model means that even within an industry or sector, each organisation finds bespoke ways (what we call *productivity recipes*) of delivering improved productivity.

To signal the need for HR directors, and HRM researchers, to be able to articulate the unique complexity of an organisation's challenge – and the strategic solutions that therefore should be pursued – we now provide a range sector examples. In doing so, we wish to draw attention to three important contextual factors that research has to take into account:

- The role of time in the HRM–productivity challenge.
- The relationship between productivity, HRM, and risk.
- The importance of understanding the most appropriate level of analysis question in examining the relationship between HRM and productivity.

10.4   The role of time in the HRM–productivity challenge

The first contextual factor that will be important is the role of time in the HRM–productivity relationship. Chapter 2 argued that future HRM research agendas need to be much more sensitive to the role of time. How might we frame the HRM issues in an industrial setting over time? We provide two examples to demonstrate how any analysis of links between HRM and productivity must be sensitive to the role of time, and how an understanding of time helps us understand the level of embeddedness that might exist from one productivity recipe to another.

- service model shifts in the fast food sector; and
- the scale of productivity challenges faced in healthcare.

The fast food sector has seen the development of new service models. The traditional quick service business model (QSR model), first emerging in the 1960s and 1970s, was based on long tills, serving multiple customers by providing a linear service, with food orders cooked on projections of what is to be sold. But now, as a consequence of the growth of individualism and developments triggered by the exploitation of data, old distinctions between casual dining, fast casual dining and quick service restaurants continue to blur.

The original service model created some natural constraints on capacity and productivity. Organisations and brands such as Subway, McDonald's, YUM, KFC, Pizza Hut, Taco Bell in the US, Café de Coral in Hong Kong, Greggs in the UK, or Seven & i Food Systems in Japan, have learned how to manage a productivity recipe that revolved around quality, service, cleanliness, and value (called QSCV). Demand was driven by demographics, consumer tastes, and personal income, and the profitability of individual companies depended on speed, price, and consistency – efficient operations and high volume sales. Globally, these organisations managed and optimised productivity from an efficiency and lean management perspective, through measures such as guest count per man hour, and store revenue per hour.

However, within the space of a few years, developments in data gathering technologies, such as low-cost sophisticated point-of-sale systems and data from social media, have meant that organisations can rapidly adjust their menu offerings based on information gathered about drive-thru customers, such as car make and model, number of passengers, items ordered or decision times. They can tailor offerings "on the fly" for particular groups of customers at particular times. This creates new opportunities for both customer engagement, and the exploitation of business intelligence, "build your own" offerings, and changes to the ordering and pick up counter process (Meredith et al., 2012).

So fast food organisations have to quickly understand how you drive productivity under a new service model. It now requires a balance between the personalisation potential offered by data with the level of uniformity that is seen to fulfil a brand promise. A complex equation.

For HR directors, this need to deliver improvements in productivity under a new ethos of customer centricity also has important implications. The productivity gains become dependent on:

- Productivity is a function of how quickly retail outlets can be converted or adapted to new service models and return to productivity. Change management protocols have to be identified and transitions delivered within relatively short time frames.

- As staff face customers with very different need states they have to manage a greater range of interactions and move from a less speed and transactional-driven service relationship to one in which more is known about the customer, productivity can only be delivered with associated changes in the sorts of skills, confidence and empathy levels of staff.
- The changes in service model come hand in hand with changes in the way you use space, design, store layout, the way technology, data, and systems are used. As these have to be managed in combination, and debated inside the business, this changes who needs to get brought together. To get customer centricity right, organisations have to start to work in a more cross-functional manner, linking up marketing, innovation and IT, corporate communications, HRM and operations. This changes the way organisations need to structure themselves to support the strategy.
- Customer centricity changes the relationship between the store environment and its service platforms, staff behaviours, the way customers are treated, the way in which teams should be organised to ensure customer service is delivered, and even staffing patterns.
- The new multi-role staff models and the new ways of working impact the staff employee value proposition.

The old service model, with its implicit style of management and reliance on known resources, is superseded by the need for new leadership, operational models, and shifts in mindset. The dining space is relatively expensive and productivity is a function of the guest count through that space, but the new service models involve seeing the dining area as not only a cost management challenge, but as an investment for growth. This totally changes the HRM context, and research agenda.

When considering the role of time in the HRM agenda associated with changes in productivity, the scale and pace of shifts requited must also be seen in context. We use the example of the changes in productivity that have been set for the National Health Service (NHS) in the UK. A longitudinal perspective shows that these are extremely challenging, to say the least. In order to close the gap between the need for services and available funding, the NHS faces the most ambitious programme of productivity improvement since its foundation (Appleby, Galea and Murray, 2014). These productivity gains also have to be achieved at a time of major reorganisation of the NHS. The organisation has to resolve conflicts between the need to deliver services with smaller budgets, whilst responding to a range of quality recommendations from various recent public enquiries. From 1997 to 2009 spending on the NHS, as a percentage of gross domestic product (GDP) rose from around 5.2 per cent to just over 8 per cent – the highest proportion since 1948. Since then, marginal 0.1 per cent real increases per year have not matched growth in service demand.

Current planning assumptions foresee a continued squeeze on resources until 2021/2, with NHS spending falling from its peak of 8 per cent of GDP in 2009 to just over 6 per cent by 2021, equivalent to spending in 2003. Under a scenario of no real funding growth, meeting the growing demands and expectations on the service requires productivity improvements of up to 6 per cent per year, whilst also coping with future increases in pay, the extra costs of capital to improve the estate, and the costs of significant reductions in waiting times. The Quality, Innovation, Productivity and Prevention (QIPP) initiative identified the need for £20 billion efficiency savings. Closing the "income–expenditure gap" at local level also requires significant efforts to increase income (rather than just reduce costs). Since then a funding gap of £30bn between 2013/14 and 2020/21 has been signalled, on top of the £20bn of efficiency savings already being met. Historically, productivity across the UK NHS, as measured by the Office for National Statistics (ONS, 2015), has averaged around 0.4 per cent a year between 1995 and 2010.

In HRM terms, this means that the traditional productivity policy levers of internal cost-reduction efforts – such as freezing pay and salami slicing of budgets – are not sustainable over the next few years. Solving the productivity equation will require local health economies to think much more collectively about how they can provide services within budget. The reactions of the workforce to changes intended to address this challenge have to be seen in this longitudinal context.

Reflecting the discussion of the role of time in Chapter 2, productivity is then something that can be looked at incrementally – continuously improved – or through periodic but radical periods of change. The productivity recipe needs insight into the complexity of productivity given the strategic context, what it means, how it should be thought about, and measured. There may be major business model changes or innovations being discussed as potential game changers in relation to productivity, such as new store or service formats, or new technical interventions. It is not always clear who in the organisation is involved in, or truly understands the implications of these.

10.5   The relationship between productivity, HRM and risk

The second contextual factor that will be important is the relationship between productivity, HRM, and risk. Changes in business model not only mean that we incorporate more awareness of how productivity recipes change over time, and the subtle changes in HRM focus this entails. They also require that we consider the role of risk in our HRM research.

We use the example of the oil and gas sector to demonstrate the importance of risk, and the macro context factors that determine the organisational HRM agenda. This sector faces an environment that combines considerable opportunity combined with a high degree of volatility and risk. Competitive pressures are forcing management to explore options for fundamental change to improve the overall productivity and efficiency of the businesses under their control (KPMG, 2013; Alix Partners, 2015).

The capital intensity of the industry naturally focuses attention away from labour productivity, towards the return on capital employed (ROCE). There have always been strong links between productivity, innovation and growth. In recent times the industry has focused on increasing shareholder returns via throughput gains and increased production volumes.

But because of the high capital costs in some industries, and the increasingly collaborative nature of many operations, there is often now the need to seek mutual productivity gains across multiple organisations. The collapse and subsequent volatility in oil price, coupled with the operation of increasingly complex projects, is leading to a broader set of actions to address the issue of productivity.

The challenge, especially for those with an integrated business model, is to maximise production whilst minimising risks. This requires a complex balance between:

1.   Increasing oil and gas throughput, tracking and aligning this with macroeconomic changes and changes in demand more closely;

2. Efficiency gains in project execution, through better selection criteria and use of gate posts, and alterations in the project economic model, spurring greater productivity from subcontractors;
3. Portfolio management (how they decide on future projects, and how they manage existing operations depending on their performance, that is, stopping or selling unprofitable operations);
4. Managing and reducing operational costs; and
5. Building an internal culture that focuses on efficiency and productivity.

In HRM terms, whilst attention to traditional gains in labour productivity remain dominant, productivity is also now framed through the need for better flexibility, problem-solving, risk management, and the use of lessons learned. There are many connections between the various end-to-end participants within the oil and gas value chain – across the upstream and downstream activities of exploration, extraction, refining, transporting, marketing and retailing, as well as between service providers such as construction, logistics, material, engineering and drilling. There is pressure to lift productivity on what have become megaprojects, across operations, and in the back office.

However, we need to think even more radically about the nature of risk and the HRM–productivity relationship. The HRM issues involved may need to be framed in terms of the macro-level transfers of costs taking place between the organisation and its consumers.

The supermarket sector is also a good example of this. The various productivity recipes in the sector remind us that productivity gains can be deceptive, as gains in one part of the system may simply transfer inefficiencies to another part of the system. Analysis of the links between HRM and productivity in this sector requires a need to understand debates about:

- competing service formats, technical developments, and service offerings; and
- the transfers of costs and risks between the organisation and the consumer.

In the mid-2000s attention was given to the general impact of trends towards larger supermarkets and retail formats, a new industry structure, operating practices and IT-driven trading-partner relationships (King and Park, 2004). However, in both HRM and business terms, relatively little was known about how these changes affected productivity at the store level. Studies began to show that productivity advantages could be traced to store format, service offerings, and disruptions associated with remodelling, as did the possession of warehouse, super warehouse, and super-centre stores, and stores without a full-service pharmacies.

When concern over poor levels of service productivity grew in the early 2000s, researchers began to exploit the wealth of data in the supermarket sector at the firm and establishment level. This showed the complexity of factors at play (Griffeth and Harmgart, 2005). Whilst retail productivity is generally thought of in terms of sales or value added per worker or per hour worked, along with factors such as land and capital usage, it is actually driven by a complex mix of urban characteristics, consumer preferences and market hegemony versus competitive rivalries.

Today, even with the advantage of improved analytics and store-level data, the need to understand complex HRM trade-offs remains. Technically productivity is being impacted by developments in digital technologies that span e-commerce, mobile-commerce, web analysis, testing, development and maintenance, social media, smart phones and apps, use of geo-locational social networks, and in-store digital ordering. These have impacted many retailing and service business models.

We also see growth of the "packaged Internet" – whereby the fragmentation of digital channels across apps, smart TVs, tablets, e-readers, gaming devices and other emerging platforms has started to erode the dominance of websites, but has also required more coordinated management of these touch points. This has created the opportunity for new service models that not only offer multi-channel shopping, but offer a system of distributed commerce across multiple touch points.

Given these technical developments, there are complex transfers of costs that have to be considered, and these frame the subsequent HRM agenda. Sector-level productivity data show that supermarkets are facing a significant fall in productivity in order to keep their online customers happy. In supermarkets, if customers scan their shopping, this is a productivity gain as they need to employ fewer people for the same amount of goods passing through the checkouts. But it is a productivity loss for the customer, as they waste time performing the task less efficiently than a full-time member of staff. At the same time, online retail results in staff trundling up and down aisles filling trolleys and preparing the orders for customers, who shop online and have their groceries delivered. Filling somebody else's shopping order is not a skilled task. This represents a productivity gain for customers, who spend 15 minutes on the Internet rather than an hour or so in the store, but a productivity loss for the supermarket, as they have to employ more people to process the same revenue. The real economic cost of selecting food from the aisles, bagging it, loading it on a van and delivering it is far higher than £1 charged, and this feeds into both profit and measured revenue picked up in GDP. Whilst the net efficiency gain (or loss) for the supermarkets from the combination of self-service checkouts and online shopping shows up in government productivity figures, the net gains or losses to customers tend not to, as the economic advantages or disadvantages of their time usage are not recorded.

The HRM issues involved in its relationship to productivity not only invoke macro-level transfers of costs between the organisation and its consumers, but sometimes enhancements of productivity at the organisational level might also be delivered by transferring costs between organisations and society. Productivity recipes might be very effective at the level of the host organisation, but can create fundamental inefficiency once we cross the boundaries between this organisation and the broader system or network.

Consider a drive down a UK motorway. You drive through tracts of motorway, sometimes with lanes blocked off 15 miles in length, with only a handful of sporadic vehicles and teams working, if any, at any one time. The model is designed to enable construction firms to switch activity and labour on and off at times that suits their portfolio of projects on the go. Within the construction firm, and at the level of the contract price, it might look like a productive use of assets, but the productivity impact is on every commuter, and firm, that has to absorb the increased travel time.

Another way of thinking about the implicit transfers of cost between an organisation and society is to understand how productivity gains are really being made. We use the example of the competitive impact of on demand business models to demonstrate this. These models include firms like Uber offering chauffeur and ride-sharing services, Freelancer.com and Elance-oDesk brokering links between freelancers and organisations, Handy supplying cleaners, SpoonRocket offering restaurant meals, Medicast supplying doctors, and Axiom supplying lawyers. In effect such models allow two types of people to trade (those who have money but little time, trading with those who have time but little money) (Brewster et al., 2016).

An analysis by *The Economist* (2015) demonstrated that such examples illustrate that in the game of productivity trade-offs, the social and risk consequences can be considerable. The owners of these businesses compete on their ability to arrange connections and oversee the quality of work, but do not need to employ people full-time nor guarantee pay and benefits, and regulatory concerns such as health and safety become a matter for debate. Productivity gains are made through transfers of risk (*The Economist*, 2015). For example, the financing of social benefits such as pensions and healthcare is pushed back from the global employer to the individual. The potential beneficiaries beyond the techno-entrepreneurs responsible for the global start-ups are consumers, taxpayers (to the extent that the efficiency of public resources used can be improved) and those employee segments who value flexibility of work over security. The potential losers include: those employee segments that value security over flexibility; and taxpayers that might have to provide financial support to contract workers who do not or cannot source their own pensions. The transfer of risks is almost totally from the organisation (the broker) to the individual, and also from the organisation to the state. Unless significant changes occur in regulatory regimes, then the model requires that individuals have to assume all welfare responsibilities, become responsible for becoming multi-skilled technically and keeping such skills up-to-date, and develop selling, networking, social media, and personal branding skills. On-demand business services also imply the need to shift a range of government measurement systems for employment and wages. Most welfare systems are delivered through employers but on demand business service models imply that they might need to be tied to the individual instead, and also be made more portable. Skill development systems also shift from employers to individuals (or to nation states that wish to create vocational education systems that enable individuals). National taxation models would also presumably need to change in order to recoup the costs for this re-distribution.

Given ongoing technical developments, HRM functions and HRM researchers are likely to face many such business developments, e-enablement, innovations in customer processes, or the opening of new channels to business to sit alongside existing channels, may all invoke business model developments and the need for productivity improvements that trigger significant risks or costs to be borne elsewhere.

10.6   The levels of analysis question in examining the relationship between HRM and productivity

The third contextual factor that we consider is the importance of understanding the most appropriate level of analysis question in examining the relationship between HRM and productivity. Given that productivity recipes may involve transfers of risks and costs across various components of a larger network, many of the productivity recipes being pursued carry implications for the best level of analysis that we should use as HRM researchers. We use the aerospace industry, and also the nuclear industry, to show that in some situations it makes little sense to focus research on the level of one sole organisation. We need to understand the inter-dependencies that exist across the broader industrial network in which they sit, such as their supply chain. In many settings, productivity is dependent on the surrounding industrial and institutional structures.

For example, the aerospace industry faces the challenge of building more aircraft and bringing them to market within a shorter time. New planes have to be lighter, faster and more efficient. The sector needs to engineer dramatic increases in the complexity of aircraft, and cope with massive increases in the volume of data managed during the whole product life cycle. This creates demands for productivity across the whole of the value chain, from the application of industrial software and automation technologies and shared development work in product design, to increases in production rates and improvements in production planning reorganising product development in order to synchronise it with manufacturing at an early stage on a global scale, by extending capacities, improving processes in engineering and execution, and through to services.

There are also different priorities built into the strategy, with drives for productivity balanced with other considerations such as innovation, more customer-centric design, and collaborative working. Leading manufacturers such as Airbus, Boeing, GE-Pratt & Whitney and Rolls-Royce, are ramping up demands for productivity across their whole supply chain. In the UK Airbus increased the production rates for

A320 wing that it sets for its suppliers from 35 a few years ago to 42 per month, with a target of 50 per month by 2018. Critical mass in the supply chain is a major element of productivity, along with the skills across this whole supply chain.

Another example to show that the management of productivity is often highly dependent on surrounding institutions and industrial sector is the nuclear industry. The Nuclear Energy Institute notes that 30 countries worldwide are operating 444 nuclear reactors for electricity generation, and 63 new nuclear plants are under construction in 15 countries.

However, in a major nuclear plant there are typically two sides of the business – the project decommissioning side (that is, project managing and engineering and operational plant elements) – and the project management side. These two elements look at productivity differently. This is important, because as the balance of activity shifts from decommissioning activities to new build activities, so too does the mindset used to think about productivity.

In general terms productivity can be thought of in terms of the amount of nuclear material that can be reprocessed (that is, the conversion rate). It can also be thought of in terms of time – the industry must constantly search for ways in which it can safely decommission at a faster rate as currently a 150 year span of activity is likely to be needed.

At plant level in the decommissioning businesses, safety is the first priority activity, but this must be closely followed by productivity. In order to have efficient steady running of the plants, there has to be downtime (outages) during which things have to be done to maintain the health of the systems. If the health of the systems is not maintained, this impacts productivity significantly. There are so many counterbalancing drivers in the industry, so productivity is always going to be incremental productivity.

The HR function becomes involved in the management organisational culture and incentive systems and exposing people to experiences from other industries and sectors, so that both managers and staff ensure that things are done safely, but are also focused on efficiency and productivity. Given high levels of unionisation in this sector, they have to manage generic messages around the industrial and employees context in order to change working practices.

In contrast, the need for major plant developments and business transitions is driven from a different productivity mindset, one seen more in terms of schedule and cost targets. Under competitive pressure, and from experience in other civil projects, contractors have learned how to improve working standards and better construct on time and on budget. But it is also clear that the skillset for collaborative working across partners and projects, and driving productivity across partners, is a major contributor to productivity. In this setting, the productivity debate, and the pace at which gains can be made, will be very dependent on the development of new learning and new skillsets:

- Learning from lean manufacturing techniques in the project management industry as they apply to productivity in production and engineering.
- Understanding the links and trade-offs between innovation and productivity.
- The skills and competence of HR – most productivity discussion takes place within the operations sphere, so within the organisation HR must now have the ability to operate across the operations interface, meaning more people in the HR function who have the necessary capability or skills.
- Other skillsets become important for the HR function to enable this cross-functional working, such as organisational design, intelligent customer skills, and relationship management.

In relation to this third contextual factor of different levels of analysis, researchers need to understand where attention to either organisational productivity or broader national productivity sits within the organisation, and how the issue of productivity fits into the HR strategy. At a macro level, any analysis of HRM may need to be framed in the context of national or industry-level developments that impact productivity, such as skills development, or process improvements across supply chains.

10.7   Conclusions

The above discussion of contextual factors and the different sector examples show that productivity may be embedded in broader service formats and offerings, for others it may be dominated by the return on capital employed. In other contexts it is dependent on the surrounding industrial and institutional structure. It often requires shifts in the mindset around HRM issues such as flexibility, and a sensitivity to the historical scale of the challenges involved.

The discussion in this chapter also has significant implications for the issue of HR Analytics. Given the discussion in Chapter 2 of human capital management, the various forms of human capital that become important in the management of productivity may also be broken down into different elements, such as human, social or intellectual capital (Greve, Benassi and Sti, 2010).

We need a more balanced set of data and set of metrics that help assess some of the fundamental performance capabilities of an organisation. Recently there have been calls for much better use of human capital metrics and HR analytics so that organisations, and important stakeholders such as the financial community, can get a better fix on the true health and future value of an organisation. Metrics that capture an organisation's productivity potential coming from a total factor productivity perspective – whether used from the inside out by Chief Executives to demonstrate the deep capabilities of their organisation or a more critical perspective from the outside in from investors and governments – can help build such confidence. However, as Chapter 9 makes clear, we are a long way from being able to demonstrate such detailed HR analytics.

Moreover, as our different examples of productivity context make clear, on the one hand there can be hidden importance of the HR strategy once we begin to analyse the business model in more detail – and these contributions are for HR directors to identify and sell within the top team – but also the level of human asset intensity and the links between people factors and total factor productivity clearly differ across industrial settings. The chapter also makes it clear that if HR functions are to demonstrate their worth they need to work much more closely with the functions that make the major interventions – for example be this with operations over skills issues or, or with customer management over service models. We have shown how the pursuit of productivity has to be a multi-functional responsibility, and it also needs internal management functions to work much more closely with major institutions. Both of these needs place pressure on the formal HR structure and raise questions as to where functions that adopt a broader organisational effectiveness should be placed.

Finally, as we try to navigate our way through what must be done to solve the national and organisational productivity challenges, a number of assumptions about the role of HRM may need to be challenged. For example, in the actions that organisations take around flexibility, the HR function may become part of the problem. Enforced flexibility is actually a poor strategy for productivity. The function's fixation with flexible work and certain employee segments may in some instances be condemning future generations to a low skill future. The HR function should expect that it will once more have to deal with split loyalties, balancing what might be seen to please the top team or other powerful functions with what it considers to be ineffective and unproductive.

References

Alix Partners (2015). Capital productivity in the oil and gas industry. www.alixpartners. com (accessed 2 May 2017).

Appleby, J., Galea, A. and Murray, R. (2014). The NHS productivity challenge: experience from the front line. The Kings Fund. http://www.kingsfund.org.uk/sites/files/kf/field/field_publication_file/the-nhs-productivity-challenge-kingsfund-may14.pdf (accessed 2 May 2017).

Brewster, C., Houldsworth, L., Sparrow, P.R. and Vernon, C. (2016). *International Human Resource Management* (4th edition). London: Chartered Institute of Personnel and Development.

Chowla, S., Quaglietti, L. and Rachel, L. (2014). How have world shocks affected the UK economy? *Bank of England Quarterly Bulletin*, 54(2): 167–179.

Greve, A., Benassi, M. and Sti, A.D. (2010). Exploring the contributions of human and social capital to productivity. *International Review of Sociology*, 20(1): 35–58.

Griffeth, R. and Harmgart, H. (2005). Retail productivity. *International Review of Retail, Distribution and Consumer Research*, 15(3): 281–290.

Hughes, A. and Saleheen, J. (2012). UK labour productivity since the onset of the crisis – an international and historical perspective. *Quarterly Bulletin*, 138–146.

King, R.P. and Park, T.A. (2004). Modeling productivity in supermarket operations: incorporating the impacts of store characteristics and information technologies. *Journal of Food Distribution Research*, 35(2): 42–55.

KPMG (2013). Driving value in upstream oil and gas: lessons from the energy industry's top performing companies. http://download.pwc.com/ie/pubs/2013_driving_value_in_upstream_oil_and_gas.pdf (accessed 2 May 2017).

Madrick, J. (1997). *The End of Affluence: The Causes and Consequences of America's Economic Dilemma*. New York: Random House.

Meredith, R., Remington, S., O'Donnell, P. and Sharma, N. (2012). Organisational transformation through business intelligence: theory, the vendor perspective and a research agenda. *Journal of Decision Systems*, 31(3): 187–201.

Office for National Statistics (ONS) (2015). http://visual.ons.gov.uk/productivity-puzzle/ (accessed 2 May 2017).

Reinhart, C. and Rogoff, K (2009). *This Time Is Different: Eight Centuries of Financial Folly*. Princeton, NJ: Princeton University Press.

Sparrow, P.R., Hird, M. and Cooper, C.L. (2015). *Do we need HR? Repositioning People Management for Success*. London: Palgrave.

Spilsbury, M. and Campbell, M. (2009). *Ambition 2020: World Class Skills and Jobs for the UK*. Wath-Upon-Dearne: UK Commission for Employment and Skills.

The Economist (2015). The future of work: there's an app for that, and workers on tap. *The Economist*, 414(8919): 13-16.

11 'We are not creative here!' Creativity and innovation for non-creatives through HRM

*Helen Shipton, Veronica Lin, Karin Sanders and
Huadong Yang*

11.1 Introduction

Although buried deep in the human psyche is a drive to think creatively in order to solve everyday problems, given workplace demands
and pressures this innate orientation may be suppressed or misaligned
with organisational goals. In this chapter, building on an emergent literature, we argue that Human Resource Management (HRM) has the
potential to release the creative propensity of "ordinary" employees.
In contrast to perspectives viewing innovation as driven by technical experts and Research and Development specialists, we argue that
those performing day-to-day jobs present an unfathomable well of
ideas. Recognising, leveraging and releasing the creative and innovative behaviours of employees across specialisms and levels of hierarchy
can therefore offer a major source of competitive advantage (Barney,
1991). We argue that HRM – when viewed as the effective management of people – presents a powerful lever for innovation and change.

We see innovation as the intentional introduction of ideas which are
valuable and novel within a specific context (West and Farr, 1990).
Innovation is often further categorised according to four related substages: problem identification, idea generation, idea evaluation and
implementation. The first two stages are primarily individual activities,
and are generally oriented towards the creativity phase of an innovation, while phases three and four are suggestive of the collective
activities required to achieve innovation implementation (Farr, Sin
and Tesluk, 2003). In its simplest form, a creative idea might arise
through an actor's reaction to stimuli presented within a work setting.
More complex determinants might govern whether or not influences

from the external environment cause an organisation to embrace a new technology or a novel technique (for example, cross-functional work systems). Influences might arise from the bottom up (initiated by individuals) or top down (triggered by contextual factors). Some may be set in motion by management (a reward structure that recognises risk and experimentation) whilst others are likely to occur by accident (an informal discussion at a conference about a new product or idea). Thus, in teasing out any effect that HRM may have on organisational innovation, a multi-level perspective is useful (Gupta, Tesluk and Taylor, 2007).

In what follows, we start by defining creativity and innovation in order to set the stage for our analysis of any role that HRM might play. After reviewing extant work on HRM and innovation, we bring out two areas where we believe the field would benefit from more focused attention. First, as suggested in recent analyses (for example, Montag, Maertz and Baer, 2012) extant work has been reticent in distinguishing between environments where creativity and innovation is overtly required, as opposed to job roles where creative outcomes, while valuable, are not expressly called for as part of the job. We target this gap and bring out potential differential effects that HRM might have for the former versus the latter categories of employees. Our second contribution, again largely neglected in extant work, is to consider any differential effect that HRM might have for the two main stages described above: creativity, followed by innovation implementation. Given that the first stage is by and large an individual-level activity, while the second entails collective-level considerations, it would not be surprising if certain HRM practices are more or less conducive to one phase or the other. We draw on extant work focused on bottom-up emergence (Kozlowski and Klein, 2000) in order to shed light on the way in which HRM might support and underpin employees' efforts not just to generate ideas but also to to foster their implementation.

11.2   Innovative behaviours and organisational innovation

Inherent in most conceptualisations of innovation is the notion of value (Gupta, Tesluk and Taylor, 2007). The innovation or change must add something that is beneficial for the organisation, either complementing existing practice or adding something that supersedes what has happened before. Rather than offering absolute novelty, innovation is instead original within a context; newness is relative and bounded. Viewed as a two-stage process, innovation requires creativity followed by innovation implementation (Anderson, Potocnik and Zhou, 2014). Based on Piaget (1970) creativity entails extending and broadening existing cognitive repertoires in order to visualise new options. This process of accommodation can be contrasted with the assimilation phase, where connections are made with what is already known in order to effect change. Thus, creativity pushes out the boundaries of knowledge and makes *potential* new insights available to organisations. Innovation implementation by contrast involves making appropriate connections across employee groups and building joint understanding so that new ideas are incorporated into organisational functioning.

Recent work has suggested that the distinction between the two phases may not be clear-cut. Employees operate within a context where rationality and applicability (implementation considerations) are inevitably weighted alongside originality as new ideas are put forward (Fay et al., 2014). Furthermore, implementing ideas may require creativity. A new technology for ascertaining customer feedback, for example, will not add value to an organisation unless it is implemented imaginatively, taking into account likely customer reactions. While it is not straightforward to distinguish between creative and innovative behaviours, our four-stage conceptualisation of innovation (Farr, Sin and Tesluk, 2003) is suggestive of a distinction pertaining to levels of analysis. Individually-oriented aspects primarily entail problem identification and idea generation while the following stages – idea evaluation and implementation – are collectively-oriented. In this chapter, we shed light on potential antecedents, especially from an HRM perspective, that may be more or less conducive to these two main stages.

Taking an organisational-level perspective, innovation is often defined depending upon its incremental or radical nature. The former entails fairly minor adjustment to strategic functioning, while through the latter significant and major amendments are proposed or have occurred (March, 1991). Organisations face inherent tensions: on the one hand seeking to push out the boundaries of knowledge to pursue new and risky alternatives and on the other, to refine and improve existing ways of working in order to deepen and enhance strategic functioning. The balance achieved varies across organisations depending on many factors including the volatility of the external environment, managerial orientation, employee skills and attitudes, including motivation and the nature of trust (Kang, Morris and Snell, 2007). Although it is possible that day-to-day employees whose job remit does not encompass creativity may sow the seeds for radical innovation, it is more likely that they will, given a supportive context, yield incremental innovation through their efforts. This is because their job role may be limited, hence suggestions are modest rather than suggestive of revolutionary change. By contrast, it is highly likely that those performing a job role where creativity is inherent may yield radical innovation, as well as that which is incremental. This group of employees will most likely have an overview of the organisation and beyond which will help them to envisage the potential for radical innovation and change.

11.3 Creativity and innovation – discretionary or not?

Although there has been reference in the literature to creative performance that is expected versus that which occurs without being overtly required, on the whole in the literature both these forms of creative activity have been treated in the same way (Unsworth, 2001). Montag, Maertz and Baer (2012) compare this situation with the way in which job performance literature distinguishes between in-role versus extra role behaviours, pointing out that there may be different (hidden) predictors of expected versus unexpected creative/innovative outcomes, in particular, differential motivators for each type of job in turn. It makes intuitive sense that some jobs embody more creativity and innovation than others. Those employed in creative industries – for example, manufacturing games for the computer industry, or employees engaged in high-technology sectors charged to keep ahead of new developments – are expected to move forward with new developments, while those employed on an assembly line, or in a call centre or fast-food restaurant, will be expected to perform a specific job function that most likely will not entail a requirement for creative or innovative behaviours.

In what follows, once we have briefly reviewed the HRM-innovation literature we turn to the question of any differential impact, first, on creativity that is expected versus that which is emergent and, second, on any role that HRM might play for the first two phases of the innovation process – problem identification and idea generation – which are individually oriented – as opposed to the final two stages – idea evaluation and implementation, which have a collective component. We then consider what this means for future research efforts in this area, and also practical implications.

11.4   Human resource management and innovation

Rather than reviewing this literature comprehensively (see Shipton et al., 2017, for an overview) we instead capture key themes relevant for the chapter. HRM is defined as all the activities organisations can utilise in order to effectively manage their employees (Wright and McMahan, 1992). Generally, it has been argued that HRM bundles rather than HRM practices per se impact on performance outcomes, such as innovation (Combs, Hall and Ketchen, 2006). The combined effect of inter-related practices more than any specific variable achieves the desired effect (Combs, Hall and Ketchen, 2006). Scholars investigating the link between HRM and innovation have followed a similar line to that pursued by SHRM researchers, identifying clusters of practices linked to performance outcomes including innovation. There is evidence of positive relationships between so-called "high performance" HRM practices and organisational innovation (Collins and Smith, 2006; Beugelsdijk, 2008; Prieto, Perez-Santana and Sierra, 2010; Jimenez-Jimenez and Sanz-Valle, 2008; Shipton et al., 2006).

A key distinction across these literatures is that some scholars have reflected upon the synergies inherent in adopting the main indicators of "high performance" (for example, training and development, discretionary reward, sophisticated selection, participation and communication, job design and so on) (for example, Collins and Smith, 2006; Chang et al., 2014), while other have instead proposed that, for innovation, some specific HR practices, especially those oriented towards the creativity-related aspects of employee performance, deserve more emphasis than others (for example, Beugelsdijk, 2008; Shipton et al., 2006; Zhao and Chadwick, 2014. Based on Oldham and Cummings (1996), for example, Beugelsdijk (2008) concentrates on two key contextual elements that promote the creative performance of employees: job complexity and supervisory style. As he argues, complex jobs can be expected to promote employee creativity, through actively developing the knowledge and abilities that lie at the heart of the development of new products and ideas. This will in turn enhance organisational innovation. Pursuing a related but slightly different argument, Shipton et al. (2006) argued that selected HR practices, including training and development, early socialisation, reward management and job design are important for organisational innovation to the extent that they occur in conjunction with an orientation described as "exploratory learning". Defined as the extent to which opportunities exist for cross-boundary working and knowledge sharing, job rotation and project-oriented activities, exploratory learning exposes employees to new experiences and perspectives, in a way that challenges existing pre-conceptions and stimulates new ideas. It is the combined effect of each specific HR practice together with employees' experience of exploratory learning that leads to higher levels of organisational innovation.

Notwithstanding valuable insights, there are hints at inconsistencies in the literature. For example, Zhao and Chadwick (2014) found that *motivation*, capturing employees' willingness to work collaboratively and take risks in developing new ideas, was more strongly associated with incremental innovation than employees' latent abilities. According to this argument, HR practices such as performance appraisal are viewed as precursors for employee motivation, while training and development is amongst the most potent enablers for collective ability. Beugelsdijk's (2008) research focusing on creativity-based HRM practices also reported mixed results, where incremental innovation is associated positively and significantly with most of the HR variables, but performance-based pay, where combined with flexible hours or task rotation was significantly and negatively linked with radical innovation. In a related line of argument, Shipton et al. (2006) showed that contingent reward had a significant and negative effect on organisational innovation across a sample of manufacturing organisations.

Also lacking in extant work is reflection upon the multi-level implications that innovation presents. Jiang et al. (2012) highlight growing interest in the way in which top-down perspectives influence employee-level attributes, especially the abilities, motivations and opportunities that HRM might release. Building on these perspectives, it has been suggested that control versus entrepreneurially-oriented HRM might have differential impacts on the way in which innovation unfolds at the employee level (Shipton et al., 2017). Entrepreneurial HRM is more conducive to employee innovative activity that challenges and questions existing ways of thinking and operating, while control-oriented HRM would instead engender ideas that the initiator believes are acceptable within a given institutional context. Furthermore, HRM might play a role not only from the top down, that is, setting out the strategic remit especially around innovation, but also in enabling bottom-up emergence. Two distinctive patterns of bottom-up emergence – composition and compilation – discussed further in what follows – may be more or less to the forefront given an orientation towards radical as opposed to incremental innovation.

In an effort to develop further insight into these areas, and point to a future research agenda, we start by highlighting any top-down implications that HRM presents for job roles where creativity is expected versus those where there is no express requirement. We then turn to the question of bottom-up emergence, arguing that our focus on this area helps shed light on the collective aspects that innovation entails (idea evaluation and implementation; Farr, Sin and Tesluk, 2003).

11.5   Individual-level HRM where creativity/innovation is overtly required

As stated earlier, in some jobs creativity and innovation are inherently expected, whereas in other jobs, although desirable, they are considered as extra-role behaviours. While ability, motivation and opportunities are crucial for good performance in any types of job (Appelbaum et al., 2000), the three elements may carry varying weights and mean different things in different job settings.

Creative people are generally highly intrinsically motivated, more highly trained and inclined to work autonomously than those who are not expressly conditioned to work in this way (Montag, Maertz and Baer, 2012). Thus, for jobs where creativity is explicitly expected, experience and ability are suggested to be good predictors (Gong, Huang and Farh, 2009; Shin and Zhou, 2007). Drawing on the componential theory of creativity (Amabile, 1983), a number of studies argue for the importance of employee knowledge, skills and abilities (KSAs) for creativity (Jiang et al., 2012). These KSAs are largely acquired from outside of the firm through recruitment and selection. Internal training can support, and bring out these latent qualities, and therefore receives less emphasis. Recruitment and selection for creative jobs is, however, complex and may entail sophisticated techniques, typically focused on the cognitive ability and flexibility of the job applicants. For example, Internet companies like Google, Facebook and Apple are well known in asking brain teaser questions to identify creative job applicants. Similarly, training aimed to foster employee creativity may also focus on enhancing employee skills in thinking creatively.

In jobs where creativity is explicitly expected and assessed, extrinsic motivation is important. In fact, monetary rewards are often contractually specified (Montag, Maertz and Baer, 2012; Unsworth, 2001). Extrinsic motivators encourage task-oriented thinking (Amabile,

Hennessey and, Grossman, 1986). Hence, in jobs where creativity is essential, extrinsic motivators direct individuals towards acting creatively. In the studies of Shalley (1991, 1995), it was found that when no creativity goal was set for the participants, their creative performance was significantly worse than other groups to whom a creativity goal was set and evaluation was expected.

Opportunities for individuals to be exposed to new knowledge and new perspectives (Shipton et al., 2006) are critical for expected creativity. Indeed, it has been argued that innovation results from the collective ability of employees to exchange and combine knowledge (Nahapiet and Ghoshal, 1998). Any ways in which HR practices can increase interaction and information exchanges are important to this end. Job rotation within an organisation and contact with people outside the organisation enables individuals to learn new knowledge and combine it with existing knowledge. Such HR practices can be used to intentionally enhance employee knowledge-sharing and to expand social networks. Added to these perspectives are dyadic exchanges such as those offered through coaching and mentoring activities, as well as an individual commitment to keeping up to date with the latest developments in one's profession.

It is worth highlighting that opportunities like those described above are (even more) important also in contexts where creativity is not explicitly required. Probably, for *required* creativity, the exposure to new perspectives within the organisation boosts the latter two phases of the innovation process – idea assessment and implementation, through opening channels of communication and helping people to understand what new ideas might mean for them. The underlying mechanism for exploratory, job-related learning might be different where creativity is *not* explicitly called for. In this case, such activities are likely to represent the main or only potential sources of new ideas for employees. Thus, these and other forms of informal learning may inform the creative, as well as the implementation-oriented, phases of innovation as depicted above (problem identification and idea generation). Such activities will also enable the latter phases too for this category of employees, as discussed below and are therefore especially crucial.

11.6   Individual-level HRM where creativity/innovation is discretionary

In jobs where creativity is not expected and is only displayed as extra-role behaviours, abilities and skills for creativity are less likely to be a criterion for recruitment and selection. Instead, skills and qualifications for relatively routine task performance are assessed. Given that creativity is not overtly required, rewards are often not specified or agreed on beforehand. If any reward is offered, it is usually awarded on an ad-hoc basis. Creativity in these jobs as an extra-role behaviour is primarily driven by intrinsic motivation for the job (Montag, Maertz and Baer, 2012) or by pro-social motivation to help others and the organisation (Grant and Berry, 2011). To foster discretionary innovation in this context, organisations can design jobs in such a way that it offers task identity, task significance, autonomy, feedback from job and the opportunity to use a variety of skills (Hackman and Oldham, 1975). Meta-analysis shows that jobs with these characteristics provide strong internal work motivation (Fried and Ferris, 1987). From a relational social exchange perspective, HRM practices signalling organisational support (such as extensive training, internal mobility and employment security) induce pro-organisational motivation and lead employees to reciprocate with organisational citizenship behaviours (Sun, Aryee and Law, 2007), including innovative behaviours (Sanders et al., 2010).

Employees make careful assessments of the environment before committing themselves to extra-role actions that could entail negative social evaluations (Bednall, Sanders and Runhaar, 2014; Yuan and Woodman, 2010). Because discretionary creativity and innovative behaviours are not part of one's job duties, they can be easily "killed". Indeed, a certain level of latitude and control is important for individuals to display and sustain these behaviours (Montag, Maertz and Baer, 2012). Organisations, hence, should give employees opportunities to make their own decisions and induce a sense of empowerment. A psychologically safe environment in which employees feel comfortable voicing their new ideas is also crucial (Gong et al., 2012).

In contexts where creative and innovation-oriented behaviours are discretionary, informal, workplace learning is likely to be at a premium. Brown (2016) asks how individuals at work can develop and actively demonstrate the capability to be innovative by focusing on the processes of individual learning that foster innovative capabilities, not through external interventions such as creativity training, but through knowledge updating and re-contextualisation. Here, technically-based and experience-based learning can develop and interact across an individual's life-course. These enabling capabilities can be generalised across multiple employment, training and education contexts.

For this category of employees we need to understand how individuals actively participate in working processes, perform roles and tasks, and learn to improve their performance. According to Brown (2016) the required knowledge includes technical know-how, along with the ability to capture different types of knowledge across several contexts. But innovative capabilities also enable the development of know-what (where and when knowledge can be applied), know-who, and know-why. These all combine to form a type of adaptive competence. Indeed, research shows that informal learning, such as a determination to keep up-to-date with professional developments – carried out individually without assistance from colleagues or supervisors – is an important antecedent for discretionary, extra-role creative activities (van Rijn, Yang and Sanders, 2013).

11.7 Collective-level HRM where creativity/innovation is discretionary

For innovative behaviours and creativity that occurs without being overtly required, a challenge or sticking point arises where idea evaluation and idea implementation are concerned. Research on staff suggestion schemes for example reveals that employees do not lack ideas, rather that suggestions are often not seriously considered and rarely implemented (Axtell et al., 2010). Like other collective-level outcomes – such as the achievement of operational targets or quality demands – idea evaluation and idea implementation depend upon collective activities and support from others, and gain traction through bottom-up emergence (Kozlowski and Klein, 2000).

In contexts where employees are not expected to be creative, innovation is likely to be a by-product of other workplace goals (such as the achievement of operational goals). In other words, through discussion about team targets, employees may see the opportunity to discuss an idea to improve future prospects around team targets, leading to a related innovation being implemented in due course. Because the dominant "institutional logics" of a team or organisation most likely surround operational goals, the range of alternative options are restricted or out of discussion. It is expected that only few innovative ideas can survive the collective evaluation, unless they are highly consistent with the main objectives of the team or organisation. With this prospect in mind, employees will be reticent in putting forward suggestions for radical innovation and change, and will instead focus more on ideas that are suggestive of incremental change, that is, slight deviations from the norm that align with the general direction of thinking and behaving. Because incremental changes appear more feasible within existing institutional framework, they are more likely to be collectively endorsed and implemented. This kind of bottom-up emergence has parallels with what Kozlowski and Klein (2000) describe as composition. Bottom-up emergence through composition holds that employees respond in a similar way to the environment to which they are exposed and the emergent phenomenon at the level of the collective is very similar or even identical to its constituent elements.

These slight deviations and incremental innovation, while limited in scope, nonetheless may where realised offer a more fruitful way of working leading in turn to competitive advantage over time (Easterby-Smith, Crossan and Nicolini, 2000). To foster innovation embedded in operational goals, a "hybrid" HRM strategy is needed (Paauwe and Boselie, 2005). The hybrid model of HRM on one hand emphasises the control over quality and quantity *outcomes*, while, on the other hand, offers a certain level of freedom on how to achieve these outcomes. Bernstein (2012) showed that when workers in a mobile phone factory were offered privacy, they used innovative methods to produce mobile phones and improved their performance, because privacy supported productive deviance and localised experimentation.

11.8   Collective-level HRM: where creativity is required

When innovation is an integral part of an organisation's strategy and creativity is a legitimate endeavour, deviance from existing practices and procedures is expected. As a result of the random variation within a unit (Staw, 1990), multiple institutional logics likely co-exist and there is no single dominant one. The dialogue or competition among different logics means that there is no substantial constraint on what is "appropriate" and innovative ideas can significantly vary from each other. Such variance provides input for innovation. While the selection of one or a few ideas promotes incremental creativity, creative synthesis of the divergent ideas has the potential to produce radical collective creativity (Harvey, 2014). Creative synthesis refers to a process that integrates unit members' perspectives into a shared understanding that is new to them. It relies not only on diverse input, but more on finding a novel convergence of the diverse ideas.

This process of integration and synthesis does not necessarily exclude composition which occurs through employees' thoughts and actions emerging in response to shared perceptions of the wider context, but does mainly follow a compilation process. In a compilation process, individual attitudes and behaviours configure to form idiosyncratic patterns, which compile in unique ways to shape emergent phenomena (Kozlowsi and Klein, 2000). Compilation requires reconciliation of diverse perspectives and suggests a (relatively) reflective stance (Kozlowski and Klein, 2000). Entrepreneurial HRM could foster such a process. Insights from institutional theory reveal that spontaneous actions, which do not fit into prescribed patterns are likely to be expressed given a context where there is no paramount isomorphic pressure (DiMaggio and Powell, 1983). Entrepreneurial HRM opens opportunities for employees to move beyond accepted wisdom to bring unique knowledge, experience and extended networks to inform any outcomes that subsequently arise at the level of the organisation. To the extent that team leaders, line managers and senior parties are open to perspectives that diverge from institutionally-driven parameters, bottom-up emergence may occur through compilation. Furthermore, in the process of integration, coordination of individual efforts becomes critical so that the emergence of collective innovation can be enabled. Teamworking skills (Collins and Smith, 2006), including communication skills and the ability to identify other team members' needs should be developed to facilitate this process. Rewards also need to be geared towards recognising contribution to collective innovation efforts, such as knowledge sharing (Zhao and Chadwick, 2014).

11.9 Conclusion

In conclusion, we propose four new research avenues. First, most research on the relationship between HRM and innovation does not take into account whether innovation is a major organisational strategy and whether creativity is explicitly required from the employees. We contend that this should constitute an important consideration in this stream of research. The SHRM literature has made clear that organisational strategy determines the choice of HRM practices. Although innovation is valuable even if it is incremental, it should be acknowledged that organisations could have other priorities, depending on strategic positioning and the external environment. In this chapter, we discussed that for expected and discretionary innovation, the implications for HRM are different. It is critical that future research takes the organisational strategy and job requirements into account.

Second, there is a lack of attention to the way in which bottom-up emergence occurs. Although Kozlowski and Klein (2000) distinguish between two discrete patterns of emergence-composition and compilation, research to date has (implicitly) adopted a compositional framing and compilation has been more or less left out of the story. For radical creativity which relies on variety in input, a compositional model is less effective. In particular, a compositional model overlooks the complexity involved in the integration and synthesis process. Theoretically, there could be multiple patterns of compilation. Future research needs to explore what these patterns are and how divergent ideas coevolve in these patterns, because how individual innovative ideas/actions are synthesized has implications for collective innovation (Harvey, 2014).

Third, acknowledging that emergence arises from contextual factors future research needs to examine the HR facilitators of different patterns of emergence. Bottom-up emergence through *compilation* occurs through two complementary processes. The first, similar to the "opportunity" dimension of the AMO framework (Appelbaum et al., 2000) entails exposure to alternative perspectives and offers the scope for individuals to apply their knowledge and skills in ways that suggest new options. The second involves reconciling these diverse insights, experiences and capabilities to form a collective whole (Kozlowski and Klein, 2000, through the use of autonomy, discretion, empowerment and so on, with these processes facilitated by those in leadership roles. Several activities have the potential to foster compilation. Communities of practice are an important mechanism for emergence (Brown and Duguid, 1991). The activity-based nature of knowing and expertise, where knowledge evolves through an ongoing process of practice, application and experience (Swan et al., 1999) means that innovation is dependent on the active participation by employees in working and learning processes that focus on the role of changes in work process knowledge and practices. Teams with distributed leadership could be another effective mechanism. Where leadership is distributed and decentralised, and only exerted through an internal model of autonomy across the constellation of members at any point in time, there is a continual adaptation of values, rules, structures and behaviours, and relationships that are contemporaneously cooperative and competitive (Battistella, Biotto and De Toni, 2012). HRM policies, reward system and management efforts would indicate their support for this activity, eventually resulting in stronger teams that self-regulate and achieve higher-level strategic goals (Kozlowsi, Chao and Jensen, 2010).

Fourth, although widely used in studying task performance, the AMO framework can also be a useful one for innovation research. The differential implications of expected and discretionary innovation for HRM and the three components need to be empirically tested and verified. Especially, little research attention has yet been devoted to explore the notion of "opportunity" (Jiang, Lepak and Baer, 2012). Opportunities could involve both privacy for experimentation (Bernstein, 2012) and engagement with the collective to be exposed to new perspectives and experiences (McGrath and Zell, 2001). A balance between these two types of opportunities needs to be struck, as there might be conflict between the two (Mumford and Hunter, 2005). Taking a multi-level perspective, opportunities for individual autonomy might come at the expense of team integration. Hence, a balanced, multi-level view towards the study of opportunities is needed.

References

Amabile, T.M. (1983). The social psychology of creativity: A componential conceptualization. *Journal of Personality and Social Psychology*, 45(2): 357–376.

Amabile, T.M., Hennessey, B.A. and Grossman, B.S. (1986). Social influences on creativity: The effects of contracted-for reward. *Journal of Personality and Social Psychology*, 50(1): 14–23.

Anderson, N., Potocnik, K. and Zhou, J. (2014). Innovation and creativity in organisations: A state-of-the-science review, prospective commentary, and guiding framework. *Journal of Management*, 40(5): 1297–1333.

Appelbaum, E., Bailey, T., Berg, P. and Kalleberg, A. (2000). *Manufacturing Advantage: Why High-performance Work Systems Pay Off*. Ithaca, NY and London: Economic Policy Institute, Cornell University Press.

Axtell, C., Holman, D., Unsworth, K., Wall, T., Waterson, P. and Harrington, E. (2010). Shopfloor innovation: Facilitating the suggestion and implementation of ideas. *Journal of Occupational and Organizational Psychology*, 73(3): 265–285.

Barney, J. (1991). Firm resources and sustained competitive advantage. *Journal of Management*, 17(1): 99–120.

Battistella, C., Biotto, G. and De Toni, A.F. (2012). From design driven innovation to meaning strategy. *Management Decision*, 50(4): 718-743.

Bednall, T.C., Sanders, K. and Runhaar, P. (2014). Stimulating informal learning activities through perceptions of performance appraisal quality and human resource management system strength: A two-wave study. *Academy of Management Learning & Education*, 13(1): 45-61.

Bernstein, E.S. (2012). The transparency paradox: A role for privacy in organizational learning and operational control. *Administrative Science Quarterly*, 57(2): 181-216.

Beugelsdijk, S. (2008). Strategic human resource practices and product innovation. *Organization Studies*, 29(6): 821-847.

Brown, A. (2016). The role of career adaptability and flexible expertise in developing individual innovative behaviour. In H. Shipton, P. Budhwar, P. Sparrow and A. Brown (eds), *Human Resource Management, Innovation and Performance* (pp. 249-265). London: Palgrave Macmillan.

Brown, J.S. and Duguid, P. (1991). Organizational learning and communities-of-practice: Toward a unified view of working, learning, and innovation. *Organization Science*, 2(1): 40-57.

Chang, S., Jia, L., Takeuchi, R. and Cai, Y. (2014). Do high-commitment work systems affect creativity? A multilevel combinational approach to employee creativity. *Journal of Applied Psychology*, 99(4): 665-680.

Collins, C.J. and Smith, K.G. (2006). Knowledge exchange and combination: The role of human resource practices in the performance of high-technology firms. *Academy of Management Journal*, 49(3): 544-560.

Combs, J., Hall, A. and Ketchen, D. (2006). How much do high performance work practices matter? A meta-analysis of their effects of organizational performance. *Personnel Psychology*, 59: 501-528.

DiMaggio, P. and Powell, W.W. (1983). The iron cage revisited: Collective rationality and institutional isomorphism in organizational fields. *American Sociological Review*, 48(2): 147-160.

Easterby-Smith, M., Crossan, M. and Nicolini, D. (2000). Organizational learning: Debates past, present and future. *Journal of Management Studies*, 37(6): 783-796.

Farr, J.L., Sin, H.P. and Tesluk, P.E. (2003). Knowledge management processes and work group innovation. In L.V. Shavinina (ed.), *International Handbook on Innovation* (pp. 574–586). Amsterdam: Elsevier Science.

Fay, D., Shipton, H., West, M. and Patterson, M. (2014). Teamwork and organizational innovation: The moderating role of the HRM context. *Creativity and Innovation Management*, 24(2): 261-277.

Fried, Y. and Ferris, G.R. (1987). The validity of the job characteristics model: A review and meta-analysis. *Personnel Psychology*, 40(2): 287-322.

Gong, Y., Cheung, S.Y., Wang, M. and Huang, J.C. (2012). Unfolding the proactive process for creativity: Integration of the employee proactivity, information exchange, and psychological safety perspectives. *Journal of Management*, 38: 1611-1633.

Gong, Y., Huang, J.C. and Farh, J.L. (2009). Employee learning orientation, transformational leadership, and employee creativity: The mediating role of employee creative self-efficacy. *Academy of Management Journal*, 52(4): 765-778.

Grant, A.M. and Berry, J.W. (2011). The necessity of others is the mother of invention: Intrinsic and prosocial motivations, perspective taking, and creativity. *Academy of Management Journal*, 54(1): 73–96.

Gupta, A., Tesluk, P. and Taylor, S. (2007). Innovation at and across multiple levels of analysis. *Organization Science*, 18(6): 885–897.

Hackman, J.R. and Oldham, G.R. (1975). Development of the job diagnostic survey. *Journal of Applied Psychology*, 60(2): 159.

Harvey, S. (2014). Creative synthesis: Exploring the process of extraordinary group creativity. *Academy of Management Review*, 39(3): 324–343.

Jiang, K., Lepak, D., Hu, K. and Baer, J. (2012). How does human resource management influence organizational outcomes? A meta-analytic investigation of mediating mechanisms. *Academy of Management Journal*, 55(6): 1264–1294.

Jimenez-Jimenez, D. and Sanz-Valle, R. (2008). Could HRM support organizational innovation? *The International Journal of Human Resource Management*, 19(7): 1208–1221.

Kang, S-C., Morris, S. and Snell, S. (2007). Relational archetypes, organizational learning and value creation: Extending the human resource architecture. *Academy of Management Review*, 32(1): 236–256.

Kozlowski, S.W., Chao, G.T. and Jensen, J.M. (2010). Building an infrastructure for organizational learning: A multilevel approach. In S.W. Kozlowski and E. Salas (eds), *Learning, Training, and Development in Organizations* (pp. 363–403). Mahwah, NJ: LEA.

Kozlowski, S. and Klein, K. (2000). A multilevel approach to theory and research in organizations: Contextual, temporal, and emergent processes. In K. Klein and S. Kozlowski (eds), *Multilevel Theory, Research and Methods in Organizations: Foundations, Extensions, and New Directions* (pp. 3–90). San Francisco, CA: Jossey-Bass.

March, J. (1991). Exploration and exploitation in organizational learning. *Organization Science*, 2(1): 71–87.

McGrath, C. and Zell, D. (2001). The future of innovation diffusion research and its implications for management: A conversation with Everett Rogers. *Journal of Management Inquiry*, 10(4): 386–391.

Montag, T., Maertz, C. and Baer, M. (2012). A critical analysis of the workplace creativity criterion workplace. *Journal of Management*, 38(4): 1362–1386.

Mumford, M.D. and Hunter, S.T. (2005). Innovation in organizations: A multi-level perspective on creativity. *Research in Multi-Level Issues*, 4: 11–74.

Nahapiet, J. and Ghoshal, S. (1998). Social capital, intellectual capital, and the organizational advantage. *Academy of Management Review*, 23(2): 242–266.

Oldham, G.R. and Cummings, A. (1996). Employee creativity: Personal and contextual factors at work. *Academy of Management Journal*, 39(3): 607–634.

Paauwe, J. and Boselie, P. (2005). HRM and performance: What next? *Human Resource Management Journal*, 15(4): 68–83.

Piaget, J. (1970) *Science of Education and the Psychology of the Child*, trans. D. Coltman. Oxford: Viking Press.

Prieto, I., Perez-Santana, M. and Sierra, C. (2010). Managing knowledge through human resource practices: Empirical examination on the Spanish automotive industry. *International Journal of Human Resource Management*, 21(13): 2452–2467.

Sanders, K., Moorkamp, M., Torka, N., Groeneveld, S. and Groeneveld, C. (2010). How to support innovative behaviour? The role of LMX and satisfaction with HR practices, *Technology and Investment*, 1(1): 59–68.

Shalley, C.E. (1991). Effects of productivity goals, creativity goals, and personal discretion on individual creativity. *Journal of Applied Psychology*, 76: 179–185.

Shalley, C.E. (1995). Effects of coaction, expected evaluation, and goal setting on creativity and productivity. *Academy of Management Journal*, 38: 483–503.

Shin, S.J. and Zhou, J. (2007). When is educational specialization heterogeneity related to creativity in research and development teams? Transformational leadership as a moderator. *Journal of Applied Psychology*, 92(6): 1709.

Shipton, H., Sparrow, P., Budhwar, P. and Brown, A. (2017). Human resource management and innovation: Looking across levels. *Human Resource Management Journal*, 27(2): 246–263.

Shipton, H., West, M., Dawson, J., Patterson, M. and Birdi, K. (2006). Human resource management as a predictor of innovation. *Human Resource Management Journal*, 16(1): 3–27.

Staw, B.M. (1990). An evolutionary approach to creativity and innovation. In M. West and J.L. Farr (eds), *Innovation and Creativity at Work: Psychological and Organizational Strategies* (pp. 287–308). Chichester, UK: Wiley.

Sun, L.Y., Aryee, S. and Law, K.S. (2007). High-performance human resource practices, citizenship behavior, and organizational performance: A relational perspective. *Academy of Management Journal*, 50(3): 558–577.

Swan, J., Newell, S., Scarbrough, H. and Hislop, D. (1999). Knowledge management and innovation: Networks and networking. *Journal of Knowledge Management*, 3(4): 262–275.

Unsworth, K.L. (2001). Unpacking creativity. *Academy of Management Review*, 26: 289–297.

van Rijn, Yang and Sanders, K. (2013). Understanding employees' informal workplace learning: The joint influence of career motivation and self-construal. *Career Development International*, 16(6): 610–628.

West, M. and Farr, J. (1990). Innovation at work. In M.A. West and J.L. Farr (eds), *Innovation and Creativity at Work* (p. 9). Chichester: Wiley.

Wright, P.M. and McMahan, G.C. (1992). Theoretical perspectives for strategic human resource management. *Journal of Management*, 18(2): 295–320.

Yuan, F. and Woodman, R.W. (2010). Innovative behavior in the workplace: The role of performance and image outcome expectations. *Academy of Management Journal*, 53(2): 323–342.

Zhao, Z.J. and Chadwick, C. (2014). What we will do versus what we can do: The relative effects of unit-level NPD motivation and capability. *Strategic Management Journal*, 35(12), 1867–1880.

12 Globalisation and human resource management

Chris Brewster, Adam Smale and Wolfgang Mayrhofer

[G]lobalisation/regionalisation, migration and reverse migration (also referred to as "brain circulation"), the ascendancy of emerging markets, the demand for people with a global mindset, and the worldwide war for talent have brought about fundamental changes to the nature, magnitude, and raison d'être for human resource management (HRM) in a global context.

(Tung, 2016: 142)

12.1 Introduction: globalisation and HRM

Globalisation has obvious implications for HRM. Beer and his colleagues, in one of the earliest scholarly analyses of HRM, paid considerable attention to the influence of context (Beer et al., 1984). However, most HRM research since that time has been conducted in single countries. The international HRM (IHRM) literature has eschewed this narrow focus and integrated the international context in various ways. Here we examine globalisation in connection with two of the main streams of research in IHRM (we exclude expatriation and mobility): comparative HRM (CHRM), examining the commonalities and differences in HRM between regions and nations; and HRM in multinational enterprises (MNEs), examining the HRM policies and practices of organisations operating across national boundaries.

In this final chapter of the book, we first outline the significance of globalisation for HRM and then briefly review how it has been incorporated into each of the two streams. We use the notions of context, time and process to structure the review. The final section sets out a research agenda and examines how synergies can be created from bridging the two streams.

Given what is happening in the world of business and politics, we suggest that an understanding of HRM increasingly needs to take an international and comparative view. Discussions of globalisation are as lively in the management literature as they are in the political and cultural literature. Globalisation is arguably a factor for all organisations. This is obviously true for MNCs, but smaller organisations in most countries (particularly in the European Union) are also impacted by competition from foreign organisations. In the public sector, there are not only the traditional diplomatic agencies that governments have (and staff) in other countries, but also the emergence of governmental and non-governmental international organisations such as the United Nations or the Red Cross. Increasingly, government departments are working with other agencies across their region or across the world. An increased knowledge about the specifics of management across borders, including knowledge of how HRM issues are handled in various countries (Dickmann, Brewster and Sparrow, 2008) has become a prominent issue for social scientists as it has become a key issue for all kinds of managers.

As international integration and the growing interconnectedness of business increases (Dunning, 2004/1993), globalisation may act to strengthen the specific advantage of particular locations or subsidiaries (Rugman and Verbeke, 2001) or it may act to increase standardisation around the globe (Kostova and Roth, 2002). This standardisation may take place between regions, countries or country clusters, as HRM policies diffuse around the world, or it may take place within MNEs, as they attempt to harmonise HRM practices and ensure local responsiveness as well as consistency across their foreign operations (Pucik et al., 2017). More generally, this speaks to the convergence and divergence of HRM at the global level as well as the different consequences of globalisation for HRM in different countries and regions – classical issues in both the CHRM and HRM in MNEs literatures.

Globalisation, an all-pervasive phenomenon with ample coverage in the research literature (for example, Michie, 2003), has given momentum to heated debate about long-term developments towards convergence or divergence at the macro level of nation states and the meso level of organisational practices. The "globalisation thesis" proposes that countries become increasingly similar (a convergence thesis) with respect to their tastes, behavioural patterns, cultural values and governance systems due to drivers such as patterns of industrialisation, trade barrier diminution, globalised media, homogeneous consumer demand, digitalisation, financial markets, and information and capital flows.

Arguably the most elaborate view comes from the world-polity approach within sociological neo-institutionalism (for an overview see Greenwood et al., 2008). It argues that, especially since 1945, Western cultural patterns and institutions dominate global developments so that core individual and collective actors, including organisations and nation states, are subject to isomorphic pressures to follow the Western model of rationalisation (Drori, Meyer and Hwang, 2006). Underlying these considerations is the view that the role of nation states will further decrease (Ohmae, 1995) and that a world-society (Krücken and Drori, 2009) emerges which is the primary locus of rationalisation.

This does not necessarily mean complete uniformity. There is room for local variation and distinctiveness. For instance, research on the translation of business and political practices across cultural and national borders emphasises that both freedom for social action as well as isomorphic pressure co-exist (see, for example, Czarniawska and Sevón, 2005). As practices travel across the world and become institutionalised, they are edited and customised to specific contextual settings.

Nevertheless, the convergence thesis has not remained uncontested. The contesters come from the cultural as well as the institutional camps. The cultural view emphasises that national and regional cultures are the result of substantial differences in norms, values and belief systems (Hofstede, Hofstede and Minkov, 2010; House et al., 2004). This makes convergence at all levels highly unlikely. There is a substantial body of literature showing that management practices differ enormously across countries and cultures and that there are no convincing reasons why these differences should vanish in the future.

From an institutional perspective, there are also significant doubts about converging tendencies. Theories of comparative institutionalism in the varieties of capitalism literature (for example, Hall and Soskice, 2001; Whitley, 1999) argue that given the differences in institutional arrangements at the national level and their relative inertia, it is hard to see existing differences between systems of economic organisation disappear. Whitley (1999) argues that "[n]ation states constitute the prevalent arena in which social and political competition is decided in industrial capitalist societies". This suggests differences, not convergence, and limits to globalisation (Guillén, 2001: 19).

This global/local tension underlies not only international business in general, but also extensive research in the field of IHRM. A much-cited article from the 1990s (Rosenzweig and Nohria, 1994) points out that this tension is of heightened relevance for HRM since of all the management functions, HRM is the most sensitive to local conditions. So globalisation, via both convergent and divergent forces, impacts HRM within organisations, MNEs in particular, but HRM also remains stubbornly rooted in its own national context. Among others, this has given rise to research along two streams within IHRM – comparative HRM and HRM in MNEs. We briefly review each in turn. To do so we adopt the concepts of context, process and time, familiar from the business strategy literature to structure the discussion (Brewster, Mayrhofer and Smale, 2016). We detail how each of these concepts has been used in each of the streams below.

12.2   Comparative HRM

CHRM examines HRM between countries or between clusters of countries or geographical regions (Brewster and Mayrhofer, 2012). In some contrast to the tenets of the "globalisation thesis", this literature has identified persistent commonalities and differences between countries in the way they conceive HRM, the way they evaluate it and the way that HRM is practiced.

12.2.1   Context

Context in the general business literature, often captured by the notion of contingency, refers to the differences in management processes created by the size of the business, the sector(s) in which it operates and the situation in which it is embedded. It is the last of these, particularly geographic context, that is by definition a key issue in the CHRM stream. As discussed above, theories underlying CHRM are based around the impact of cultural or institutional differences between nations. Culturalists argue that there are deep-rooted differences in values and beliefs between nations (Hofstede, Hofstede and Minkov, 2010; House et al., 2004) and these are inevitably reflected in the way people are managed at work, for example, in terms of leadership (Moran, Harris and Moran, 2011) or career management (Shen et al., 2015). Institutionalists on the other hand believe that it is the structures and mechanisms of social order that support and constrain the behaviour of businesses. Synthesising and developing these ideas, the comparative capitalisms literature (Hall and Soskice, 2001; Whitley, 1999) suggests that the elements of the system external to the business tend to be reflected in internal relationships – or HRM.

In CHRM research, contextual explanations drawing upon institutionalism seem to have taken over from those based on cultural differences. This may reflect the critique of the cultural literature (Avloniti and Filippaios, 2014; Gerhart and Fang, 2005) or simply that each culture contains a more or less normal distribution of people who fit the stereotype in question and organisations can select or avoid people "typical" of that culture (Vaiman and Brewster, 2015). There is much less they can do to avoid the effects of institutions.

The overwhelming conclusion within the CHRM stream is that context matters, since patterns and models of HRM are consistently shown to vary between countries and institutional contexts (for example, Wood, Brewster and Brookes, 2014; Morley, Heraty and Michailova, 2009). Much of the data coming from the ongoing Cranet (www.cranet.org) surveys have identified clear differences in HRM practices between countries ranging from the professionalism of the HRM function (Farndale, 2005) to compensation practices (Lowe et al., 2002), to training (Goergen et al., 2012).

12.2.2   Time

In organisation theory, time has had a prominent place in calls for better theory building (for example, Mitchell and James, 2001). In CHRM this is focused on the debates around convergence. Time is embedded in questions concerning whether differences between countries and regions are increasing, static or decreasing, and calls for longitudinal analyses. Cranet, which has collected 25 years of broadly representative country data at roughly five-year time intervals, has made some advances in this regard.

Since time is so important to the CHRM stream (since if country differences are decreasing there is less value in studying them), defining constructs such as convergence is an appropriate starting point (Mayrhofer et al., 2002). Directional convergence points towards similar trends. Even if the same trend is apparent in many countries, different starting points and different rates of change may mean that countries remain as far apart as ever or even diverge further. For final convergence, countries would have to become more alike in the way that they manage their HRM over time.

However, the empirical evidence shows little evidence of final convergence. Whether based on cultural or institutional analyses, or on a combination of the two, the research has tended to reveal continuing differentiation. While we see instances of directional convergence/similarity (for example, Mayrhofer et al., 2011), no convincing case for final convergence has been made.

12.2.3 Process

Process, or the means and mechanisms through which management operates, is a surprisingly neglected perspective in the study of IHRM:

> [T]he literature has presented only limited accounts of what actually happens in the process of constructing and negotiating HR[M] systems in the context of so many potentially conflicting institutional rationales. (Rupidara and McGraw, 2011: 175)

Indeed, it is argued that since "Western" cultural patterns and institutions dominate global developments, actors including organisations and countries are subject to strong isomorphic pressures to follow that model (Drori, Meyer and Hwang, 2006). So how does convergence and divergence occur? How do these pressures manifest themselves and how do models of HRM become institutionalised?

Both cultural and institutional theories have been criticised for being rather static (for example, Oliver, 1991) and for a lack of clarity about how the broader social context impacts HRM (Edwards and Kuruvilla, 2005). Neither allow much room for agency – for individuals and organisations to "buck the trends". Given the centrality of the convergence/divergence debate within the CHRM stream and the corresponding significance of time in providing answers, a lack of theory and in-depth empirical examination into the processes and mechanisms of convergence and divergence can be seen as a serious shortcoming. We return to this and other issues in the agenda for future research.

12.3 HRM in multinational enterprises (MNEs)

The stream of HRM in MNEs deals with HRM issues that businesses face when they operate across national borders, unified in their attempts to provide answers to the main over-riding question of how people are managed in MNEs and with what outcomes (Björkman and Welch, 2015). Based on research published in top management journals, Werner (2002) summarised the territory of international management research as comprising the following key areas:

- Global business environment;
- Internationalisation;
- Entry mode decisions;
- Foreign direct investment (FDI);
- International exchange;
- International joint ventures;
- Strategic alliances and networks;
- Transfer of knowledge;
- Multinational enterprises (MNEs)/multinational corporations (MNCs);
- Subsidiary–HQ relations;
- Subsidiary and multinational team management; and
- Expatriate management.

Under this broad umbrella, the dominant research themes within HRM in MNEs can be seen as relating to the management of MNE subsidiaries and knowledge transfer. More specifically, its focus has been on the extent of, and processes involved in, the transfer of HRM practices between MNE headquarters and their foreign subsidiaries (Welch and Björkman, 2015). This has typically been explained as contingent upon a complex interaction of factors relating to the home- and host-country contexts, the strategy and structure of the global corporation and the subsidiary, and the nature of the headquarters–subsidiary relationship (Edwards and Kuruvilla, 2005).

12.3.1   Context

Context in the HRM in MNEs stream is often framed as a tension, or duality, between HRM standardisation and the constraints imposed by the local environment (Ferner et al., 2011), more specifically about the external and internal variables that explain why MNEs may "desire" to standardise/transfer HRM, and why this might not be "feasible" (Dickmann, 2003). There is an implicit assumption in much of this research that the MNE's desire to standardise their HRM is restricted by local contextual constraints that require them to compromise. The reverse scenario, that is, how the local contextual norms and arrangements regarding HRM is influenced by MNEs and MNE subsidiaries, is much less often researched even though it seems likely that, especially in societies where institutions are new or weak, MNEs may have considerable power to influence institutions in their favour (Thite, Wilkinson and Shah, 2012; Welch and Björkman, 2015). There has equally been a dearth of literature examining contextual effects at a regional level, either externally in terms of regional exogenous effects or internally in terms of regional MNE structures (for example, regional HQ), despite the regional nature of international business (Rugman and Oh, 2013) and the tendency for larger MNEs to regionalise their operations.

Departing from the dominant headquarters' view of HRM in MNEs, research adopting the subsidiary perspective and examining the contextual antecedents of reverse HRM transfer has also attracted growing attention. Context in this sub-domain is analysed from the host-country perspective, looking at conditions under which foreign subsidiaries, usually from institutionally strong host-country settings, are capable of reverse transferring HRM practices to headquarters (Edwards and Tempel, 2010), as well as laterally to other MNE subsidiaries (Edwards et al., 2015).

12.3.2   Time

Time has received much less attention within the HRM in MNEs stream. A large proportion of research in this stream is quantitative (Welch and Björkman, 2015), based on cross-sectional data and using predominantly subjective and varying measures/classifications of HRM practices. This has rendered it almost impossible to make inferences about patterns of standardisation or differentiation over time. Whilst some isolated studies comparing HRM in subsidiaries has suggested that there is a "dominance" of (US-style) HRM "best practice" that is creating an inexorable move towards convergence of practices across foreign subsidiaries (Pudelko and Harzing, 2007), much of this research is not longitudinal in design (cf. Björkman et al., 2008).

However, there has been some insightful, longitudinal-type, qualitative work in the form of case studies. These have revealed the important role that power relations and micro-political processes play in determining the use and effectiveness of different HRM control mechanisms over time (for example, Ferner, 2000) and the influence of strong local cultures (Dixon, Day and Brewster, 2014). They have also contributed a more dynamic view of HRM transfer by demonstrating that standardisation should be seen as fluctuating and subject to continual negotiation between parent and subsidiary. Whilst case studies can facilitate the study of HRM developments over time in a potentially nuanced fashion, one could still argue that case studies are inferior when it comes to identifying overall trends or showing representative change over time.

12.3.3   Process

Process perspectives in HRM in MNEs have only quite recently started to attract serious theoretical and empirical attention. A possible explanation for this lack of focus on issues of process, apart from the disproportionately high number of quantitative studies, is the dominance of contingency models (DeCieri and Dowling, 2012). Nevertheless, interest has grown in part in response to a broader critique that a lack of focus on the processes through which HRM practices are created and developed is a shortcoming in the general HRM literature (Paauwe, 2004). Process is, in a variety of ways, gradually infiltrating the HRM in MNEs stream. For instance, we are being encouraged to conceive of HRM systems as comprising different process features such as validity, visibility, consensus, and justice that send signals that are interpreted heterogeneously by individuals, which in turn leads to strong/weak HRM climates (Bowen and Ostroff, 2004).

This "process school" emphasises the role of key actors at higher levels (Rupidara and McGraw, 2011) as well as the role of psychological processes at the individual level through which employees attach meaning to HRM (Sanders, Shipton and Gomes, 2014). There have been similar calls for actor-centric research into the HRM function itself: who the key actors are and what their roles actually are in HRM development processes (Welch and Welch, 2012). Drawing on the strategy-as-practice perspective in the strategy literature, it is suggested that a similar focus on HRM practices, practitioners in a broad sense and praxis interact will advance our understanding of the processes behind how people-related decisions within organisations are made, implemented and enacted (Björkman et al., 2014).

12.4   A future research agenda for international HRM

We suggest that a future research agenda for international HRM should take account of globalisation in four different but inter-related respects: paying more attention to context, process, time and the potential synergies between the comparative HRM and HRM in MNEs streams.

12.4.1   Context

A fruitful avenue of future research for CHRM in terms of context involves researching HRM in a wider range of countries and conducting more fine-grained cross-county comparisons. Most HRM research, and most IHRM research, has been conducted in the WEIRD – Western, educated, industrialised, rich, democratic – countries (Henrich, Heine and Norenzayan, 2010). What we know so far covers a minority of the world's countries, with limited data from countries outside of the Global North in particular, though there are welcome developments in the range of countries being studied (see for example, Budhwar and Mellahi, 2006; Dessler and Tan, 2009; Dowling and Donnelly, 2013).

Research within HRM in MNEs has focused on the effects of external contextual determinants on MNE headquarters' and subsidiary HRM practices. How MNEs influence local HRM practice – for example, through the deployment of various power and political resources – is a significant research gap (Welch and Björkman, 2015). Arguably a crucial impulse and motor of development, in particular in the so-called developing economies, MNEs can play an important role in spreading HRM innovations. To the best of our knowledge, however, there is extremely little analysis on whether different degrees of MNE presence in various countries have systematic effects on developments within these countries, or whether these effects are similar in other contexts. Specifically, we know little about the effect of foreign MNEs on the institutional environment governing HRM in a country and, of particular importance with regard to the convergence/divergence debate, the long-term effect on HRM in these countries, for example, the emergence of a standardised national model. The research on CHRM, on the other hand, has taken little account of the internal context of MNEs and how that impacts the spread or variation of HRM policies and practices.

Context is a highly diverse concept used, among others, by linguists, anthropologists, and political scientists. Especially in countries such as Nepal, Pakistan, Angola, or Libya with "difficult" or "extraordinary" contextual situations in terms of geography, language diversity, political stability, intra-national relationships between different groups or tribes, we understand very little about how HRM unfolds and develops in such settings. For instance, we know next to nothing about whether MNEs choose similar HRM strategies to cope with the situation in such countries and whether these strategies change or stay stable over time. Our understanding of what happens with regard to convergence/divergence would deepen were we to apply a more differentiated view of what context means and look at areas currently "off the map" for the most part.

12.4.2   Process

Process, in particular the various ways in which HRM is diffused, negotiated, (de)institutionalised, perceived and enacted, holds substantial potential in deepening our understanding about convergence/divergence at the cross-national level as well as standardisation/localisation at the firm level. First, this necessitates stronger theoretical approaches for analysing the dynamics behind convergence/divergence and the spread of HRM policies and practices, with more in-depth discussions about theoretical discourses. In line with a renewed interest in actor-centric viewpoints in literatures about strategy (Eisenhardt, Furr and Bingham, 2010) and institutional thinking (Powell and Colyvas, 2010) we call for research that incorporates the roles of key actors in these processes. More detailed studies of the roles and activities of key actors at various levels within the MNE will clarify the dynamic interactions between MNE actors and their context in shaping HRM practices (Rupidara and McGraw, 2011).

This will also serve to complement theoretical insights from neo-institutionalism with those based around agency, power and politics in revealing the complex dynamics of the contested institutional terrain. We support a broader conceptualisation of "practitioners" (Björkman et al., 2014) or stakeholders (Beer, Boselie and Brewster, 2015) to include key individual and collective actors both internal and external to the MNE. The CHRM literature could similarly benefit from the addition of an actor perspective and bring in hereto neglected actors (for example, business schools, HRM professional associations, consultants, HRM gurus, policy makers, lobbying groups) into the empirical realm. In short, if our understanding of HRM convergence and divergence processes is to progress beyond attempts at explaining observed similarities and differences between organisational practices, we need more theoretically-grounded research and more innovative research designs that directly tackle issues of process within and across levels of analysis.

12.4.3   Time

Time should be more central to empirical research efforts within both streams – within CHRM due to convergence/divergence lying at the heart of its main research question; and within HRM in MNEs due to its conspicuous absence – even in areas such as expatriate adjustment where time spent in a country has a clear but non-straightforward impact (Hippler, Brewster and Haslberger, 2015).

This almost inevitably means more longitudinal research. Besides serving as a stronger foundation for inferences about causality – an issue that afflicts a substantial proportion of the IHRM literature – it also allows studies to capture how change occurs, the speed and direction of change and whether the rate of change is constant. We suggest the more targeted use of and improvements to existing data. For instance, in addition to HRM-specific databases such as Cranet, we believe there is also a lot of potential in using other available data such as the European Working Condition Survey (EWCS, n.d.) – two waves of data from 2005 and 2010 are available with data from the sixth round in 2015 being made publicly available soon.

We would simultaneously call for a careful treatment of time in such future studies. For instance, time spans should be related to the context they denote. Three years in a comparatively stable period, for example, 1982–1985, do not equal three years in a time of dramatic global change, for example, 2007–2010. Hence, assigning qualitative elements to time spans and taking into account sequential effects could bring valuable insights into the dynamics of convergence or divergence. There is also scope to complement existing "trend" studies with empirical studies that rely on matched samples. Practicalities may mean that these studies have to make certain concessions in terms of smaller samples, fewer countries and shorter time spans, but they will bring deeper understanding of how, when and why convergence/divergence occurs. In terms of HRM in MNEs, this kind of research might shed more light on HRM-related decisions during the internationalisation process and the factors leading up to more mature MNEs to go through "pendulum swings" in terms of their periodic focus on HRM standardisation and localisation (Farndale et al., 2010; Evans, Pucik and Björkman, 2011).

12.5   Conclusions: synergies between CHRM and HRM in MNEs

Synergies are clear from much of the preceding discussion. CHRM and HRM in MNE streams would each be improved through better acknowledgement of research in the other tradition and via greater dialogue and cross-fertilisation. Context is the topic of several discourses across a number of disciplines, reaching far beyond management or organisation studies. Against this backdrop, it seems especially fruitful to exploit these discourses in the narrower realms of international HRM. Cross-fertilisation can principally be realised through empirical examinations of the processes taking place at the intersections between MNEs and the national/global systems of HRM in which they are embedded. Indeed, it is rare that studies in HRM in MNEs place equal emphasis – either in terms of theory or research design – on MNE headquarters/home-country issues and subsidiary/host-country issues (McDonnell, Lavelle and Gunnigle, 2014). The added challenge of data access notwithstanding, such studies are much better placed to draw conclusions about HRM convergence/divergence in ways that can combine and leverage the explanations offered by each of the two streams.

Combining the insights from research in HRM in MNEs and CHRM would deepen our understanding of convergence/divergence by taking into account the mutual effects between the national and organisational levels. Given the historically greater importance attached to the role of MNEs in this regard, Welch and Björkman (2015) suggest looking to the international business literature for examples of how this could be done. As an example, the neo-institutionalist school of thought is already established in both streams. Developments within this theoretical discourse have not fully found their way into IHRM discourse, nor been used to explain convergence and divergence between countries or standardisation and differentiation within MNEs.

The neo-institutionalist school of thought has produced a number of insights which might usefully inform IHRM research concerning potential mechanisms of standardisation/convergence. A few examples may suffice, such as an individual director being a member of two or more boards provides an important means for transferring information and know-how between organisations (Shipilov, Greve and Rowley, 2010). In HRM, further exploring the role of such interlocks for spreading HRM policies and practices across different organisations and national borders would give us additional insights in the role of social networks in the processes of standardisation/convergence. Proximity plays an important part when looking at how HRM spreads. The relative position of the units of analysis such as organisations or countries between themselves often is operationalised by a variant of proximity such as geographical or cultural proximity. However, other forms of proximity with arguably an equally important role such as social or technological proximity (Knoben and Oerlemans, 2006) are rarely researched. They could provide a more detailed understanding of how "closeness" influences standardisation and convergence of HRM across the globe. The discussion on translation and diffusion (Czarniawska and Sevón, 2005) emphasises analysing the how, why and when of organisational policies and practices spreading across different organisations and countries actually refers to a complicated and multifaceted process. Far from being a simple "transfer", the policies and practices are taken apart and re-assembled, with various factors such as political interests, implicit and cultural norms, and legal regulations coming into play, leading to a new "product". Again, efforts of standardisation in HRM can hardly be understood properly without such a more in-depth understanding of how processes of translation travel rather than a mere transfer with minor amendments taking place. Neo-institutional thinking allows a coherent view of such issues partially addressed in current HRM research and links it with broader organisational phenomena.

Of course, not all of these ideas can be immediately translated into empirical research settings within CHRM or HRM in MNEs. Yet, we do suggest that a more systematic incorporation of these theoretical insights can open up new avenues for making sense of the processes underlying HRM convergence and divergence and standardisation/differentiation.

References

Avloniti, A. and Filippaios, F. (2014). Evaluating the effects of cultural difference on corporate performance: A meta-analysis of the existing literature. *International Business Review*, 23(3): 660–674.

Beer, M., Boselie, P. and Brewster, C. (2015). Back to the future: Implications for the field of HRM of the multi-stakeholder perspective proposed 30 years ago. *Human Resource Management*, 54(3): 427–438.

Beer, M., Spector, B., Lawrence, R., Quinn, M.D. and Walton, E. (1984). *Managing Human Assets: The Groundbreaking Harvard Business School Program*. New York: Free Press.

Björkman, I., Ehrnrooth, M., Mäkelä, K., Smale, A. and Sumelius, J. (2014). From HRM practices to the practice of HRM: Setting a research agenda. *Journal of Organizational Effectiveness: People and Performance*, 1(2): 122–140.

Björkman, I., Smale, A., Sumelius, J., Suutari, V. and Lu, Y. (2008). Changes in institutional context and MNC operations in China: Subsidiary HRM practices in 1996 versus 2006. *International Business Review*, 17(2): 146-158.

Björkman, I. and Welch, D. (2015). Framing the field of international human resource management research. *The International Journal of Human Resource Management*, 26(2): 136-150.

Bowen, D.E. and Ostroff, C. (2004). Understanding HRM–firm performance linkages: The role of the "strength" of the HRM system. *Academy of Management Review*, 29(2): 203-221.

Brewster, C. and Mayrhofer, W. (2012). *Handbook of Research on Comparative Human Resource Management*. Cheltenham, UK and Northampton, MA, USA: Edward Elgar Publishing.

Brewster, C., Mayrhofer, W. and Smale, A. (2016). Crossing the streams: HRM in multinational enterprises and comparative HRM. *Human Resource Management Review*, 26(4): 285-297.

Budhwar, P.S. and Mellahi, K. (2006). *Managing Human Resources in the Middle East*. London: Routledge.

Czarniawska, B. and Sevón, G. (eds) (2005). *Global Ideas. How Ideas, Objects and Practices Travel in the Global Economy*. Copenhagen: Liber, Copenhagen Business School Press.

DeCieri, H. and Dowling, P. (2012). Strategic human resource management in multinational enterprises: Developments and directions. In G.K. Stahl, I. Björkman and S. Morris (eds), *Handbook of Research in International Human Resource Management* (2nd edition, pp.13-35). Cheltenham, UK and Northampton, MA, USA: Edward Elgar Publishing.

Dessler, G. and Tan, C.-H. (2009). *Human Resource Management, An Asian Perspective*. Singapore: Pearson Education.

Dickmann, M. (2003). Implementing German HRM abroad: Desired, feasible, successful? *International Journal of Human Resource Management*, 14(2): 265-283.

Dickmann, M., Brewster, C. and Sparrow, P.R. (eds) (2008). *International Human Resource Management: A European Perspective* (2nd edition). London: Routledge.

Dixon, S., Day, M. and Brewster, C. (2014). Changing HRM systems in two Russian oil companies: Western hegemony or Russian spetsifika? *International Journal of Human Resource Management*, 25(22): 3134-3156.

Dowling, P.J. and Donnelly, N. (2013). Managing people in global markets: The Asia-Pacific perspective. *Journal of World Business*, 48(2): 171-174.

Drori, G.S., Meyer, J.W. and Hwang, H. (eds) (2006). *Globalization and Organization: World Society and Organizational Change*. Oxford: Oxford University Press.

Dunning, J.H. (2004/1993). *The Globalization of Business*. Abingdon, Oxon: Routledge.

Edwards, T. and Kuruvilla, S. (2005). International HRM: National business systems, organizational politics and the international division of labour in MNCs. *The International Journal of Human Resource Management*, 16(1): 1-21.

Edwards, T., Sanchez-Mangas, R., Bélanger, J. and McDonnell, A. (2015). Why are some subsidiaries of multinationals the source of novel practices while others are not? National, corporate and functional influences. *British Journal of Management*, 26(2): 146-162.

Edwards, T. and Tempel, A. (2010). Explaining variation in reverse diffusion of HR practices: Evidence from the German and British subsidiaries of American multinationals. *Journal of World Business*, 45(1): 19–28.

Eisenhardt, K.M., Furr, N.R. and Bingham, C.B. (2010). Micro-foundations of performance: Balancing efficiency and flexibility in dynamic environments. *Organization Science*, 21(6): 1263–1273.

European Working Condition Survey (EWCS, n.d.) https://eurofound.europa.eu/european-working-conditions-surveys-ewcs (accessed 2 May 2017).

Evans, P., Pucik, V. and Björkman, I. (2011). *Global Challenge: International Human Resource Management* (2nd edition). New York: McGraw-Hill.

Farndale, E. (2005). HR department professionalism: A comparison between the UK and other European countries. *The International Journal of Human Resource Management*, 16(5): 660–675.

Farndale, E., Paauwe, J., Morris, S.S., Stahl, G.K., Stiles, P., Trevor, J. and Wright, P. (2010). Context-bound configurations of corporate HR functions in multinational corporations. *Human Resource Management*, 49(1): 45–66.

Ferner, A. (2000). The underpinnings of 'bureaucratic' control systems: HRM in European multinationals. *Journal of Management Studies*, 37(4): 521–540.

Ferner, A., Tregaskis, O., Edwards, P., Edwards, T., Marginson, P., Adam, D. and Meyer, M. (2011). HRM structures and subsidiary discretion in foreign multinationals in the UK. *The International Journal of Human Resource Management*, 22(3): 483–509.

Gerhart, B. and Fang, M. (2005). National culture and human resource management: Assumptions and evidence. *International Journal of Human Resource Management*, 16(6): 971–986.

Goergen, M., Brewster, C., Wood, G. and Wilkinson, A. (2012). Varieties of capitalism and investments in human capital. *Industrial Relations*, 51(2): 501–527.

Greenwood, R., Oliver, C., Suddaby, R. and Sahlin, K. (eds) (2008). *The Sage Handbook of Organizational Institutionalism*. London: Sage.

Guillén, M.F. (2001). *The Limits of Convergence. Globalization and Organizational Change in Argentina, South Korea and Spain*. Princeton, NJ and Oxford: Princeton University Press.

Hall, P.A. and Soskice, D. (eds) (2001). *Varieties of Capitalism. The Institutional Foundations of Comparative Advantage*. Oxford: Oxford University Press.

Henrich, J., Heine, S.J. and Norenzayan, A. (2010). The weirdest people in the world? *Behavioral and Brain Sciences*, 33(2–3): 61–83.

Hippler, T., Brewster, C. and Haslberger, A. (2015). The elephant in the room: The role of time in expatriate adjustment. *International Journal of Human Resource Management*, 26(15): 1920–1935.

Hofstede, G.H., Hofstede, G.J. and Minkov, M. (2010). *Cultures and Organizations. Software of the Mind: Intercultural Cooperation and its Importance for Survival* (3rd edition). New York: McGraw-Hill.

House, R.J., Hanges, P.J., Javidan, M., Dorfman, P.W. and Gupta, V. (eds) (2004). *Culture, Leadership, and Organizations: The GLOBE Study of 62 Societies*. Thousand Oaks, CA: Sage.

Knoben, J. and Oerlemans, L.A. (2006). Proximity and inter-organizational collaboration: A literature review. *International Journal of Management Reviews*, 8(2): 71–89.

Kostova, T. and Roth, K. (2002). Adoption of an organizational practice by subsidiaries of multinational corporations. *Academy of Management Journal*, 45(1): 215–233.

Krücken, G. and Drori, G.S. (2009). *World Society: The Writings of John W. Meyer*. Oxford: Oxford University Press.

Lowe, K.B., Milliman, J., De Cieri, H. and Dowling, P.J. (2002). International compensation practices: A ten-country comparative analysis. *Human Resource Management*, 41(1): 45–66.

Mayrhofer, W., Brewster, C., Morley, M. and Ledolter, J. (2011). Hearing a different drummer? Evidence of convergence in European HRM. *Human Resource Management Review*, 21(1): 50–67.

Mayrhofer, W., Müller-Camen, M., Ledolter, J., Strunk, G. and Erten, C. (2002). The diffusion of management concepts in Europe: Conceptual considerations and longitudinal analysis. *Journal of Cross-Cultural Competence & Management*, 3: 315–349.

McDonnell, A., Lavelle, J. and Gunnigle, P. (2014). Human resource management in multinational enterprises: Evidence from a late industrializing economy. *Management International Review*, 54(3): 361–380.

Michie, J. (ed.) (2003). *The Handbook of Globalisation*. Cheltenham, UK and Northampton, MA, USA: Edward Elgar Publishing.

Mitchell, T. and James, L. (2001). Building better theory: Time and the specification of when things happen. *Academy of Management Review*, 26(4): 530–547.

Moran, R.T., Harris, P.R. and Moran, S.V. (2011). *Managing Cultural Differences. Global Leadership Strategies for Cross-cultural Business Success* (8th edition). Oxford: Butterworth-Heinemann.

Morley, M., Heraty, N. and Michailova, S. (eds) (2009). *Managing Human Resources in Central and Eastern Europe*. London: Routledge.

Ohmae, K. (1995). *The End of the Nation State: The Rise of Regional Economies*. New York: Free Press.

Oliver, C. (1991). Strategic responses to institutional processes. *Academy of Management Review*, 16(1): 145–179.

Paauwe, J. (2004). *HRM and Performance: Achieving Long-term Viability*. Oxford: Oxford University Press.

Powell, W.W. and Colyvas, J.A. (2010). Microfoundations of institutional theory, in R. Greenwood, C. Oliver, R. Suddaby and K. Sahlin (eds), *The Sage Handbook of Organizational Institutionalism* (pp. 276–299). London: Sage.

Pucik, V., Evans, P., Björkman, I. and Morris, S. (2017). *The Global Challenge: International Human Resource Management* (3rd edition). Chicago, IL: Chicago Business Press.

Pudelko, M. and Harzing, A.-W. (2007). Country-of-origin, localization, or dominance effect? An empirical investigation of HRM practices in foreign subsidiaries. *Human Resource Management*, 46(4): 535–559.

Rosenzweig, P.M. and Nohria, N. (1994). Influences on human resource management practices in multinational corporations. *Journal of International Business Studies*, 25(2): 229–251.

Rugman, A. and Verbeke, A. (2001). Subsidiary specific advantages in multinational enterprises. *Strategic Management Journal*, 22(3): 237–250.

Rugman, A.M. and Oh, C.H. (2013). Why the home region matters: Location and regional multinationals. *British Journal of Management*, 24(4): 463–479.

Rupidara, N.S. and McGraw, P. (2011). The role of actors in configuring HR systems within multinational subsidiaries. *Human Resource Management Review*, 21(3): 174–185.

Sanders, K., Shipton, H. and Gomes, J.F. (2014). Guest editors' introduction: Is the HRM process important? Past, current, and future challenges. *Human Resource Management*, 53(4): 489–503.

Shen, Y., Demel, B., Unite, J., Briscoe, J.P., Hall, D.T., Chudzikowski, K., . . . Zikic, J. (2015). Career success across 11 countries: Implications for international human resource management. *International Journal of Human Resource Management*, 26(13): 1753–1778.

Shipilov, A.V., Greve, H.R. and Rowley, T.J. (2010). When do interlocks matter? Institutional logics and the diffusion of multiple corporate governance practices. *Academy of Management Journal*, 53(4): 846–864.

Thite, M., Wilkinson, A. and Shah, D. (2012). Internationalization and HRM strategies across subsidiaries in multinational corporations from emerging economies: A conceptual framework. *Journal of World Business*, 47(2): 251–258.

Tung, R.L. (2016). New perspectives on human resource management in a global context. *Journal of World Business*, 51(1): 142–152.

Vaiman, V. and Brewster, C. (2015). How far do cultural differences explain the differences between nations? Implications for HRM. *The International Journal of Human Resource Management*, 26(2): 151–164.

Welch, C.L. and Welch, D.E. (2012). What do HR managers really do? HR roles on international projects. *Management International Review*, 52(4): 597–617.

Welch, D. and Björkman, I. (2015). The place of international human resource management in international business. *Management International Review*, 55(3): 303–322.

Werner, S. (2002). Recent developments in international management research: A review of 20 top management journals. *Journal of Management*, 28(3): 277–305.

Whitley, R. (1999). *Divergent Capitalisms: The Social Structuring and Change of Business Systems*. Oxford: Oxford University Press.

Wood, G.T., Brewster, C. and Brookes, M. (eds) (2014). *Human Resource Management and the Institutional Perspective*. New York and Oxon: Routledge.

Index